THE LITERARY ABSOLUTE

Intersections: Philosophy and Critical Theory
A SUNY series edited by Rodolphe Gasché and Mark C. Taylor

THE LITERARY ABSOLUTE

*The Theory of Literature
in German Romanticism*

♦ PHILIPPE LACOUE-LABARTHE and
JEAN-LUC NANCY ♦ *Translated with an
Introduction and Additional Notes by
Philip Barnard and Cheryl Lester*

State University of New York Press

Originally published as L'ABSOLU LITTERAIRE
© 1978, Editions du Seuil

Published by
State University of New York Press, Albany

© 1988 State University of New York

For information, address State University of New York
Press, State University Plaza, Albany, NY., 12246

Library of Congress Cataloging-in-Publication Data

Lacoue-Labarthe, Philippe.
    The literary absolute.

    (Intersections)
    Translation of: L'absolu littéraire.
    Bibliography: p.
    Includes index.
    1. Romanticism—Germany.   2. German literature—
18th century—History and criticism.   3. German literature
—19th century—History and criticism.   4. Criticism—
Germany—History.   5. Philosophy, German—18th century.
6. Philosophy, German—19th century.   7. Idealism,
German—History—18th century.   8. Idealism, German—
History—19th century.   I. Nancy, Jean-Luc.   II. Title.
III. Series: Intersections (Albany, N.Y.)
PT363.P6L3   1988   830'.9'145   87-10047
ISBN 0-88706-660-7
ISBN 0-88706-661-5 (pbk.)

10 9 8 7 6 5 4 3

Contents

Translators' Introduction:
The Presentation of Romantic Literature

Although Philippe Lacoue-Labarthe and Jean-Luc Nancy are not part of a self-declared school like that of the *Annales* group in history, the Frankfurt School for Social Research, or the Konstanz school in literary studies, they have been associated since the late 1960s with a group of French philosophers now well known in the United States, including most notably Jacques Derrida, Sarah Kofman, Bernard Pautrat, and (more distantly) Jean-François Lyotard, philosophers who share with them certain methodological and theoretical assumptions. Both individually and in collaboration (besides *The Literary Absolute*, they have coauthored a study of Lacan and numerous articles), Lacoue-Labarthe and Nancy have published a wide range of texts, generally concerned with the modern period in philosophy, from Descartes through Kant and idealism to Heidegger, but dealing as well with literature, art, music, psychoanalysis, and what they refer to as "the political." While they freely acknowledge their debt to Derrida, it would be a mistake to assume that their work might be qualified as "Derridean," much less that it might be resumed under the literary-critical rubric of "deconstruction" or that its philosophical nature might be assimilable to a general conception of literary theory. For if they have been a central part of this loosely defined group's many organizational initiatives—colloquia and conferences, collectively organized volumes of essays such as *Mimesis: des articulations*[1], GREPH (the "groupe de recherche sur l'enseignement de la philosophie"), the Parisian "Collège de philosophie" founded under the auspices of the Mitterand government, or the "Centre de recherches philosophiques sur le politique," which they founded in 1980—their work nonetheless retains a specificity of its own, constituting a particular project within this larger context.

In its broadest outlines, the question that informs and constitutes the specificity of their work is that of the relation between literature and philosophy, although these terms must be taken in a provisional manner. Lacoue-Labarthe and Nancy assume a post-Heideggerean understanding of philosophy that takes into account Derrida's inflection of the Heideggerean question of Being, and a concern with "literature" that is indebted to Heidegger's investigation and criticism of the philosophical-aesthetic assumptions governing the understanding of art and literature in classical and modern philosophy. *Literature* is therefore a term that for Lacoue-Labarthe and Nancy corresponds to a rigorously defined area of philosophical inquiry, but an area whose implications, for all that, remain extensive. This post-Heideggerean formulation of the question of "literature and philosophy" distinguishes their work from other investigations of the subject in Germany, where such work is generally informed by the Frankfurt or Konstanz schools, or in our own Anglo-American context. A study of this sort is particularly welcome here, for its rigorous attempt to articulate the philosophical-theoretical grounding of the romantic (and thereby modern) conception of literature has few parallels in traditional Anglo-American considerations of romanticism. Following the lead of Walter Benjamin's early study of the concept of criticism in Jena romanticism, Lacoue-Labarthe and Nancy make it clear that the study of romanticism and its theory of literature is necessarily part of a study of assumptions governing *current* literary-critical and theoretical practices, a study of the initial elaboration of contemporary literary-critical and theoretical models. To study romanticism, in light of the present investigation, is to inquire into the grounds and the initial elaboration of "our" literary-critical and theoretical concerns. The genuinely historical relevance of this investigation to ongoing critical debates is therefore at the greatest possible remove from the literary-critical historicism that characterizes most traditional thinking on romanticism.

As is the case in *The Literary Absolute*, Lacoue-Labarthe and Nancy's treatment of this relation between "literature and philosophy" has often involved the problematic of presentation or *Darstellung*. *Darstellung*, which in modern philosophy generally designates the rendering of a concept in terms of sense, or a sensibilization (*Versinnlichung*), has a long and complex history. The term translates the Latin *exhibitio*, which is itself a translation, in turn, of the Greek *hupotúposis*, a sketch, an outline, a draft of a book, a model or pattern. As a rhetorical term, homologuous to illustration or demonstration, *hupotúposis* is defined in Quintilian as a figure by which a matter is vividly sketched in words.[2] Above all, *hupotúposis* involves *sensible* presentation, and particulary presentation of a *specular* nature; it speaks to the eye rather than the ear, and forms an "image," a "tableau," or even a "scène vivante," according to Dumarsais and later Fontanier.[3] In the eighteenth century, Herder and others use *Darstellung* to translate the Aristotelian concept of *mimesis*, and it subsequently plays an important role in the aesthetics of Goethe and Schiller.

The term enters modern philosophy when, in the *Critique of Pure Reason*, Kant elaborates the concept of the transcendental schema in response to the necessity for a "third term" that could reconcile understanding with sensibility, by partaking of the orders of both the intelligible and the sensible.[4] Schemata render the pure concepts of understanding, i.e., the categories, intuitable to sense; they translate categories of understanding into forms that are intuitable to sense. Schematism is less adequate, however, when it comes to translating between sensibility and reason, for the concepts of reason, i.e., ideas, unlike the concepts of understanding, do not lend themselves to presentation, sensibilization, or intuitable formation. Thus, the schematism that attempts to link sensibility and reason, the schematism that Kant refers to as "symbolic" in ¶59 of the *Critique of Judgment*, is necessarily only an approximation. Strictly speaking, a more adequate or perfect presentation of ideas is impossible. Despite its inadequacy, therefore, the partial and approximate operation of symbolic presentation is the most adequate form of presentation to which the idea *per se* may attain.

Following this genuinely radical insistence on the incompatibility of sensible presentation and the ideas of pure reason, on the impossibility of an adequate presentation of ideas, Kant's successors in idealism and romanticism, albeit in quite distinct but ultimately related ways whose interactions are taken up by Lacoue-Labarthe and Nancy, will reinvest the concept of presentation in such a way as to transform it into the kind of adequate and ever more perfect operation they perceive to be lacking in Kant. The analysis and elaboration of this more adequate form of presentation as it appears in the romantic theory of literature is the subject of *The Literary Absolute*. In the romantic theory of literature and art, what is perceived as both the dead end and the most formidable challenge of the Kantian model of presentation is transformed into a model of art as the aesthetic activity of production and formation in which the absolute might be experienced and realized in an unmediated, immediate fashion. In literature, i.e., in the productive unity of creative formation and critical reflection, the formative power or *bildende Kraft* of the artist extends beyond a presentation of the sensible (beyond the level of representation), and, recalling Kant's concept of the sublime, accomplishes a presentation of what in Kant remained unpresentable. Art realizes an adequate presentation of the Idea, or in other words accomplishes a sensible actualization of the Idea in the realm of the aesthetic. This conception of literature, by virtue of its ability to perform this operation, comes to be situated as more basic than or superior to the realm of philosophy from which it has drawn its founding concepts.

As Nancy argues in an earlier essay that relates the general problem of presentation to the problem of "style" and of philosophical self-presentation in Kant, the problems concerning philosophy's adequate self-presentation that had already appeared in the *Critiques* prepared the way for the elaboration of the literature-philosophy opposition that underlies the post-Kantian development of the romantico-modern concept of literature:

> How is philosophy to be presented? This question is repeated throughout
> the history of philosophy. . . . But there is a moment when this question
> *arrives* as a question, is engaged as such, and begins to pose and articulate
> itself in an express manner, producing its own terms: it is the moment when
> philosophy explicitly designates its own exposition as *literature* [comme *la
> littérature*], or as being *literary* [comme *de la littérature*]. In other words, no
> longer as the philosopher's own hand (his autography), but as his other, or
> as . . . all the rest.
>
> Thus, there comes a moment when, in a certain sense, philosophical
> autography can no longer certify itself, can no longer authorize or authenti-
> cate itself—but when philosophy designates *itself*, implies *itself*, exhibits
> *itself*, and disavows *itself* under the aegis of what will rapidly become the
> modern notion—and thus a notion *outside* philosophy—of 'literature.'
> This is the moment of Kant. Our task consists simply in attempting to
> establish this proposition: it is only after Kant that the express distinction of
> philosophy and literature (and therefore the division and coupling of the
> terms and concepts, as well as the positing of the question) becomes
> possible and necessary. [5]

Only after and in reaction to Kant's critical system, then, do the problems raised
by the auto-production of philosophy provoke the explicit development of the
notion of a literary form of presentation capable of raising itself to the level of a
presentation adequate to the Idea. Although the problems inherent in the
literature-philosophy distinction are an integral part of philosophy from Plato
on, it is nonetheless only after Kant that "Literature" can be posited and can
posit itself as such. [6] To understand the question of literature in this manner is
clearly to enter into a reconsideration of the moment of romanticism, and to
rethink the romantico-modern concept of literature that it inaugurates.

The Literary Absolute is a study of the initial appearance of this concept of
literature in the texts of the Jena romantics. As its subtitle indicates, it proposes
an analysis of the "theory of literature in German romanticism." It does not
primarily concern the German early romantics in a literary-historical sense,
although the authors take full account of this aspect of the problem and constantly situate their own analysis vis-a-vis Roger Ayrault's still-authoritative work on
the subject. Rather, *The Literary Absolute* concerns the specific manner in which
the Jena romantics, and especially Friedrich Schlegel, pose the question of
literature as the question of the presentation of philosophy, or in other words, in
this case, as the question of the aesthetic presentation of the idea along lines
determined by philosophy.

Before discussing the manner in which this ensemble of problems is posed in
The Literary Absolute, it would perhaps be helpful to approach them by way of
an example from the literary canon. Mary Shelley's *Frankenstein* (1818), a text

fully informed by the romantic context in question, will serve here, although the problems in question cannot be restricted to the so-called Romantic Period. Our example is drawn from the series of letters that form the novel's introduction and frame. The implications of the introduction's epistolary form and of the particular logic of the frame at work in it, not to mention that of the *novelistic* genre of the book as a whole, cannot be addressed here, but we may note that they add considerable complexity to the particular inscription of the literature-philosophy relation that we have in view. In the second of these letters, the narrator, who has undertaken the task of self-cultivation, finds himself isolated in the polar wastes and regrets the incompletion of his literary and intellectual formation. The stage for the narrator's reflection on his present situation is set in the formless and colorless polar expanse to which his efforts have led him:

> It is true that I have thought more, and that my daydreams are more extended and magnificent [than those of schoolboys of fifteen], but they want (as the painters call it) *keeping*; And I greatly need a friend who would have sense enough not to despise me as romantic, and affection enough for me to endeavour to regulate my mind.[7]

The narrator seeks cultivation, but fears that his thoughts and magnificent representations, his rich and perhaps even excessive poetic capacity, or in short, his romantic disposition, may be mistaken for mere disorder and enthusiasm. His disposition wants "keeping," as he puts it, using a term from eighteenth-century aesthetic theory. Initially part of the vocabulary of painting, *keeping* designates "the maintenance of harmony of composition," or more simply, "agreement, congruity, harmony." Whether in reference to outline and form, or tone and color, *keeping* concerns "the proper subserviency" or "proper relation" in "every part of a picture, so that the general effect is harmonious to the eye."[8] What his formation lacks, and what he seeks in reflection, in the form of a mirrored interlocutor or friend—"a man," he writes in the same paragraph, "who could sympathize with me, whose eyes would reply to mine"—is therefore the kind of regulation that would bring order and proportion to his representations. The narrator conceives of his fulfillment or perfection by analogy to the perfection of a work of art, but a work of art that could behold itself. In his fulfillment, he would in fact become both work of art and artist; as the product of *Bildung*, he would become both a completed *Bild*, or picture, and his own beholder. With the longed-for friend and collaborator, the narrator would continue to "perfectionate" his "unfashioned" or "half made up" disposition, as Frankenstein puts it a few pages later. In short, he would become what Lacoue-Labarthe and Nancy call the "subject-work," the paradigmatic model of the romantic subject's auto-production in the (literary) work of art. The arduous process of self-cultivation that he has undertaken is coextensive with this auto-production; it is his all-consuming "project," to use the romantic term employed by Shelley.

Engaged as he is in the task of auto-production, the narrator's disposition as the subject-work is *fragmentary* in nature; that is, it assumes and continually points toward a perfection and completion that lie beyond it, yet also underlie its self-productive activity. Thus the narrator's attempt to describe the "extraordinary" merits of Frankenstein, in whom he sees some of the qualities of the companion or keeper he seeks, points toward the nature of that more perfect regulation which could refashion the narrator as a total subject-work:

> Will you smile at the enthusiasm I express concerning this divine wanderer? You would not if you saw him. You have been tutored and refined by books and retirement from the world, and you are, therefore, somewhat fastidious; but this only renders you the more fit to appreciate the extraordinary merits of this wonderful man. Sometimes I have endeavoured to discover what quality it is which he possesses, that elevates him so immeasurably above any other person I ever knew. I believe it to be an intuitive discernment; a quick but never-failing power of judgment; a penetration into the causes of things, unequalled for clearness and precision; add to this a facility of expression and a voice whose varied intonations are soul-subduing music.[9]

Whereas the narrator presents the fragmentary model of an auto-productive subject, his description of Frankenstein presents what seems to be an example of such a subject's perfection, completion, or harmony. The fulfillment Frankenstein represents involve the remarkable development of his rational and critical powers—his "ability to supply causes," his "intuitive discernment," and his "judgment"—which characterize him, in however allusive a fashion, as an exemplary subject of philosophy, and more precisely of the critical philosophy formulated by Kant. Superadded to these "philosophical" attributes, and explicitly placed in the position of a supplement, is Frankenstein's "soul-subduing music," or, to speak less hyperbolically, his "facility of expression." This portrait seems to suggest not only that Frankenstein possesses the regulative powers missing in the narrator, but also that the capacity for critical reflection they imply has had the additional effect of intensifying the poetic capacity he shares with the narrator. Frankenstein thus accomplishes a fully developed operation of reflection, one that raises the poetic capacity to its highest power, where it becomes capable both of producing itself and of reflecting on and theorizing its own production. As will be shown, this gesture of completion is what Lacoue-Labarthe and Nancy refer to as "critical perfecting."

Taken together in the relation of reciprocal mirroring that Shelley carefully elaborates, what we have called the model of the auto-productive "subject-work" provided by the narrator and that of the movement of "critical perfecting" carried out by Frankenstein constitute the general structure of the romantic concept of literature as it is analyzed in *The Literary Absolute*. It is this fundamental concept of a productive or formative literary consciousness forming its own theory, positing itself as a totalizing auto-presentation of the subject that ultimately completes the work of philosophy, that is in question in the "Promethean" staging of Shelley's novel—which is subtitled "The Modern Prometheus." But of course, as the novel attests, this remarkable project is never fulfilled; for intrinsic reasons, it never reaches perfection. The novel's account of the project's failure, of what Lacoue-Labarthe and Nancy might call its "redhibitory defect" or inherent flaw, suggests, if nothing else, that the seemingly far-reaching powers of such a model of literature are not sufficient to regulate or control what its reflective operation engenders and that when the regulatory power of this literary subject fails, the results—at least according to this somewhat moralistic scenario—are catastrophic. One might say that when monstration is controlled by the totalizing reflection of Literature, it becomes, in the terms of this narrative, monstrous. One should recall here that Frankenstein's goal within the staging of the novel's framework is to arrest the "literary" (in an entirely different sense here) or irretrievable effects of his project, which has grown so distant from his initial idea that it seems to have altogether escaped his control.[10] The project of the Jena romantics, as discussed in *The Literary Absolute*, is engaged in the elaboration of such a concept of literature and, despite itself, in the attainment of its limits.

In light of *The Literary Absolute*'s articulation of a concept of literature derived from a philosophical context, the question that arises, from a literary-critical standpoint, is why the general reader—or "critic," to use an appellation whose romantic determination is amply demonstrated by Lacoue-Labarthe and Nancy—of literature should consult a book by two philosophers on the "theory of literature in German romanticism" rather than a more straightforward "literary" treatment of romanticism's conceptual background. Or in other words, why should such a reader concern himself or herself with a study that approaches this particular moment in this particular philosophical manner? Would it not be simpler and more effective as well to forego this detour through philosophy, which after all ought to be rendered unnecessary by one's institutional formation, and to treat literature on its own terms and its own ground? It would be, if only literature's terms and ground were indeed its own, if only they were properly literary and could be adequately delimited by a "literary theory" proper to them. But literature lacks propriety, and this absence of the proper is precisely what inhibits efforts to establish a positive methodology for literary studies and encourages a proliferation of "approaches to" literature, all of which, appealing to the enviable methodological security and liberal plurality of the social sciences, at least implicitly suppose that the question of literature has been put to rest. If this study leaves the reader with little else, it should make it apparent not only that the term literature cannot be taken for granted, but also that a lack of awareness of the philosophical roots of this term and its concept can only inhibit attempts to come to terms with the questions it raises.

Thus one of the notable virtues of *The Literary Absolute* is that it raises and insists on the question of literature as such. As the authors' analyses show, literature as it is most often understood, i.e., the romantico-modern concept of literature, literature as the object of a duly legitimated and institutionalized discipline, is thoroughly determined as a response to a certain philosophical "crisis." The received notion of literature, in other words, which assumes in particular that literature is different from or external to philosophy in various ways (and can thus perennially bemoan "external" incursions on the part of philosophy or "theory" into properly literary problems), is in fact philosophical through and through. The moments at which literature makes its most comprehensive gestures of authenticity invariably correspond to its greatest dependency on philosophy. This study clearly demonstrates that this romantic concept of literature is still in full force today, despite the claims often made for a "modern," much less "postmodern" literature that would postdate it. The specific nature of such claims, in fact, their ready acceptance of notions of literature and of language that ultimately remain unquestioned, often turns out to be the best evidence that the concept of literature of which Lacoue-Labarthe and Nancy speak is far from behind us. Thus, the philosophical nature of this study is not one among a number of alternatives, a sort of intellectual-historical addendum to the study of literature, but a thorough-going and consequent exploration of the philosophical determinations of the concept of literature, as these determinations appear not exclusively, by any means, but with particular explicitness, in the writings of the Jena romantics. Continuing the project of the few studies that have preceded it in this area, notably those of Walter Benjamin and Peter Szondi, this sort of undertaking is an indispensable preliminary to any attempt at a rigorous formulation of that in "literature," or that literature, which is not merely subservient to philosophy.

What *The Literary Absolute* demonstrates is first of all that the concept of literature arises as a response to the problems posed by Kant's critical enterprise. While discussions of the conceptual genealogy of the Jena romantics often concentrate on Fichte's concept of the I and the beginnings of speculative dialectics, this study situates their texts more generally, and perhaps more pertinently, with respect to the "crisis" that arises in the aftermath of Kant. To condense the argument of Lacoue-Labarthe and Nancy, the problem of presentation that concerns us here, the presentation of philosophy and the subject of philosophy (of what Lacoue-Labarthe and Nancy refer to as the "system-subject"), is opened up by Kant. Kant bequeaths this crisis of presentation to his successors by effectively depriving the subject of its being-subject, i.e., of its adequate presentation of itself to itself, reducing the subject to little more than the logically necessary, purely regulatory idea of the unity of its representations. This crisis of presentation provides an initial context for the development of idealism and romanticism alike: "One must set out from this problematic of the subject unpresentable to itself and from this eradication of all substantialism in order to understand what romanticism will receive, not as a bequest but as its 'own' most difficult and perhaps insoluble question" (30). Idealism and Jena romanticism represent divergent yet intersecting responses to this crisis, responses that cannot be distinguished as simply philosophical on the one hand, and literary on the other. The imbrication of their responses is in fact already suggested by the two manners in which Kant's third *Critique* had earlier begun to sketch out a potential resolution of the problems of the subject. The *Critique of Judgment* points toward a form of auto-presentation in reflective judgment, i.e., in the subject's synthetic function; at the same time, it suggests that a (simply regulatory) presentation of the subject occurs by means of the Beautiful in works of art, in the formative power of nature, and in history and culture, or the *Bildung* of humanity.

Both romanticism and idealism set out along these reflective paths toward a restoration or redefinition of the subject of philosophy. But whereas idealism embodies the fulfillment of the Subject in the labor of the Concept, constructing the living System of Philosophy, the Jena romantics (along with the romantico-modern period in general) envision the production of the Subject (the Subject's auto-production) in the work of art, which is to say both in the artwork and in its generative or operative productivity (its "creativity"). In one sense, as Lacoue-Labarthe and Nancy point out, Friedrich Schlegel even envisages the completion of philosophy in the work of art. The adequate presentation of the subject is thus accomplished through what Lacoue-Labarthe and Nancy call *eidaesthetics*, or the (attempted) subsumption and presentation of the Idea within the work of art. This is why Hegel finds the romantic solution, the romantic dissolution (*Auflösung*) of the Subject in the work of art, lacking in the rigor and seriousness that in conceptual labor should lead beyond art to the speculative Idea. In sum, and somewhat crudely, one might say that faced with a subject frozen in Kantian antinomies, like Frankenstein in the polar ice, idealism invents the speculative dialect while romanticism invents literature. Thereafter, the opposition is a fluid and volatile one, a dialectic (in the Heideggerean sense referred to by Lacoue-Labarthe and Nancy, that of the thinking of identity through the mediation of nonidentity) in which philosophy summons literature just as effectively as literature summons philosophy.

Setting out from this program for the presentation of a system-subject, discussed in relation to the "Earliest System-Programme of German Idealism" in the book's first chapter, the "Overture," Lacoue-Labarthe and Nancy's examination of the romantic concept of literature takes the form of careful analyses of particular texts by Friedrich Schlegel and other members of the Athenaeum group (texts that were included in translation in the French edition of *The Literary Absolute*). These discussions are not exegetically oriented readings or interpretations, in the literary-critical sense, of the texts of the Jena romantics, but rather are attempts to articulate and define the conceptual determinations, *topoi*, or motifs that structure the concept of literature as it appears there.

The four central chapters (situated between the book's "Overture" and "Closure") organize this concept around its two most constraining and general determinations: literature as productivity and literature as reflection. The fragmentary model of the work that develops in Jena is the subject of "The Fragment: The Fragmentary Exigency" and "The Idea: Religion within the Limits of Art." It is in these two chapters' discussion of the fragment—which is not the same as the genre of aphorism or fragment, but rather romanticism's productive model of the literary work-subject—that this study's most immediate and apparent connections with traditional Anglo-American treatments of romanticism and its fascination with the creative subject and with "form" will be found. The "fragmentary exigency" is the exigency of auto-production, that is, the demand that the literary work organize and produce itself as *organon*, that it *operate* in view of an essential totality and completion. In its fragmentary work, literature is determined as the productive capacity of *poiesis*, and manifests the synthetic totality that lies behind or before each of its particular manifestations. One of the primary implications of this fragmentary model, as seen here in an analysis of Friedrich Schlegel's fragment-collection *Ideas*, his *On Philosophy* (To Dorothea), and Schelling's satirical poem "Widerporst," is the becoming-religion of art. Long before Arnold's celebrated dictum, "religion and philosophy will be replaced by poetry," literature's moral and pedagogical function, its exemplary function as the becoming-*artist* or completed individuality of every subject, was understood by the Jena romantics in relation to its formative force as *Bildung*. As the adequate presentation of this model of the subject-work creating itself, literature becomes what Lacoue-Labarthe and Nancy call a "metaphysics of art," a *religious* art in the sense that it represents the remainderless presentation of the truth, the joining (according to an etymological interpretation of *religio*) of differences into the Same. Within this discussion, Lacoue-Labarthe and Nancy's examinations of *Witz*,[11] the pedagogical function of the artist, and the motifs of "chaos" and "love" clarify the relation of these romantic *topoi* to the philosophical assumptions that govern their usage from the eighteenth century to the present.

Whereas this treatment of the *productive* determination of romantic literature has well-established parallels in Anglo-American discussions of romanticism (however different their assumptions and goals may be), Lacoue-Labarthe and Nancy's exploration of literature's *reflective* determination in the chapters entitled "The Poem: A Nameless Art" and "Criticism: The Formation of Character" leads into less familiar territory. Because the question of reflection and the role it plays in the determination of the concept of literature is less well known in a critical community informed by new-critical and structuralist assumptions, assumptions, in other words, that have never thought their constitution *in* romanticism, it may well be that *The Literary Absolute*'s most important contributions are to be found in this section of the book.

The fundamental insight elaborated in these chapters, an insight explored earlier, although in different terms, by Benjamin, is that criticism, the reflective function of "critical" discourse, is determined by the romantics as a constitutive element of literature as such. Indeed, perhaps even more primitively or "originally," in a certain sense, than its productivity, and behind even its most general and trivialized literary-historical determinations—literature as the harmonious effusion of the subject, literature as the harmonious fusion of discursive content and form; literature as communication and community; literature as cultural capital, or the spiritual and social value devolving from the cultural—it is literature's determination as a reflective movement (rising above and *completing* "mere" literature) that provides literature's ultimate condition. It is this reflective determination, the "progressivity" of "progressive universal poetry," that accounts for the rest, and it is this determination that most decisely engenders literature (in an asymptotic relation to idealism) as the *literary absolute*—literature ostensibly separate and sufficient unto itself, especially with regard to the unshakeable philosophical double that from now on can only intrude upon it, or in more "modern" fashion, be overcome by it. Using a term drawn from one of Novalis' "dialogues," Lacoue-Labarthe and Nancy describe this reflective excess of literature in relation to itself as the *hyperbolic* constitution of literature, or literature's infinite demand for completion (*achèvement*) and perfection (or "hyper-completion," as their term *parachèvement* might also be translated) beyond any finite instance of literature (hence literature's necessarily fragmentary presentation of totality).

In its literary effects, this "hyperbolic" reflection is nothing other than criticism, insofar as criticism, beyond any mistaking of it as a secondary function, always serves to "perfect" the program that literature gives itself, whether immanently as "irony" and incessant formalization, or exoterically, as the critical "literature" and academic institutions that surround it. In a discussion of Friedrich Schlegel's *Dialogue on Poetry* (in "The Poem: A Nameless Art"), the critical or reflective determination of literature is shown to account for the

particular mode of auto-figuration and formalization in romantico-modern writing. In the notion of genre, in particular, or the sublation of classical genres into
the *novel*, the Socratic-ironic Genre of literature as such, as well as in the related
motif of mixture (*Mischung*), Lacoue-Labarthe and Nancy describe the operation by which literature defines itself as "work and reflection of the work,
poetry and criticism, art and philosophy. And consequently a 'genre,' beyond
all genres and containing the theory of this beyond within itself—or in other
words, at once a general theory of genres and its own theory" (86). Outside the
context of the Jena romantics, one can observe that this reflective determination
of literature accounts not only for the importance of the concept of synthetic
auto-figuration as it appears in the theory of the novel from the Schlegels to
Bakhtin and Lukács, but also as it is emphasized in a tradition extending,
despite apparent differences, from Schlegel's *Lucinde* through various avant-
garde and formalist movements up to the *nouveau roman* and to figures such as
Wallace Stevens or Maurice Blanchot, whose statements on the romantics are
cited by Lacoue-Labarthe and Nancy.

But of greater interest, perhaps, from the perspective of literary studies, is
the manner in which this reflective determination accounts for what is referred to
as "literary criticism" and the tensions that constitute it. As the "highest"
manifestation of this reflection, criticism is the most visible instance of the
hyperbolic gesture by which literature not only posits and occupies the place of
the Absolute Literature beyond all literature, but actually tends to replace
"mere" literature, thereby becoming more authentically literary than "primary"
literature. As Lacoue-Labarthe and Nancy demonstrate in "Criticism: The
Formation of Character," romantic criticism institutes "the true concept of art
(of the Subject)" (104), for it is only in criticism that literature penetrates to the
heart of the formative process that constitutes it. Only in criticism, according to
a certain fidelity to the Kantian motif of the *critical*, does literature reconstruct its
operative, poetic capacity beyond any illusions of naturality. Criticism under-
takes the work of essential formation and presentation that completes all works
and all authors, and goes beyond them, as Lacoue-Labarthe and Nancy
demonstrate in their analysis of the motif of critical *characterization*, to an abyssal
auto-engenderment of literature in criticism itself. "The true critic," as Friedrich
Schlegel states in a posthumous note cited in this chapter, "is an author to the
second power." "Literature" and "criticism" are thus coextensive, two functions
of the same concept of literature. To discover, therefore, that literature constitutes its own criticism more radically than any extrinsic commentary, that
literature tends to become critical just as criticism tends to become literary, or to
claim further that literature's critical constitution is capable of subsuming or
going beyond the function of philosophy, is only to reiterate the most fundamental credo of the "romantic disposition," and to reiterate it, most often, without

awareness of the philosophical assumptions that control it. Already part of the romantic concept of literature, criticism and its modern avatar, "theory," are rigorously determined by philosophy, and most of all when they pretend to escape it.

If one grants this global reinsertion of the concept of literature and its criticism into philosophy, however, this is not yet to have answered the question of what, in "literature," is not controlled by philosophy and of what this aspect or dimension of the literary consists. It should be noted that this question arises as part of the overall argument of *The Literary Absolute*, for the authors' goal in analyzing the concept of literature is not simply and flatly to subordinate "literature" to "philosophy," but quite to the contrary, as we have suggested, to open up the question of literature and of its relation to the philosophical. For if the concept of literature that reaches explicit formulation with the romantics and is still dominant today cannot rigorously and fully account for the text of a Proust, say, or to use the paradigmatic romantic triumvirate, of a Homer, Dante, or Shakespeare—and strictly speaking, it has never been able to—then what constitutes the literary?

The Literary Absolute does not pretend to answer this question, but, in "Closure: Romantic Equivocity," the books' brief final chapter, the authors acknowledge the problem and attempt to sketch out its relation to the concept of literature they have analyzed in the preceding pages. They describe this relation as romantic "equivocity." This term should not be confused with "ambiguity," a literary-critical concept of controlled polysemy that, as one semantic mode among others, is coextensive with the totalizing reflective consciousness that constitutes the semantic ground of literary "expression."

Rather, equivocity designates a basic indetermination, or absence of determination, that appears along with literature's hyperbolic movement, yet does not coincide with it. Equivocity occurs when, in its auto-productive gesture, literature and its (philosophical) subject, of necessity, but an unaccountable necessity that begins to undermine literature despite itself, never reaches identity: "the Same, here, never reaches its sameness." This "absence" of the work recalls the problem of presentation, but now in what is finally a negative fashion, which the authors link to an "eclipse" within manifestation, related to the problem of the "literary" in Heidegger's thinking on language and Being; in Derrida's analysis of the trace, dissemination, and writing; or in Blanchot's discussion of fragmentation. Yet, at the same time—which is only appropriate, if the nature of the literary is indeed to be understood as equivocal—this sobering "negativity" may not be incompatible with what appears in the "grotesque and insignificant" as "a sort of bottomless generosity of the book and of books, a debauchery of works that would no longer make a work, a proliferation that could no longer be numbered" (127).

Lacoue-Labarthe and Nancy's final gesture, then, is to leave the reader with the question of a literary thing both receding from the categories in which it has traditionally been thought and, at the same time, appearing in excess of them, not so much "beyond" them (according to the hyperbolic gesture of romantic literature) as across or in oblique movement through them, as a traversal of literature that is the question of literature as it can be thought at present. If *The Literary Absolute* does not attempt to resolve this question, it is not as a result of any failure to grasp the question's essential dimensions, but rather because of its fidelity to its initial goal, which was to open up the question for thinking. In the last analysis, this goal may be a more appropriate response to the question than any resolution.

Philip Barnard and Cheryl Lester

Note on the Text

The original French text of *The Literary Absolute* includes appended translations of the principal texts discussed in each chapter. Thus the first chapter, "Overture: The System-Subject," includes a translation of the "Earliest System-Programme of German Idealism," and so on. These translations (accompanied by a glossary explaining the use of key terms), by Lacoue-Labarthe, Nancy, and Anne-Marie Lang, were carried out as part of the work for the original text, which generously proposed not only to analyze the theory of literature in German romanticism, but also to provide, in the same volume, French versions of the German texts in question, which were not then available. Because the greater part of these texts (the "Earliest System-Programme," Friedrich Schlegel's *Critical Fragments*, the *Athenaeum* fragments, *Ideas*, and the *Dialogue on Poetry)* already exist in English translation, and because the inclusion of the remainder, without the former, would create problems of presentation, the English version of *The Literary Absolute* consists of Lacoue-Labarthe and Nancy's analyses alone. Nancy and Lacoue-Labarthe have slightly modified the present version of their text to omit references to the translations excluded here.

Wherever English translations of the German and other French texts cited are available, we have used them, and have modified them when necessary. Publication information concerning these translations is included in the notes and bibliography. In other cases, the translation is our own. All material in brackets, which have primarily been used to clarify terminological problems by giving the French or German original, has been added by the present translators.

The following abbreviations are employed to refer to frequently cited sources: *A,* the *Athenaeum* Fragments; *CF,* the *Critical Fragments; I,* the *Ideas; KS,* Friedrich Schlegel, *Kritische Schriften;* and *KA,* the *Kritische Friedrich-Schlegel-Ausgabe.*

Because it provides a statement on the particular goals and "format" of the original text, we include here the jacket copy, signed by Lacoue-Labarthe and Nancy, that appeared on the back cover of the French edition:

> Because it establishes a period in literature and in art, before it comes to represent a sensibility or style (whose 'return' is regularly announced),

romanticism is first of all a *theory*. And the *invention* of literature. More precisely, it constitutes the inaugural moment of literature as *production of its own theory*—and of theory that thinks itself as literature. With this gesture, it opens the critical age to which we still belong.

A Poietics in which the subject confounds itself with its own production, and a Literature enclosed in and enclosing the law of its own engendering, romanticism (ourselves, in sum) is the moment of the *literary absolute*.

All this was played out around 1800, in Jena, around a journal (the *Athenaeum*) and a group (that of the Schlegels). But although nearly two hundred years have passed since this moment took place, virtually none of the major texts in which such an operation was effected have been translated into French. This book's primary ambition is consequently to allow certain of these texts to be read.

But because the constraints that romanticism exerts upon us are proportionate to the misconceptions that surround it, we have deemed it necessary to provide each of these texts with an accompaniment, and to gauge for ourselves their theoretical import. This is quite simply a matter of *vigilance*: for in the end, is it not this "literary absolute" that continues, even today, to haunt our theoretical semisomnolence and our reveries of writing?

Romanticism

O Genoa, willingly would I divide myself into thee
And a wave, in thy port, roll with the waves,
Ripen in the company of thy golden oranges,
Become the marble and audacity of thy porticos;

A hero, I would rally thy band of maidens,
I would tear the veil from their fiery eyes,
I would revel in cups of nectar,
In all of them, tarrying at none.

Done with vague longing and hazy dreams!
Let me delight in and embrace the stone statue,
The Cytherean, and not her reflection.

I dreamt—when from the foam, upsurging
Came the goddess in a fragrance of roses.
A voice resounded: "I form and transfigure!"

Zacharias Werner

From *Selected Writings, published by his friends* (Grimma, 1840–1841), vol I, 174. The translation of this poem (here slightly modified) is by Lewis Gaylord Clark, and appeared in *The Knickerbocker Magazine* XXIV (1844).

Preface: The Literary Absolute

I

"There are classifications that are bad enough as classifications, but that have nonetheless dominated entire nations and epochs . . .": we will not be the first to note that this phrase, which opens *Athenaeum* fragment 55, appears to refer to that classification, more than to any other, which singles out the rubric of *romanticism* within the history and theory of literature.[1] The "mediocrity"—or the flimsiness—of this classification is certainly indisputable when it specifically applies to the initial and initiating moment of "romanticism," which the Germans, at least, unlike the French, take care to distinguish with the appellation "early romanticism" (*Frühromantik*).

It is to this early or "first" romanticism, which *first* constituted "romanticism," and determined not only the possibility of a "romanticism" in general, but also the course that literary history (and history as such) would follow from the romantic moment on—it is to this "early romanticism" that this book is devoted. In these few pages of introduction and in all that follows, we will find more than one occasion to suggest the degree to which the denomination "romanticism" is inadequate to this object. As it is usually understood—or not understood—this name is quite inaccurate, both in what it evokes as an aesthetic category (which often amounts to an evocation of evocation, so to speak, to an evocation of flowing sentimentality or foggy nostalgia for the faraway), and in what it pretends to offer as a historical category (in a double opposition to classicism and to realism or naturalism). It is even less appropriate in that the romantics of "early romanticism" never gave themselves this name (if we will refer to them this way, not without irony, it simply will be in keeping with customary practice). Finally, this name is false, in a very general manner, in that it attempts to set something apart—a period, a school, a style, or a conception—that would belong first and foremost to a certain *past*.

Each of these assertions will be justified in turn. For we do not pretend, far from it, that they go without saying, or even that the "romantics" were not in certain respects the first to equivocate about "romanticism." Undoubtedly, a rather long history was necessary before it would become possible, and even urgent, to manifest some distance from and some vigilance toward this question. But if the misinterpretation that surrounds the word "romanticism" is fairly

1

general (with the exception of certain works, not all recent, on which we will rely), it is no doubt more profound and tenacious in France than elsewhere — primarily as a result of neglect. Although the names of the Schlegel brothers, and that of their journal—the *Athenaeum*—are not unknown, and although one encounters a certain number of citations from their texts (most often from their "fragments," in which case the detached citation reinforces the equivocity of this neglect), it is nonetheless true that the absence, in France, of translations of the most important texts of "early romanticism" is one of the most startling of the lacunae that almost traditionally make up the singular bequest of the nation's cultural and editorial institutions. [2]

What is at stake in "early romanticism"—in other words the *romanticism of Jena*, a toponymic appellation to which we will return—can also be referred to, in at least a first approximation, as *theoretical romanticism*, and more precisely as what we will have to examine as the inauguration of the *theoretical* project in literature. As the inauguration, in other words, of a project whose place we know only too well, almost two hundred years later, in modern theoretical work—and not only, far from it, in the register of literature. One need not look far for indications of this heritage, which in fact is much more than a "heritage"; it can be found on the cover of this book. What does it mean to give a collection (and a journal) the title *poetics* (*poétique*)[3] except to put back in play, by way of Valéry and several others, the term and part of the concept that summarized, in 1802, the program of August Wilhelm Schlegel's *Lectures on Art and Literature*[4]—lectures that did little but articulate a general poetics that had emerged several years earlier in the Jena circle. If, in this context, the French lacuna is all the more strange, it is not surprising that it seems necessary, here, to begin filling that lacuna in.

We will in fact only be beginning, as we go directly to the texts and themes that should be considered essential—but to them only. We will not exhaust the inquiry, but perhaps we will at least be able to discern what it involves. We will also have to deal with what the intentions of such an undertaking might be. First of all, we are not engaging in an archival enterprise: we are not concerned with the reconstitution of a past event whose only relation to us, to speak with Nietzsche, (who contributed, in this, to prolonging romanticism), would be that of a monumental or antiquarian history. Our approach does not involve a history of romanticism of any sort. For one thing—and we will return to this—it could be a history *in* romanticism. But neither do we intend to exhibit and commend any romantic *model* whatsoever—in the manner, generally speaking, of Surrealism (or, to a lesser extent, of Albert Béguin and others). [5] Romanticism does not lead us to anything that one might imitate or that one might be "inspired by," and this is because—as we will see—it "leads" us first of all to ourselves. Which is not to say that we would suggest a pure and simple identification with romanticism and in romanticism or that we mean to place ourselves *abyssally* in romanticism. We will learn only too well to what extent the romantics were the first to romanticize romanticism and how much in general they *speculated*—giving it all its modernity—on the figure and the operation of the literary *abyss*, which they encountered, among other places, in the eighteenth-century English novel.

Consequently, this lacuna should be "filled in" yet must not be *saturated*. Thus, it should be approached in a manner that allows the decipherment of the massive equivocity that underlies the term "romanticism," insofar as one can separate oneself from this equivocity.

What, then, is in question in theoretical romanticism—in what we will have to characterize as the *theoretical* institutionalization of the *literary genre* (or, if you like, of literature *itself*, of *literature* as absolute)? To pose this question is to ask: What is in question in the well-known *Athenaeum* fragment 116, which contains the whole "concept" of "romantic poetry," or in the *Dialogue on Poetry*, which contains the definition of the novel as "romantic book"? Let us turn, then, to the texts.

But one should not turn to them without having begun to dissipate, already from without, the equivocity or illusion that these texts, as they are, perpetuate—sometimes deliberately, as we shall see. In other words, one should not begin to read them under the impression that one already knows what is covered by the word "romantic," or at least by its position in these texts. One can imagine that one knows what this word means in two very different ways, by regarding it as the beneficiary of a transmitted heritage, ripened throughout the eighteenth century or, on the contrary, as an absolutely original innovation. But the "truth" is not between the two: it is elsewhere. The word and the concept "romantic" are indeed *transmitted* to the "romantics," and their originality does not consist in inventing "romanticism," but rather, on the one hand, in using this term to cover up their own powerlessness to name and conceive what they invent, and, on the other (in any case, one can suspect this of Friedrich Schlegel[6]), in dissimulating a "project" that exceeds, from all points of view, what this term transmits to them.

Let us recall then quite briefly a number of givens concerning the history of that to which the fate of the word *romantic* has been linked. We know that the *romance* languages were the vulgar languages, thought of as derived from the vulgar *romance* tongue as opposed to the *Latin* of the clergy; that the *romance* literatures were the literatures of these languages; and that different forms and genres were soon called *romant, romanze, romancero*. When the *romantic* first appeared in England and in Germany (*romantick, romantisch*) and for the most part in the seventeenth century, it most often implied depreciation, or even moral condemnation, of what was being discarded, along with this type of literature, into the shadows of the prehistory of Modern Times: marvelous prodigies, unrealistic chivalry, exalted sentiments. To say again what many others have said, the novel *Don Quixote* lays out the nascent condition of the "romantic." With the birth of a philosophy of enthusiasm (Shaftesbury) on the one hand, and of an initial form of literary criticism (particularly the Swiss: Bodmer, Breitinger) on the other, the term will begin to take on a descriptive or frankly positive sense. Throughout the theoretical history of the seventeenth and eighteenth centuries, the history of this word is thus inseparable from what is represented, respectively, by philosophy in its debate with or assumption of modern "reason," and by the problematic of a critique of taste—or, more largely, of an aesthetic.

In the course of the eighteenth century, the word takes on both an aesthetic and historical value. It brings together, in a simple way, the initial givens we evoked a moment ago (the *Dialogue on Poetry* and the "Letter on the Novel" refer to these same origins) and links them, in Germany, to the concept of the *gothic* as the historical and geographical opposite of the *ancient*—thereby constituting the historical concept of the "romantic poem" (*romantisches Gedicht*), which began to describe a genre of poetry, for example, in 1784, when Wieland (an author distant from the romantics in every respect) composes *Idris and Zenaide, A Romantic Poem.* The romantic as genre sets out to adopt two related models: the heroic "gothic" gesture, and through it the epic (where one again finds Wieland and his *Oberon,* for example), as well as the "courtliness" of the troubadours. It adopts these models both in opposition to the models of the "classics" and simply as other models, chosen according to circumstance. But Shakespearean drama—with all its difference from classical or neoclassical tragedy—also becomes a model for this genre or spirit.

With the genre, an entire climate takes form, as it were. Romantic — especially in its English provenance—is the landscape before which one feels the sentiment of nature, or the epic grandeur of the past, or a mixture of both: ruins in a wilderness. But romantic, as well, is the sensibility capable of responding to this spectacle, and of imagining, or better, recreating—*phantasieren*—what it evokes. At the end of the eighteenth century, and particularly in Germany, this literary sensibility, at times, "romanesque," at others "poetic," carries with it what can be considered one of the first effects of *fashion,* in its properly modern and "spectacular" sense. "Romantic" is the word one has to write, the genre one has to give one's book—in short, romantic literature around 1795 is what today, a few "medias" later, might be called "pop literature." Nothing remains to be said about it, then, and early romanticism is not constituted in its aftermath; rather, as one sees in the "Letter on the Novel," it proposes the *ironic* reading of those works that might be called, employing a quasi-tautology, "romanesque romanticism."

Early romanticism represents the sudden appearance of a *crisis* that romanesque romanticism, which displayed some of its symptoms, would only have hidden. In the sudden vogue of "romanticization" and in the soberly categorical use of "romantic" as a form or a particular literary subject (one finds both characteristics in the movement of the 1770s and 1780s that came to be called *Sturm und Drang*, "storm and stress," and consequently in Herder, the early Goethe, and the early Schiller), everything might seem to have taken place like the ultimately simple and natural discovery of a new literature—in other words, as a simple progression or maturation, even if in reaction against the *Aufklärung*, whose innovations did not deeply question the general awareness of *progress*— economic, social, political, and moral.

In many respects, then, early romanticism corresponds to the profound economic, social, political, and moral crisis of the latter years of the eighteenth century.[7] This is not the place to study it, but it is nonetheless indispensable to recall that the Germany of this period, suffering from economic crisis and profound social problems accompanied by continual revolts, found itself, to schematize the situation from our own point of view, plunged into a triple crisis: the social and moral crisis of a bourgeoisie, with new-found access to culture (consuming romanesque romanticism, like those cultured managers [*gebildete Ökonom*] who read Jean Paul, according to Friedrich Schlegel)[8] but who are no longer able to find positions for those sons traditionally destined for the robe or the rostrum (unless the sons no longer wanted these jobs, notably that of pastor[9]); the political crisis of the French Revolution, a model that disturbed some and fascinated others, and whose ambiguity becomes ever more apparent with the French occupation; and the Kantian critique, finally, which is unintelligible for some, liberating but destructive for others, and which seems urgently in need of its own critical recasting. The characters we will see assembling at Jena participated in this triple crisis in the most immediate manner. Thus their project will not be a literary project and will open up not a crisis *in* literature, but a general crisis and critique (social, moral, religious, political: all of these aspects are found in the *Fragments*) for which literature or literary theory will be the privileged locus of expression. The reasons for such a privilege—which opens the entire history, up to the present, of the relations literature is supposed to have with society and politics—will appear in all that follows, and above all in the reading of the texts themselves. But we would be reading these texts badly were we to forget, at the start, that the theoretical romanticism of Jena characterized itself as the *critical* question of literature with all the historical and conceptual overdetermination we have just evoked—or perhaps even as the most properly critical (with all the values and limits of the term) formulation of *the* crisis of modern history.

For just this reason, the "romantics" will not give themselves this name, will not advocate the return to or invention of yet another genre, and will not erect a doctrine out of yet another aesthetic preference. Regardless of the form it takes, their literary ambition is always the result of their ambition for an entirely new social function for the writer—that writer who was, for them, a character still to come, and in the concrete form of a profession, as we read in *Athenaeum* fragment 20—and consequently for a different society. The "romantic poetry" that will concern us throughout this book was always meant to signify what it signifies—somewhat ironically and ambiguously—in this statement of Dorothea Schlegel: "Since it is altogether contrary to bourgeois order and absolutely forbidden to introduce romantic poetry into life, then let life be brought into romantic poetry; no police force and no educational institution can prevent this."[10]

The Jena romantics did not call themselves romantics. At the most, Novalis will use the word *der Romantiker*, which a posthumous fragment defines as follows: "Life is something like color, sound, and force. The romantic [*Romantiker*] studies life like the painter, musician, and mechanic study color, sound, and force."[11] In several other posthumous fragments, *Romantik* is the rubric for a "science" analogous to *Poetik*, *Physik*, or *Mystik*. But we will note frequently that this is precisely one of the characteristics that separates Novalis from Jena romanticism.

It is first of all their adversaries (pamphlets against them were published from 1798 on) and then their earliest historians (Jean Paul as early as 1804) and critics who will give them their name and describe them as a "romantic school"; all of these, however, will continue to distinguish carefully between the later stages of the "school," after 1805, and the initial moment, which we are referring to as that of the crisis.

The actors in this crisis will use *romanticism*—or more precisely, because they never speak of an *-ism*, the *romantic*—in two ways. Its first and most frequent use is the *classic* usage of the period (we will see that this is far from paradoxical), that of Wieland, Goethe, or Schiller. It is one literary category among others, and not even the supreme category, as is indicated for example in *Critical Fragment* 119, where the *lyric* is more highly esteemed than the *romantic*.

Their "own" usage of the term constitutes the *properly indefinite* program of the texts we will be reading, all of which should be coupled with the irony of Friedrich's letter to his brother August: "I can hardly send you my explication of the word Romantic because it would take—125 pages."

reading proofs but of thinking but requires to id itself [handwritten marginalia]

II

Such an ironic definition—or the irony of such an absence of definition — seems worth holding up as a symbol. The entire romantic "project" is in it: the romantic "project," or in other words that brief, intense, and brilliant *moment of writing* (not quite two years and hundreds of pages) that by itself opens an entire era, but exhausts itself in its inability to grasp its own essence and aim—and that will ultimately find no other definition than a place (Jena) and a journal (the *Athenaeum*).

Let us, then, call this romanticism the Athenaeum.

Its initiators, as everyone knows, are the two Schlegel brothers: August Wilhelm and Friedrich. They are philologists and have already made names for themselves in classical research. The texts they published (the *Letters on Poetry, Meter, and Language* by the one, *On the Study of Greek Poetry* by the other), as well as the journals to which they contributed (Goethe and Schiller's *Die Hören* and Reichardt's *Lyceum der schönen Künste*) indicate their success. In short, they are both very young and, from 1795–1796 on, appear to have very promising academic careers ahead of them.

In many ways, however, they are neither simply "future academics" nor pure philologists. First of all, both August and Friedrich (the latter no doubt more than the former) have explicit ambitions as *writers*. It is not by chance that they frequent Weimar. They are also paying very close attention to the movement which, in the "aftermath of Kant," is beginning to overtake German philosophy and will soon give birth to speculative Idealism. They attend Fichte's courses, read Ritter, discuss Jacobi, and try to establish contact with Schelling. Friedrich, in Berlin, becomes friendly with Schleiermacher. Finally, they are perceived as politically "advanced" (which during this period means "revolutionary," "republican," or "Jacobin"): the mistress of the elder brother and Egeria of the younger, Caroline Michäelis, marries Böhmer and is jailed in Mayence for subversive activities or, at least, for sympathy toward the occupying (French) army. But above all, they are involved in the "literary" and social circles of Berlin (the "Jewish" salons of Rahel Levin and of Dorothea Mendelssohn-Veit, Friedrich's future wife), which makes them, according to the French model of the period, perfect "intellectuals"—if indeed this type was born in the second half of the eighteenth century and was spreading across Europe from the Paris of the Encyclopedists.

It is within this milieu that the Athenaeum begins to take shape.[12] What initially takes shape is the group—a close-knit and relatively closed circle, which was founded, at least in the beginning, on intellectual fraternity and friendship, and on the desire for collective activity, for a certain "community" life as well. It is by no means the "committee" of a journal (we will soon see, moreover, that the journal itself is directed almost exclusively by the two brothers). Nor is it simply a circle of friends (there are women, amorous or erotic relationships, a heightened sense of moral "experimentation" that will encourage dreams, for example, of a "four-way marriage"[13]) or a "coterie" of intellectuals. It is, rather, a sort of "cell," marginal (if not altogether clandestine), like the core of an organization destined to develop into a "network" and serve as the model for a new style of life. Friedrich, who is the most taken with this form of community and who will be the real force behind it, will ultimately tend to describe it as a secret society. He will at least entertain the utopic idea that an "alliance" or "league" of artists could develop from the Athenaeum and be organized like the more or less "Masonic" sects whose importance, in Germany, to the spread of ideas and political struggle during the Revolution is well known. In many respects, the Athenaeum undoubtedly remains imprisoned by models inherited from the *Aufklärung*. Nonetheless, it clearly anticipates the collective structures that artists and intellectuals from the nineteenth century to the present will adopt. In fact, and without any exaggeration, it is the first "avant-garde" group in history. At no point, in any case, does one discern the least departure from this nearly two-hundred-year-old form on the part of what calls itself "avant-garde" today (and is distinct, as was the Athenaeum, from the older concept of a "school"). The Athenaeum is our birthplace.

But in order to be precise, we must make distinctions within the group itself. In the restricted sense, the group consists of ten persons at most: the initial trio (August, Friedrich, Caroline) transformed into a quartet with the arrival of Dorothea, along with Schleiermacher, Novalis (whom they met in 1792), Tieck, and Schelling.[14] Hülsen is on the fringes of the group. One should note that Schelling's participation begins relatively late, that he will never publish in the journal, and that one of his principle motivations, after all, will be Caroline (whom he will marry in 1803, shortly after the group's dissolution). But from a wider perspective, and considering what it was—a kind of center of attention in both Berlin and Jena—the group was somewhat larger. People will gravitate around the group, pass in and out of it, frequent the same places, visit one or the other of the two brothers. Tieck's sister Sophie will introduce her husband, the linguist Bernhardi; Wackenroder will be there during the last months of his life; the poetess Sophie Mereau will become closely involved with Friedrich before marrying Brentano, who himself will share the life of the group just before its dissolution; his sister Bettina (future wife of von Arnim) will be there as well; Steffens becomes part of the group in Dresden and Jean Paul will visit from Berlin; and then there will be the letters, many letters, between the members of the group, between Berlin, Weimar, and Jena, exchanged with Fichte, as well as with Baader and Ritter. An enormous correspondence, to which at least some of them, Caroline, for example, consign the best of romanticism.

But the journal is still the essential thing. Barely six issues and two years of existence (it is true that many others have appeared since), a "level" that is not always even, a certain tone of arrogance (which later, of course, becomes *de rigueur*), the petty insolence of the "avant-gardes."[15] But also a "mode of operation" that deliberately breaks with everything that could be compared with it or opposed to it and that determines, for the future, all of its power as a model. The journal is based on "fraternization": the introductory "Notice" speaks of "the fraternization of knowledge and talents." And in the last analysis, fraternization means collective writing: "We are not simply the directors, but also the authors of this review . . . . We accept outside contributions only when we esteem that we can adopt them as our own . . . ." As Ayrault observes, after citing these lines, "this affirmation carries considerable weight at the head of an issue containing, under the name Novalis, the series of aphorisms entitled 'Grains of Pollen'."[16] Clearly, a certain amount of "monolithicism" is involved, as well as a kind of dictatorial practice, notably on the part of Friedrich (who dreams that he and his brother may become the "critical dictators" of Germany). Already one can see the well-known "papal" phenomenon developing, and before long, the soon-to-be "classic" (so to speak) scenario will be in place, with its annexations, its sensational ruptures, its exclusions and excommunications, its quarrels and spectacular reconciliations, etc.; everything, in sum, that on a small scale constitutes the politics (for it is clearly a politics and a very precise one) of this sort of organism. Including, moreover, its intrinsic weakness: recantations and an undeniably "arriviste" mentality. It will take only six years to convert to Catholicism; a little more than ten to dine with Metternich. But in point of fact, things are not this simple (even with regard to the romantics' politics, widely criticized in France as reactionary, probably because it was opposed to Napoleon, but which is still instructive today). Things are not this simple because it is precisely this mode of operation that leads to the entire "experience" of romantic writing (the use of all genres, the appeal to the "fragment," the questioning of literary property and of "authority" by the challenge of anonymity), and that founds group "theoretical practice" (continual discussions, regimented work sessions, collective readings, "cultural" outings, and so forth), a practice that accounts for the prodigious amount of work accomplished during these two brief years, for the constant inventiveness, the rapid development, the radicality of the entirely unprecedented, in fact, "theoretical breakthrough."

Of course it does not last. The Athenaeum cannot withstand such an "expenditure" (nothing and no one could). It does not become exhausted so much as dislocated from itself. Internal dissent, jealousies, and theoretical disagreements (which can be traced even in the texts) have a lot to do with it, undeniably. But what is important is that everything was said and done very quickly, in the fever of things, "furiously" as one says today. It was almost as if each (even Schelling, who was already an academic) had realized that there was no future in it or that the world (not simply *Letters*) was slipping into another period or turning on itself, no doubt opening up a limitless perspective, but still offering nothing immediately adequate to the presaged and unreservedly welcomed event (even if it was still unnameable and faceless, a pure "thing" in the midst of being born and coming to the light of day).

This is why the Athenaeum, although it displayed all the characteristics of a modern "clique," cannot be considered a genuine "movement." The Athenaeum does not claim to represent a rupture. It makes no pretense of starting out with a *tabula rasa* or of ringing in the new. It sees itself, much to the contrary, as a commitment to the critical "recasting" of what is (hence its relation to Goethe, for example). It is not by chance that it originated in philology and criticism.

In the beginning, its great concern—around which, in 1794, everything will pivot and suddenly "gel"—is Antiquity, the poetry of Antiquity. The Schlegels' early work (and thus everything that will form the axis of the Athenaeum) gropes vaguely toward a new vision of Antiquity. We will see to what degree Winckelmann becomes their constant point of reference—not simply in an effort to continue in his path or to exploit it, but because serious theoretical work on the Greeks can be undertaken only on the basis of what he managed to establish. What comes to light is well known: a previously imperceptible hiatus in Greek "classicism," the traces of a savage prehistory and terrifying religion, the hidden, nocturnal, mysterious, and mystical face of Greek "serenity," an equivocal art barely detached from madness and "orgiastic" (one of the Schlegels' pet words) fury. In sum, tragic Greece. Like Hölderlin during the same period— but differently, although Schelling ensures the transition, and in a "dialecticizing" mode that will follow a well-known course from Hegel to the young Nietzsche—the Schlegels invent what becomes known (under various names) as the opposition of the Apollonian and the Dionysian. And what they also establish, because they have arrived (however unwittingly) at the "matrix" that produces it, is indeed—as Heidegger emphasizes—the philosophy of history. For the Schlegels, it is true, this philosophy will be less rigorous (less dialectical) than it is in Idealism properly speaking. Although simpler in many ways and closer to the "Rousseauistic" model (loss of the origin, necessary mediation by rationality, future reconciliation of a divided humanity), it is nonetheless complicated by a certain attention to (and taste for) the phenomena of decadence (Alexandrianism) and by a great precision in the analysis of movements of dissolution and transition—mechanical, chemical, or organic—from one period to another. Rome, for example, will be an important model. And the aim of all this, a distinctive trait of what we will thus call romanticism, is nothing other than the *classical*—the chances for and possibility of the classical in modernity.

This critical recasting is coupled with a constructive theme: the constant horizon of the project is to make (or remake, in the modern mode) the great classical work that the period lacks, despite Goethe. More particularly, and because the philosophy of history will emerge precisely from a critical problematic of *imitation* (throughout the last years of the century), it involves doing better or more than Antiquity: at once surpassing and fulfilling the unfinished or incomplete aspects of Antiquity, wherever it failed to effectuate the classical ideal it envisaged. This amounts, in the end, to performing the "synthesis" of the Ancient and the Modern—or, if you like, to anticipate the Hegelian word (although not the concept), to sublate, *aufheben*, the opposition of the Ancient and the Modern.[17] But that such a logic impels the romantic project in no way suggests that the romantics limit themselves to the "application" of a scheme derived from post-Kantian philosophy. It is rather in conjunction with the first stages of Idealism (both within and outside Idealism) and in its own realm (philology, criticism, art history) that romanticism assumes an analogous task, the task of a completion, in the strongest sense of the word. The goal is to have done with partition and division, with the separation constitutive of history: the goal is to construct, to produce, to effectuate what even at the origin of history was already thought of as a lost and forever inaccessible "Golden Age." And so, if dialectics is invented in romanticism's philosophy of art just as much as in speculative physics, it is perhaps because the attempts to reconcile Kant and Plato turns out to be difficult to distinguish from the enterprise that would conjugate Homer and Goethe.

This is the reason romanticism implies something entirely new, the *production* of something entirely new. The romantics never really succeed in naming this something: they speak of poetry, of the work, of the novel, or . . . of romanticism. In the end, they decide to call it—all things considered—*literature*. This term, which was not their own invention, will be adopted by posterity (including their own, most immediate posterity) to designate a concept—a concept that may still be undefinable today, but which the romantics took great pains to delimit. They, in any case, will approach it explicitly as a new *genre*, beyond the divisions of classical (or modern) poetics and capable of resolving the inherent ("generic") divisions of the written thing. Beyond divisions and all de-finition, this *genre* is thus programmed in romanticism as *the* genre of *literature*: the genericity, so to speak, and the generativity of literature, grasping and producing themselves in an entirely new, infinitely new Work. The *absolute*, therefore, of literature. But also its *ab-solute*, its isolation in its perfect closure upon itself (upon its own organicity), as in the well-known image of the hedgehog in *Athenaeum* fragment 206.

At the same time, however, the stakes turn out to be even larger. The absolute of literature is not so much poetry (whose modern concept is also invented in *Athenaeum* fragment 116) as it is *poiesy*, according to an etymological appeal that the romantics do not fail to make. Poiesy or, in other words, production. The thought of the "literary genre" is thus less concerned with the production of the literary thing than with *production*, absolutely speaking. Romantic poetry sets out to penetrate the essence of poiesy, in which the literary thing produces the truth of production in itself, and thus, as will be evident in all that follows, the truth of the production *of itself*, of autopoiesy. And if it is true (as Hegel will soon demonstrate, *entirely against* romanticism) that auto-production constitutes the ultimate instance and closure of the speculative absolute, then romantic thought involves not only the absolute of literature, but literature as the absolute. Romanticism is the inauguration of the *literary absolute*.

This is not, once again, the romanticism one ordinarily hears about. Madame de Staël foresaw it, in her own manner. Despite her somewhat curt (and very "French") resistance to theory, she had at least understood that what was new, in the Germany of 1800, was not "literature" but criticism or, as she also puts it, "literary theory."[18] A "romantic literature" existed, of course—she was the last to ignore it—just as a "romantic sensibility" existed, which had already spread across virtually all of Europe. There were even writers and poets around the Athenaeum (or in the Athenaeum itself), and the Schlegels, for example, clearly recognized Tieck's or Jean Paul's novels, Wackenroder's tales, and Sophie Mereau's poetry as modern (or romantic) works that they could discuss on the same level as Diderot or the English novel. But they also knew that this was not yet "it." This was the fantastic or the sentimental, but not fantasy or reflection. These were works capable of "playing with themselves," but not works that comprised their own theory. Goethe was not far from incarnating the great ideal (as Dante, Shakespeare, and Cervantes—the "trinity" of the Athenaeum—did historically), but his lack of philosophy was a little too much. He was not yet, not altogether, equal to the period. In short, there were only indications of what they were awaiting as romanticism or what they were attempting to forge as romanticism.[19] Hence, their critical position toward both Weimar and Berlin, toward both the classicist ideal and fantastic literature. Jena wanted to be their *sublation* [*relève*].

What this amounts to saying—and this is what Madame de Staël fails to understand (condemning the French university and everything it affects, practically until today, to ignorance on this subject)—is that romanticism is neither mere "literature" (they invent the concept) nor simply a "theory of literature" (ancient and modern). Rather, it is *theory itself as literature* or, in other words, literature producing itself as it produces its own theory. The literary absolute is also, and perhaps above all, this absolute *literary operation*.

In the end, Jena will be remembered as the place where it was claimed that the theory of the novel must itself be a novel. This demand, with which our "modernity" is still grappling, is expressed, a year before the journal is founded, in *Critical Fragment* 115, and it furnishes the entire program of the Athenaeum: "The whole history of modern poetry is a running commentary on the following brief philosophical text: all art should become science, and all science art; poetry and philosophy should be made one."

If only for this reason, it seemed to us necessary (in other words *still* urgent) to undertake a properly philosophical study of romanticism. This undertaking results neither from a vaguely fashionable taste for theoretical technicality, nor from any sort of predetermined "professional angle" on the question. As should be evident by now, it results from a necessity inherent in the thing itself. Which is to say, inherent in literature itself. For it was not just yesterday, nor even in Jena—although it was indeed Jena that taught us to think it—that literature's destiny was tied to that "brief philosophical text" in which, since Plato and Aristotle at least, the union of poetry and philosophy is postulated and called for. Madame de Staël, to refer to her one last time (although in this respect she is admittedly a paragon of critical unintelligence), raised the question, having become perplexed by the Schlegels' work, whether Homer, Dante, or Shakespeare "needed this metaphysics in order to be great writers." She resorted to this feeble question (for Homer is one thing, remaining as much a mystery for the Schlegels as for every one else, but the other two . . .) in order to justify her tempered enthusiasm with regard to "philosophical systems applied to literature."[20] In many ways, and in spite of everything, the same feeble question still confronts us. As proof of this, one might ask: how many people, even among the best intentioned, are repeating Jena today—because they have not been able to read it?

But the decision to take a philosophical approach to these texts (a more precise justification will be given in the "Overture") in no way indicates that we have become concerned with the "philosophy of the romantics." It exists, quite clearly, and is in fact, broadly speaking, better known in France than "literary theory." It has been necessary, obviously, for us to suppose that it lies behind each of our attempts at analysis. But the object of our study is exclusively the *question of literature*, and, as a reading of the entirety of the fragments will reveal, this focus has obliged us to abandon or eliminate a variety of other motifs (concerning science and politics especially, but also aesthetics—music in particular).

This accounts for our choice of texts and for our plan.

As for the texts—with the exception of the "Earliest System-Programme of German Idealism," which seemed to impose itself as an introductory text that would circumscribe the "anticipatory force" ["*avant-coup*"] of the question of literature—our decision to concentrate on the central theoretical texts of the

Athenaeum years imposed itself. This is why the limit-dates of the *Athenaeum* (1797–1798 to 1800) are hardly exceeded, except by what most closely pertains to them. Actually, we have based our choice on Friedrich's own itinerary, which we follow from his first attempts at the fragment (the *Critical Fragments* of the *Lyceum*) to his clarification of the very concept of "criticism" ("On the Essence of Criticism"), or in other words, from 1797 to 1804.

Our study will therefore be concerned with twelve texts, one of which is admittedly quite short (Friedrich's sonnet, "Athenaeum," which appeared, with two or three others, in the last issue of the journal). Five of these texts are drawn from the *Athenaeum* itself: the *Athenaeum Fragments*, of course, but also *Ideas*, *On Philosophy* (better known as the "Letter to Dorothea"), the famous *Dialogue on Poetry* and, finally, the sonnet just mentioned. With the exception of the latter, these are in fact the most important texts to appear in the journal,[21] and it is no accident that all of them, partially or not, are by Friedrich Schlegel. Partially or not because the *Athenaeum Fragments*—this extreme limit of romantic writing, which Friedrich valued particularly—are a collective and anonymous ensemble, jointly authored by the two Schlegel brothers, their wives, Novalis, and Schleiermacher. Although they undeniably bear Friedrich's mark, they are to such an extent the work of the entire group that, for historical criticism, one hundred or so of the fragments remain inextricably bound up in problems of attribution.

In addition to the five texts drawn from the *Athenaeum*—and aside from the 1795 "*Systemprogram*," which is also of complex, anonymous authorship—we will rely on the two other above-mentioned texts by Friedrich Schlegel (the *Critical Fragments* and "On the Essence of Criticism"), one text by August (his 1801 lecture), two (or three) texts by Schelling (*Heinz Widerporst's Epicurean Confession of Faith*, a satiric and speculative poem; the introduction to his 1802 lectures; and, if one attributes it to him, the "*Systemprogram*"), and, finally, one text by Novalis (the first two of five *Dialogues* that he wrote for the *Athenaeum* but that the journal never published).

Our plan, on the other hand, is quite simple. As far as possible, we have attempted to reconstitute the internal evolution of romanticism and to retrace romanticism's "years of apprenticeship" (which by no means makes our study a "novel"). This is why a certain rational progression [*progression raisonée*] is intended to coincide, with the exception of a few minimal discrepancies, with the chronology of the Athenaeum.

Thus, having set out from the question of the fragment as a genre (or as "genre"), or in other words, from the moment the question of literature is first raised ("The Fragment: The Fragmentary Exigency"), we took the speculative "step" necessarily raised by the question itself ("The Idea: Religion within the Limits of Art"), before approaching this question for itself and in itself ("The

Poem: A Nameless Art"), thereby attaining the properly romantic moment of reflection or of "literature raised to the second power" ("Criticism: The Formation of Character").

III

One is nonetheless quite correct in suspecting that our reasons for undertaking and presenting this work are not "archaeological" in nature—or even historical, as we have said—but are precisely related to our situation and interests today.

Not that our goal is to establish the "contemporary relevance of romanticism." The usual results of this sort of program are well known: a suppression pure and simple of history, the dubious immortalization of what is supposedly given "contemporary relevance," the (far from innocent) occultation of the specific characteristics of the present. Very much to the contrary, what interests us in romanticism is that we still belong to the era it opened up. The present period continues to deny precisely this belonging, which defines us (despite the inevitable divergence introduced by repetition). A veritable romantic *unconscious* is discernable today, in most of the central motifs of our "modernity." Not the least result of romanticism's indefinable character is the way it has allowed this so-called modernity to use romanticism as a foil, without ever recognizing— or in order not to recognize—that it has done little more than rehash romanticism's discoveries. To suspect a trap in the imprecision of the Schlegels, and to comprehend that the trap had worked perfectly, required all the lucidity of a Benjamin.

This trap still works, in fact, whenever our period decides to verify the "contemporary relevance of romanticism." Thus (according to the latest fashion), one finds the motif of "romanticism" in fundamental revolt against Reason and the State, against the totalitarianism of Cogito and System. A romanticism of libertarian and literary rebellion, literary because libertarian, whose art would incarnate insurrection. This motif is not simply false, of course. But it would not be far from it, were one to overlook its reverse (or obverse . . .) side. For the literary Absolute aggravates and radicalizes the thinking of totality and the Subject. It *infinitizes* this thinking, and therein, precisely, rests its ambiguity. Not that romanticism itself did not begin to perturb this Absolute, or proceed, despite itself, to undermine its Work [*Oeuvre*]. But it is important to carefully distinguish the signs of this small and complex fissuring and consequently to know how to read these signs in the first place—as signs of a romantic, not romanesque, reading of romanticism.

Today, in fact, romanticism is known only through—or deliberately limited to—what was indirectly transmitted by either the English tradition (from Coleridge, who read them closely, to Joyce, who knew everything and always more than one suspects), by Schopenhauer or Nietzsche (who did not discuss what they derived from it), or—but here the path is even more indirect and for good reason—by Hegel and Mallarmé (or even by what, in France, takes on the specifically romantic name of "Symbolism"). But in almost every case, when the essential is not deliberately obscured or distorted, it still goes unperceived. If it nonetheless appears, it is repeated without comprehension and with no awareness of what is at stake.

This essential, however, is of great concern to us. It is precisely what determines the age we live in as the *critical* age *par excellence* or, in other words, as the "age" (almost two hundred years old, after all) in which literature—or whatever one wishes to call it—devotes itself exclusively to the search for its own identity, taking with it all or part of philosophy and several sciences (curiously referred to as the *humanities*) and charting the space of what we now refer to, using a word of which the romantics were particularly fond, as "theory."

Thus it is not difficult to arrive at the derivatives of these romantic texts, which still delimit our horizon. From the idea of a possible formalization of literature (or of cultural productions in general) to the use of linguistic models (and a model based on the principle of the auto-structuration of language); from an analytic approach to works based on the hypothesis of auto-engendering to the aggravation of the problematic of a subject permanently rejecting subjectivism (that of inspiration, for example, or the ineffable, or the function of the author, etc.); from this problematic of the (speaking or writing) subject to a general theory of the historical or social subject; from a belief that the work's conditions of production or fabrication are inscribed within it to the thesis of a dissolution of all processes of production in the abyss of the subject. In short, we ourselves are implicated in all that determines both literature as auto-critique and criticism as literature. Our own image comes back to us from the mirror of the literary absolute. And the massive truth flung back at us is that we have not left the era of the Subject.

It goes without saying that this observation is not made for the pleasure of recognizing ourselves in romanticism, but on the contrary in order to gauge what in fact functions as a genuine denegation and also to guard against a fascination and a temptation. For insofar as we are, we are all preoccupied with fragmentation, the absolute novel, anonymity, collective practice, the journal, and the manifesto; as a necessary corollary, we are all threatened by indisputable authorities, petty dictatorships, and the simplistic and brutal discussions that are capable of interrupting questioning for decades; we are all, still and always, aware of the *Crisis*, convinced that "interventions" are necessary and that the least of texts is immediately "effective" ["*opératoire*"]; we all think, as if it went without saying, that politics passes through the literary (or the theoretical). Romanticism is our *naiveté*.

This does not mean that romanticism is our error. But rather that we have to become aware of the necessity of this repetitive compulsion. That is why this book involves an exigency, but one we do not wish to speak of as "criticism," for good reason. At the most we might call it "vigilance." We know very well that one cannot simply dismiss romanticism (one cannot dismiss a naiveté). All the same, for this is not a superhuman task, one can exhibit a minimum of lucidity. These days, this would already be a great deal.

Chronology

The few dates in the history of philosophy and literature provided here are intended only to enable the reader to "situate" the brief romanticism of Jena.

Pre-1790:

1755   Winckelmann, *Gedanken über die Nachahmung der griechischen Werke in der Malerei und Bildhauerkunst* [*Thoughts on the Imitation of Greek Works in Painting and Sculpture*].

1759–65   Lessing, *Literaturbriefe* [*Letters on Literature*].

1766   Lessing, *Laokoon*.

1767–68   Lessing, *Hamburgische Dramaturgie*.

1772   Hemsterhuis, first writings, in French (first translated into German in 1782); Herder, *Über den Ursprung der Sprache* [*On the Origin of Language*].

1774   Goethe, *Die Leiden des jungen Werthers* [*The Sorrows of Young Werther*].

1780   Lessing, *Die Erziehung des Menschengeschlechts* [*The Education of the Human Race*].

1781   Kant, *Kritik der reinen Vernunft* [*Critique of Pure Reason*]; Schiller, *Die Räuber* [*The Robbers*]; Voss, translation of *The Odyssey* (and *The Iliad* in 1793).

1782   Posthumous publication of the first part of Rousseau's *Confessions* (the rest is published in 1789).

1784   Herder, *Ideen zur Philosophie der Geschichte der Menschheit* [*Ideas on the Philosophy of the History of Mankind*] (beginning).

1788   Moritz, *Über die bildende Nachahmung des Schönen* [*On the Plastic Imitation of the Beautiful*].

19

1790   Kant, *Kritik der Urteilskraft* [*Critique of Judgement*]; Goethe, *Versuch, die Metamorphose der Pflanzen zu erklären* [*Essay in Explanation of the Metamorphosis of Plants*].

1790–1798:

1791   Moritz, *Götterlehre oder Mythologische Dichtungen der Alten* [*Mythological Poetry of the Ancients*].

1792   Schiller, *Über den Grund des Vergnügens an tragischen Gegenstand* [*On the Ground of Pleasure in the Tragic Object*].

1793   Adelung begins the *Versuch eines vollständigen grammatisch-kritischen Wörterbuchs der hochdeutschen Mundart* [*Attempt at a Complete Grammatical and Critical Dictionary of High German*]; Kant, *Die Religion innerhalb der Grenzen der blossen Vernunft* [*Religion within the Limits of Reason Alone*].

1794   Fichte, *Über den Begriff der Wissenschaftslehre* [*On the Concept of the Science of Knowledge*] (first version).

1795   Goethe and Schiller found the journal *Die Hören*; Jean Paul, *Hesperus*; Schelling, *Vom Ich als Prinzip der Philosophie, oder über das Unbedingte im menschlichen Wissen* [*On the I as Principle of Philosophy, or on the Absolute in Human Knowledge*]; Schiller, *Über die ästhetische Erziehung des Menschen in einer Reihe von Briefe* [*Letters on Aesthetic Education*], *Über naive und sentimentalische Dichtung* [*On Naive and Sentimental Poetry*]; Tieck, *Geschichte des Herrn William Lovell*; Chamfort, *Pensées, Maximes, et Anecdotes* (published posthumously); August W. Schlegel, *Briefe über Poesie, Sylbenmass und Sprache* [*Letters on Poetry, Meter, and Language*; Friedrich Schlegel, *Vom Wert des Studiums der Griechen und Römer* [*On the Value of the Study of the Greeks and Romans*] (unpublished text).

1796   Wackenroder (and Tieck), *Herzensergiessungen eines kunstliebenden Klosterbruders* [*Effusions of a Monk Friendly to the Arts*]; Diderot, *Jacques le fataliste*; Goethe, *Wilhelm Meister* (first part).

1797   Schelling, *Ideen zur Philosophie der Natur* [*Ideas on the Philosophy of Nature*]; Tieck, *Der blonde Eckbert*; Hölderlin, *Hyperion I*; Friedrich Schlegel, *Kritische Fragmente* [*Critical Fragments*] (in the journal *Lyceum*).

1798–1800:

1798 Baader, *Über das pythagoräische Quadrat in der Natur, oder die vier Weltgegenden* [*On the Pythagorean Square in Nature*]; Ritter, *Über Galvanismus* [*On Galvanism*].

1799 Goethe, *Die Propyläen*; Herder, *Verstand und Erfahrung. Eine Metakritik zur Kritik der reinen Vernunft* [*Understanding and Experience. A Metacritique on the Critique of Pure Reason*]; Wackenroder, *Phantasien über die Kunst, für Freunde der Kunst* [*Fantasies on Art, for Friends of the Arts*]; Hölderlin, *Hyperion* II; Schleiermacher, *Reden über die Religion an die Gebildeten unter ihren Verächtern* [*On Religion: Speeches to Its Cultured Despisers*]; Novalis, *Die Christenheit, oder Europa*; Friedrich Schlegel, *Lucinde*.

1800 *Jean Paul, Titan* (completed in 1803); Schelling, *System des transzendentalen Idealismus* [*System of Transcendental Idealism*].

1800–1810:

1801 Schelling, *Darstellung meines Systems im Ganzen* [*The Exposition of My System as a Whole*] and course on the philosophy of art; August W. Schlegel lectures on art and literature.

1802 Hegel and Schelling found the *Kritische Journal der Philosophie*; Novalis, *Heinrich von Ofterdingen*; Friedrich Schlegel, *Alarcos*.

1803 Friedrich Schlegel founds the journal *Europa* (which lasts until 1805).

1804 Jean Paul, *Vorschule der Aesthetik* [*Introduction to Aesthetics*]; Hölderlin, translations of Sophocles' *Antigone* and *Oedipus Rex*, with remarks on these tragedies.

1805 Arnim and Brentano, first volume of *Des Knaben Wunderhorn* [*The Boy's Enchanted Horn.*]

1807 Hegel, *Phänomenologie des Geistes* [*Phenomenology of Spirit*].

1808 Kleist, *Penthesilea*. Friedrich Schlegel, *Über die Sprache und Weisheit der Indier* [*On the language and Wisdom of India*]. Friedrich converts to Catholicism.

1809 Goethe, *Die Wahlverwandtschaften* [*Elective Affinities*].

Summary of the Athenaeum

The following complete summaries of the contents of each issue of the journal will inform the reader of the context of various texts mentioned or treated in this study. Where no author is given, the name of the author does not appear in the original. Those articles or reviews that lack titles have been indicated by a brief description, which is enclosed in brackets.

1798

Volume 1 (1):

Notice (A. W. and F. Schlegel)

Languages: A Dialogue on Klopstock's Grammatical Dialogues (A. W. Schlegel)
Grains of Pollen (Novalis)
Elegies translated from Greek (A. W. and F. Schlegel)
Contributions to the Most Recent Criticism of Literature (A. W. Schlegel)

Volume 1 (2):

Fragments

On Goethe's Wilhelm Meister (F. Schlegel)

1799

Volume 2 (1):

On Philosophy. To Dorothea (F. Schlegel)
The Paintings. A Dialogue (A. W. Schlegel with Caroline Schlegel)
On the Natural Equality of Man (A. L. Hülsen)

Volume 2 (2):

The Art of the Greeks. To Goethe. An Elegy. (A. W. Schlegel)
On Drawings Based on Poems, and on the Silhouettes of John Flaxmann (A.W. Schlegel)
The Eleventh Song of "Orlando Furioso" (A. W. Schlegel)
Postscript of the Translator to Ludwig Tieck (A. W. Schlegel)
Notes (A. W. Schlegel)
[*Discourses on Religion*] (F. Schlegel, review)
Anthropology by Emmanuel Kant (F. Schleiermacher, review)
[On the ancient songs of the bards] (A. W. Schlegel)
[Lichtenberg]
[Femininity in Art]
[Godwin's biography of Mary Wollstonecraft]
[Johannes Müller's letters] (Caroline Schlegel)
[Anton Wall] (A. W. Schlegel)
[La Fontaine's "Romulus"], [On the playwright Schink], [Thümmel's journeys in southern France], [Kotzebue's "Hatred of Men and Repentance"] (K. G. Brinckmann)
[Mme. de Genlis' "Reckless Vows"] (Dorothea Schlegel)
[Tieck's translation of *Don Quixote*] (F. Schlegel)
[Cervantes]
The Literary Indicator of the Empire, or Archives of the Epoch and its Taste (A. W. Schlegel, series of critical notes)

1800

Volume 3 (1):

To Heliodora (F. Schlegel)
Ideas (F. Schlegel)
Considerations of Nature during a Voyage in Switzerland (A. L. Hülsen)
Dialogue on Poetry I (F. Schlegel)

Notes:
The Last Writings Published by Garve (F. Schleiermacher, review)
[On Matthisson, Voss, and Schmidt] (A. W. Schlegel, review)
List of Reviews published by A. W. Schlegel in the Universal Journal of Literature

Volume 3 (2):

To the Germans (F. Schlegel)
Dialogue on Poetry II (F. Schlegel)

Hymns to the Night (Novalis)
Conception of Life (Sophie Bernhardi)
Idylls translated from Greek (A. W. and F. Schlegel)

Sonnets:
To Ludwig Tieck (A. W. Schlegel)
Discourses on Religion — The Soul of the World of Schelling.
The Athenaeum — Zerbino (F. Schlegel).

Notes:
The Moral Stories of Ramdohr (Dorothea Schlegel)
[Philosophers for the World, by Engel] (F. Schleiermacher, review)
[The "War of the Gods," by Parny] (A. W. Schlegel, review)
Understanding and Experience. A Metacritique of the Critique of Pure Reason, by J. G.
    Herder (A. F. Bernhardi, review)
[The "Destination of Man," by Fichte] (F. Schleiermacher, review)
[The translation of Don Quixote by Soltau] (A. W. Schlegel, review)
[On the "journal of belles-letters"] (A. W. Schlegel)
On Incomprehensibility (F. Schlegel)

Overture:
The System-Subject

> Next to the complete presentation of critical
> Idealism, which always comes first, the fol-
> lowing seem to be the most important desider-
> ata of philosophy: a materialist logic, a poeti-
> cal poetics, a positive politics, a systematical
> ethics, and a practical history.
>
> —*Athenaeum fragment 28.*

Given our principles, it should come as no surprise that under the guise of an overture we have chosen to analyze a text that does not belong, strictly speaking, to the romantic *corpus* itself—if only because of its status, which at least seems to be altogether philosophical.

But would it have been possible to avoid inscribing romanticism under the sign of paradox one way or another?

The "Earliest System-Programme of German Idealism"—since this is the title it has been given—is an enigmatic text.[1] These brief and incomplete pages have given rise to an abundant literature since their discovery by Rosenzweig in 1917, among a bundle of Hegel's papers.[2]

The fact is, no one knows who wrote it.

According to the most probable hypothesis, the manuscript, which is in Hegel's handwriting, is a copy of a text composed earlier (in March or in the summer of 1796) by Schelling (whose style at least the critics agree to recognize). But Schelling seems to have composed it, at least partly, under the direct influence of Hölderlin, whom he had met in Stuttgart in 1795 in the absence of Hegel.

This is not then a text "without an author" or with a "collective author," oscillating between anonymity and "symphilosophy" in accordance with one of the distinctive traits of romantic writing. None of its three putative authors can be characterized, rigorously speaking, as romantic. Not even Schelling who, despite his intimate relations with the Jena group, never ended up writing for the *Athenaeum* and remains in many respects an "outsider" of romanticism *stricto sensu*.

Nonetheless, as we note elsewhere, it is Schelling who is called upon to complete or rather to attempt to complete the systematic aspects of this "System-Programme."[3] For neither Hölderlin (whose poetic gesture, as Heidegger justly points out, "remains entirely foreign to the metaphysics of German Idealism"— *Schelling* 190), nor Hegel (who will, in a certain way, overturn German idealism), nor even the Jena romantics (who will not attain the System, properly speaking) will try or manage to realize it. It is worth noting in advance that even Schelling, the only person besides Hegel with the necessary will and power, will not be able to follow this program through. Not because he was incapable of erecting a (or the) System, but because he will continually struggle, to the point of losing his capacity to write, with the composition of the great speculative poem, which was intended to be the completion of philosophy, and which was announced in the program of 1795–1796 as a "new mythology of reason."

In sum, the fact that this "System-Programme," within the strange framework of romanticism it proposes, comes to us in a fragmentary state is perhaps a symbol. A symbol of the incompletion that still constrains us, to which the will to completion, moreover, was deliberately dedicated. From this perspective, a better "exergue" cannot be imagined, if an exergue is understood, as Novalis put it, as "the musical theme of a book." An overture, then, in more than one sense.

Why start out from this text? Or, to make the question more precise: Why take a *philosophical* text as an overture?

As all that we have said suggests, this text is neither entirely nor simply philosophical. First, the mute presence of Hölderlin is in or "behind" it. We bear Heidegger's observation in mind when we say that Hölderlin did in fact participate in the genesis of German idealism (and thereby in a certain genesis of romanticism[4]). Yet it is nonetheless true that the poetic and dramatic task he claims as his own from this period on, his almost exclusive dialogue with the aesthetics of Schiller, and the emphasis this bias leads him to place on a "return to Kant" separate him from the properly philosophical (in other words speculative) efforts developing during this period. Even if these same factors separate him from what is already occurring in romanticism under the title of "literature." But secondly, supposing that Hölderlin's role is relatively restricted, the conjunction of Hegel *and* Schelling at the origin of this text is still far from constituting a philosophical unity. This is the least one might say.

But despite all this, and regardless of its problematic character, it is imperative that this text be accounted for *philosophically*, that it be articulated with the philosophical itself, for in its fundamental provenance and consequences, it is philosophical through and through. This is precisely why it has seemed not only desirable but also inevitable to invoke this text as an overture to our discussion: although it is not entirely or simply philosophical, romanticism is rigorously comprehensible (or even accessible) only on a philosophical basis, in its proper and in fact unique (in other words, entirely new) articulation with the philosophical. Neither a simple "literary movement" nor—still less—the appearance of some "new sensibility," nor even the recasting (in any sense) of the classical problems of the theory of art or aesthetics, romanticism cannot be approached with a model of seamless evolution or progress (which would amount to tracing its "genesis" to the schemes of the *Aufklärung* against which it arises) or with a model of organic maturation (which would already be romantic and would thus encourage a sort of auto-interpretation of romanticism). If romanticism as such is approachable, it is in a certain manner approachable only in the "in-between," by means of an extremely narrow passage, given the constraints imposed by the aforesaid "models," such as *eruption, event, sudden appearance* [*surgissement*], or *surrection* ("revolution," as it were) or, in brief, by means of everything that one speaks of in terms of something like *crisis*. If romanticism is approachable, in other words, it is approachable only by means of the "philosophical path," if it is true that crisis is fundamentally philosophical and that the crisis at stake here, as we will see, is opened by nothing other than Criticism itself.

It is still necessary to point out that the "System-Programme," if it is philosophical (and opens romanticism only on this account), introduces, within the philosophical, a distance from the philosophical, a distortion and a deviation, which inaugurates the genuinely *modern* position of the philosophical (which is still our own, in more ways than one). At the appropriate moment, we will examine this more closely.

Philosophy, then, controls romanticism.

In this context, and crudely translated, this means that Kant opens up the possibility of romanticism. Or further, since it is certainly worthwhile to insist: however accurate historico-empirical geneses of the origins of romanticism may be (and they sometimes are, in which case one must take them into account), one cannot pass from Diderot to Schlegel, or even from Herder to Schlegel, or derive the first texts of the *Athenaeum* by way of *Sturm und Drang* or, more indirectly, through Lessing, by way of Wieland or the successors of Baumgarten. The romantics have no predecessors. Especially not in what the eighteenth century insistently held up under the name of *aesthetics*. On the contrary, it is because an entirely new and unforeseeable relation between aesthetics and philosophy will be articulated in Kant that a "passage" to romanticism will become possible. Yet this relation, in Kant, cannot be reduced to anything like a simple "putting into relation." In reality, an abyss opens up where a bridge should have been built and, if some connections are woven—between art and philosophy, for example—they also appear in the paradoxical figure of disconnection [*déliaison*] or, as Heidegger would say, of absolution. This explains, then, why the "passage" that leads to romanticism allows *nothing* to pass through, except the distance that separates the *Observations on the Feeling of the Beautiful and Sublime* (the obligatory professorial contribution to the questions of aesthetics henceforth inscribed in university programs) from the third *Critique* (which, because it is an "aesthetic" presentation of the *problem* of reason, bequeaths the question of art as the question *of* philosophy), along with the crisis concerning the possibility of the philosophical in general that transcendental Aesthetics initiates.

What does the transcendental Aesthetic represent? Not the traditional division of the sensible and the intelligible but rather the division between *two* forms (*a priori*) within the "sensible" or intuitive itself. The first and most fundamental result is that there is no *intuitus originarius*. Whether it was situated as *arche* or as *telos*, within the divine or within the human (as either pure intellectual self-consciousness in Descartes or pure empirical sensibility in Hume), what had heretofore ensured the philosophical itself disappears. As a result, all that remains of the subject is the "I" as an "empty form" (a pure logical necessity, said Kant; a grammatical exigency, Nietzsche will say) that "accompanies my representations." This is so because the form of time, which is the "form of the internal sense," permits no *substantial* presentation. As is well known, the Kantian "cogito" is empty.

One must set out from this problematic of the subject unpresentable to itself and from this eradication of all substantialism in order to understand what romanticism will receive, not as a bequest but as its "own" most difficult and perhaps insoluble question. From the moment the subject is emptied of all substance, the pure form it assumes is reduced to nothing more than a *function* of unity or synthesis. Transcendental imagination, *Einbildungskraft*, is the function that must form (*bilden*) this unity, and that must form it as a *Bild*, as a representation or picture, in other words as a phenomenon, if by phenomenon one means that which is neither of the order of appearance (of the "mere phenomenon") nor of the order of manifestation, of *Erscheinung* in the strong sense, which can found an ontology of "that which is." What is formed or constructed by the transcendental imagination is thus an object that may be grasped within the limits of *a priori* intuition but is nothing that can be thought under the concept of *eidos* or *Idea*, an originary and genuine form of reason itself. (It is well known that the Idea in Kant will be relegated as an unproductive and unattainable regulatory principle to a secondary role with regard to

Knowledge [*savoir*].) What results from this is a cognition [*connaissance*] within the limits of possible *a priori* experience, but such a cognition is incapable of restoring anything like a subject. Except, of course, for those who are satisfied with a "subject of the cognition of appearances," whose progeny will extend, from positivism to pragmatism and from pragmatism to structuralism, to the last years of the present century.

This weakening of the subject is accompanied by an apparently compensatory "promotion" of the *moral subject* which, as we know, launches a variety of philosophical "careers." Without oversimplifying or hardening the contours of a question that merits extended analysis, we cannot fail to note that this "subject" of morality can only be defined negatively, as a subject that is not the subject of knowledge (this knowledge suppressed "to make room for belief"), as a subject without *mathesis*, even of itself. It is indeed posited as freedom, and freedom is the locus of "self-consciousness." But this does not imply that there is any cognition—or even consciousness—of freedom, for freedom in turn is posited only as *ratio essendi* of the moral law within us, which, because it is only a fact (a *factum rationis*, as Kant says), can provide only a *ratio cognoscendi* of freedom, which produces no cognition. This fact (the imperative, the universality of the law) is neither an intuition nor a concept. As a moral subject, in sum, the subject recovers none of its substance. Quite to the contrary, the question of its unity, and thus of its very "being-subject," is brought to a pitch of high tension.

Kant's "successors" are well aware of all this. Even at the time, a few scant years before the beginning of the *period* that concerns us here, when the third *Critique* seemed to sketch out a gesture by means of which this tension would be resolved.

The third *Critique* sketched it out in two manners.

On the one hand, a resolution was envisaged in the *reflection* of the synthetic function of the subject, in the reflection of judgment and transcendental imagination. *Reflection*, here, does not of course mean *speculation* (Kantian reflection is not a "mirror stage"; it produces no "jubilant" assumption of the subject, no self-awareness as awareness of substance) but connotes only a pure referral or reflecting back, obtained by a simple, optical pattern and presupposing, moreover, the mediation of an inert, dead body, of a blind tain. Insofar as reflection operates in the judgment of taste as the free play of the imagination (that is, as a function of synthesis in its *pure* state, producing no object whatsoever), it brings about the unity of the subject only insofar as the subject sees itself in the image (*Bild*) of something without either a concept or an end.

But on the other hand, the resolution was envisaged in the *Darstellung* (the presentation, the figuration, the staging—to point to a highly equivocal word) of the never substantial "substance" of the "subject" by means of the *Beautiful* (in art, nature, or culture). Or rather, because we have already intruded upon romanticism in characterizing these three instances as instances of the Beautiful, let us say that the resolution was envisaged in the *Darstellung* of the "subject" by means of the Beautiful in works of art (the formation of *Bilder* able to present liberty and morality analogically), by means of the "formative power" (*bildende Kraft*) of nature and life within nature (the formation of the organism), and finally by means of the *Bildung* of humanity (what we retain under the concepts of history and culture). It is necessary to emphasize the *Bilden*, here, in a more rigorously Kantian manner, in order to underline (1)the solely analogical character of *Darstellung* (analogy having become very distant from its traditional concept, as attested, for example, if one can even call it an example, by the role of the *sublime*, taken as the presentation of the unpresentable); (2)the strictly unknowable character of life, of the formative power, insofar as for us it has no *analogon*; and (3)the infinite character of the process of human *Bildung* (with which Kant, in the eighteenth century, departing radically from the *Aufklärung*, represents the first view of history that refers its telos to infinity).

Consequently, if this tension is resolved, it is a result of this double analogical and historical tension; or what amounts to the same thing, according to a (specifically Kantian) mode of "resolution" that corresponds to no logic of identity or identification and that is particularly inassimilable to either *Aufhebung* or *Auflösung*, to sublation or dissolution or solution. In other words, to use the vocabulary that will be claimed by speculative idealism, the Idea, insofar as it is the idea of the subject or, that is, its unpresentable form, remains for Kant a *regulatory idea*. Thus, in the absence of a subject whose self-presence is guaranteed by originary intuition and whose *mathesis* of this first evidence organizes the totality of knowledge and the world *more geometrico*, the system as such, although it is deeply desired by Kant (witness the notes collected in his *Opus posthumum*) is continually lacking precisely where it is in greatest demand. The hiatus introduced at the heart of the subject will vainly exacerbate the will to system [*la volonté du système*].[5]

Thus, the crisis inaugurated by the question of the subject will preoccupy Kant's successors, if indeed one can be "successor" to a crisis. And romanticism, among others, will "proceed" from it.

Romanticism *among others*, for romanticism is by no means alone in experiencing this crisis, or rather in taking this crisis as the occasion and possibility of its paradoxical birth. Again, this is why the text of the "Earliest System-Programme," given its origin in a unique and momentary constellation of "authors" and given the differentiated stamp with which it is marked, is especially well suited to indicate the direction romanticism will choose to take as it sets out, not from a "crossing of paths" (as they were fond of saying in Jena), but from the *trivium* of possibilities offered by the *aftermath of Kant*. This text, in other words, is especially well suited to showing how, from Königsberg to Jena *and* by way of Tübingen, a path was forged—not by speculative idealism or by the "poetry of poetry" (in the sense Heidegger gives this expression in reference to Hölderlin[6]), but between both, and often barely distinguishable from them—by romanticism; that is to say, by *literature*.[7]

As its quite appropriate title indicates, the text of the "Earliest System-Programme" is entirely oriented toward a sort of goal or guideline common to all post-Kantianism and thus to all that can be classified as *speculative idealism*, if one understands this denomination more or less rigorously as the project of reconquering the possibility of effective speculation, the possibility, in other words, of the auto-recognition of the Ideal as the subject's own form.

This general line, as one might suspect, corresponds to what must be called, giving equal weight to each term, *the will to System* [du Système]. And such a will to System is visible from the first paragraphs of the text forward. It is indicated by the ontological position reserved for the Idea in general (and even, as part of an invocation of a "natural primacy," for the idea of the subject as self-consciousness). It is indicated by the linking, or better, the adjoining [*l'ajointment*] of all the rubrics of *metaphysica specialis* (beginning with the idea of a knowledge of the world as ideal knowledge—"a greater physics"—in other words, the subject's self-presentation of the true form of the world[8]). It is indicated, finally, by its announcement in the future, by the announcement of the "programmatic" fact according to which the System is envisaged in the name and in the form of an exigency, a desire, or a will; the System is not there (does not exist). It is "to do" (the goal is "practical" as well), but only as the last thing to do, the last task and the last work of humanity.

This entire movement, then, sets out to be an overcoming—which is also to say, a reversal—of Kant. It clearly presupposes, first of all, a conversion of the Kantian subject (i.e., the moral subject) into the ideal of a subject absolutely free and thereby conscious of itself. In the shadow or in the wake of Fichte, the absolute Self as *Selbstbewusstsein* is affirmed. Such a conversion, however, presupposes in turn an extremely complicated maneuver, which takes place behind Kant's back, so to speak, and which consists in positing the absolute freedom of consciousness as a corollary or even as the possibility of the System. But this is not all. For in the second place, this systematic programming makes the world itself into a corollary of the subject. This gesture would be in complete conformity with Kant if only this subject, once again, were not the free subject itself, and consequently, if only the world were not posited here as *creation*, as the subject's work—or, in other words, as a world organized in terms of absolute freedom, and therefore of morality (by the simultaneous effect of a fulfillment and a perversion of Kantian teleology). This, in turn, is what gives the "greater physics" the status of a "creation," an easily recognized Cartesian motif, if indeed the Cartesian subject already knew the world from only the perspective of its at least possible Creator. Finally, once the idea of mankind itself is "premised"—which obviously means that man as such is premised—it goes without saying that an at least implicit answer is given to the question: *What is man?* As is well known, Kant said that philosophy is forever incapable of answering this question. But the very possibility of an answer here, which in any case can never exceed the circumscription of subjectivity in general, immediately implies the exigency of a sociality grounded in freedom. And consequently, as is almost always the case in this sort of "speculative Rousseauism," it implies the exigency of an overcoming of politics itself by a pure moral sociality or, more precisely, by a social ontology grounded in the subject insofar as it possesses the "intellectual world" in itself, in its ideality—in other words, insofar as it possesses all truth and, by the same token, all authority.[9]

All of this, in which the essential elements of the metaphysics of German idealism (politics aside) is sketched out, constitutes by right and in fact the impassable horizon of romanticism. What has not yet appeared, however, is what properly constitutes romanticism; that is, what most narrowly delimits romanticism *within* idealism but at the same time distinguishes it from both Hegel (who has not yet appeared) and Fichte, whose ontology of the absolute Self has nonetheless initiated the movement as its most proximate cause.

Where then does this difference come from? *Within* idealism, where—and how—does romanticism become itself? In short, does romanticism have real specificity—and if so, what is it?

The decisive character here appears in the proposition around which the entire second half of the "System-Programme" pivots and is organized: *"the philosophy of the Spirit is an aesthetic philosophy,"*(§4).

"The philosophy of the Spirit" clearly designates the philosophy (henceforth the System) of the Subject itself, in its ideality, or, in other words, in its absoluteness. Ultimately, it designates what could be called, with considerable precision, the *System-subject*. This, then, is precisely where romanticism articulates itself within speculative idealism.

But as is suggested by the entire logic of the final development of the "System-Programme," "Spirit" also refers to the concept of the organism. The "philosophy of Spirit" is indeed the System-subject, but it assumes this status only insofar as it is alive, as it is the *living System*—and as such, in keeping with the entire tradition of metaphysics, it is opposed to the philosophy of the letter alone (to dead philosophy) and to system as a simple "pigeon-holing" by tables and registers. Here again, we encounter what is undeniably a fundamental motif of speculative idealism. Everyone knows that in Hegel the Concept is life, life is the "life of the Spirit," the System is an organic totality, etc. From this angle, then, there appears to be little distance between romanticism and idealism. However, the life implied here is *beautiful*, and the organism which it animates or within which it occurs (it would be better to speak, as Schelling later does, of an *organon*[10]) is essentially the *work of art*. And this, of course, changes everything—or almost everything.

It changes everything, first, with regard to the "relation to Kant." For if, as the "System-Programme" announces in the name of "aesthetic philosophy" (of the System-subject converted into Speculative Aesthetics), "*truth and goodness only become sisters in beauty*," then what is at stake is the very unity sought for by Kant in the *Third Critique*. Moreover, as in Kant, this unity is primarily sought in art and not, as is the case with idealism properly speaking, in politics and the State (this proposition is simplistic but, in its broad outlines, is not false). Nevertheless, it is necessary to consider (and admit) that the Idea as such, that is, the idea of the Subject or the Subject in its ideality (the "first Idea" or the very principle of the System of Ideas), is still organized, through a kind of internal folding of ideality in general, in terms of beauty—the "Idea that unites the rest," as the familial metaphor suggests, in a profoundly organic unity. Beauty, as a result, is the very generality of the Idea. With all the conditions necessary to the functioning of speculative logic already present, one could say even more rigorously that beauty is the unifying Idea or the generality of the Idea, the ideality of the Idea, insofar as it *sublates* all the organic oppositions—beginning, as could easily be demonstrated, with the most fundamental of all, the opposition of System and freedom.

Second, this sublation, at any rate as it inscribes itself here, in filigree, takes place in, by, and as *Darstellung* itself. Although the word never appears and the formulation is highly elliptical, this is nevertheless affirmed with great clarity: "*the philosopher must possess just as much aesthetic power as the poet*." In other words, because the idea of beauty is the very ideality of the Idea, the speculative Aesthetics in which the System-subject culminates must necessarily reverse itself in aesthetic speculation; it must adopt a presentation or exposition which is itself aesthetic. Philosophy must fulfill itself in a work of art; art is the speculative *organon par excellence*.

That the idea of beauty should be the ideality of the Idea implies that the Idea itself be determined as the *beautiful Idea*. And if the being-idea in general is the presentation of the thing of which there is an idea—if the idea, in consequence, fundamentally remains the *eidos*—then the idea of the Idea, as the beautiful Idea, is the very "presentability" of presentation (as beautiful presentation). It is the *bildende Kraft* as *aesthetische Kraft*: formative power *is* aesthetic power. This explains why the aim of the Idea should be an *act* (which implies both power or will and the subject) and how the aim of the idea of beauty, the aesthetic act, can be called "*the highest act of Reason*." It is a question here of effectivity and of effectuation—of *Wirklichkeit* and *Verwirklichung*.

This is fundamentally why, programmatically, the philosophical *organon* is thought as the product or *effect* of a *poiesis*, as work (*Werk*) or as poetical *opus* (for such is the weight of a bimillenary poetic constraint). Philosophy must effectuate itself—complete, fulfill, and realize itself—as poetry.

Yet the problem of *Darstellung* is at no moment treated explicitly.

Indeed it is affirmed that "*poetry [Dichtkunst] alone will survive the other sciences and arts*," and consequently, that it will replace philosophy (as well as history). In spite of its clarity, this affirmation is immediately inflected toward ethics and pedagogy, or in other words, toward politics. Since, even when raised to the level of the speculative, the historico-systematic scheme and its implicit philosophy of history remain profoundly "Rousseauistic," poetry will in the end (of history) regain a "*higher dignity*" only to the extent that it once more become "*the teacher of mankind*." It is a question of *Bildung* again, but in the most general and least penetrating sense of the word, in which the concept brings together shaping and molding, art and culture, education and sociality, and ultimately history and figuration. As always, an obsessive concern with *efficacity* is concealed within the problem of effectuation. And the *organon* easily becomes *organization*.

From the speculative point of view, however, the question of politics is the question not only of the State but also of religion. In his enumeration of the conditions of possibility of the System (in the sense that speculative idealism gives it), Heidegger speaks of "the downfall of ecclesiastical faith's exclusive domination of the configuration of knowledge" (which in no way excludes the "sublation" of the "Christian experience of being in totality"). This downfall is simultaneously understood as a "deliverance of man to himself." In view of a certain Jacobin (or Girondin?) "radicalism," in view of the at any rate revolutionary call for "*universal freedom and equality of spirits*," it is indeed a downfall of this order that the "System-Programme" practically envisions. This is why the aestheticization of Ideas (poetry) provokes the announcement of a "*new mythology*," of a "mythology of *Reason*," that "must be in the service of Ideas." From this perspective, the speculative *organon* must sublate the opposition between monotheism and polytheism (Christianity and paganism) in a "*new religion*"—a new "light" brought by a new, heaven-sent spirit. But also, through the exchange of mythology and the philosophical, Ideas must once again become accessible to *the people*. Philosophy's *effectivity-efficacity* presupposes the mankind-subject, which is itself understood as a people (as a privileged locus of the mythological, which is itself conceived as the possibility of an exemplarity and a figurability, of a formative power, even of a determinate language), by means of which the Subject itself, in its own knowledge and self-certainty, self-consciousness itself, can come into being.

In sum, all this represents nothing other than the final repetition of Western eidetics in the element of subjectivity. From now on, in the axis of a certain Plato, or rather, of a certain Platonism, eidetics will always be able to shift into aesthetics. This eidaesthetics—if you will pardon our coining the concept— traces, within the landscape of idealism in general, the horizon proper to romanticism. The philosophical horizon of romanticism.

This horizon is what both Hegel and Hölderlin will seek to overcome, each in his own way—the one, to better fulfill idealism, and the other, undoubtedly, to reject its destiny. This is not to say, by mere difference, that the "System-Programme," which we cannot even describe as collective, would constitute *all* of romanticism. It is still absolutely necessary to indicate—or else this "over-ture" would immediately become a "closure"—that, if Schelling remains up to a certain point faithful (assembling all the possibilities of a *philosophical romanti-cism*), romanticism strictly speaking will follow yet another path. Its direction will be the same, but it will not conceive the work after the model of the philosophical work, of the speculative *organon*. Another model of the work will come into play, if indeed the ideas of the work and of the model remain intact in this adventure.

1 The Fragment:
The Fragmentary Exigency

There is so much poetry and yet there is nothing
more rare than a poem! This is due to the vast
quantity of poetical sketches, studies, fragments, tendencies, ruins, and raw materials.

—*Friedrich Schlegel*, Critical Fragment 4.

Romanticism, then, inaugurates another "model" of the "work." Or rather, to be more precise, it sets the work to work in a different mode. This does not
mean that romanticism is the "literary" moment, aspect, or register of "philosophical" idealism, or that the inverse would be correct. The difference in the
setting-to-work—or, as one could just as well say, the difference in *operation*—
between Schelling and the *Athenaeum*,[1] which must be examined in order to
circumscribe the specificity of romanticism, does not amount to the difference
between the philosophical and the literary. Rather, it makes this difference
possible. It is itself the internal difference that, in this moment of *crisis*, affects
the thought of the "work" in general (moral, political, or religious as well as
artistic or theoretical). Thus, in all of the Schlegels' fragments, one can, without
difficulty if not without surprise, find many propositions concerning all sorts of
domains or operations that are foreign to literature. And we will have many
occasions to observe that the "literary theory" of the romantics can be situated
with some accuracy only on condition that the *total* character of the enterprise be
grasped.

It nonetheless remains true, and this is our starting point, that an idea of the
literary or poetic work, setting aside for the moment its exact contents, indeed
orients and informs the enterprise, precisely with regard to its totality. This idea
orients and informs it first of all by means of the genre in which the Jena
romantics' best-known texts are written, the genre that has become almost
inevitably associated with their name: the *fragment*. To an even greater extent
than the "genre" of theoretical romanticism, the fragment is considered its

incarnation, the most distinctive mark of its originality, or the sign of its radical modernity. This, in fact, is precisely the claim made by Friedrich Schlegel and Novalis,[2] each in their own manner. Indeed, the fragment is the romantic genre *par excellence.*

Such a statement, however, is absolutely exact only on certain conditions, which must be specified before we turn to the genre for itself.

The first of these conditions consists in remembering that the genre of the fragment was not invented in Jena. Far from it. Friedrich Schlegel receives the revelation of the fragment, so to speak, from the first publication of Chamfort's *Pensées, Maximes et Anecdotes,* which was published posthumously in 1795.[3] Through Chamfort, the genre and the motif of the fragment refer to the entire "tradition" of English and French moralists (let us say, to retain only two symptomatic names, Shaftesbury and La Rochefoucauld), which in turn, *via* the publication, in complex conditions, of Pascal's *Pensées,* directs one back to the "genre" whose paradigm is established for all of modern history by Montaigne's *Essays.* We will need to return to the significance of this filiation, which we represent here in the broadest fashion. For the moment, however, let us observe that, along with the fragment, the romantics receive a heritage, the heritage of a genre that, at least externally, can be characterized by three traits: the relative incompletion (the "essay") or absence of discursive development (the "thought") of each of its pieces; the variety and mixture of objects that a single ensemble of pieces can treat; the unity of the ensemble, by contrast, constituted in a certain way outside the work, in the subject that is seen in it, or in the judgment that proffers its maxims in it. To underscore the importance of this heritage is not to belittle the originality of the romantics. On the contrary, one needs to understand it fully in order to grasp what the romantics had the originality to take to its conclusion: the very genre of originality, the genre, absolutely speaking, of the subject that cannot or can no longer conceive itself in the form of a *Discourse on Method*[4] and that has not yet truly undertaken its reflection as subject.

The second of these conditions consists in observing the established yet often neglected or ignored fact that the fragments written by members of the Jena group are far from constituting a homogeneous and undifferentiated ensemble, whose fragments would all be "fragments" in the same sense, as is erroneously suggested by common phrases such as, "one of Novalis's fragments says that . . . ." In fact, only a single ensemble, published with the one-word title *Fragments,* corresponds entirely (or as much as possible) to the fragmentary ideal of romanticism, notably in that it has no particular object and in that it is anonymously composed of pieces by several different authors. These two characteristics, in fact, distinguish the form of this ensemble from its earlier models. Without an objective and without an author, the *Fragments* of the *Athenaeum* strive to be absolutely self-posited. But they are alone in representing the "purity" of the genre, and, regardless of their total volume, their unique, paradoxically punctual status is not without importance in characterizing the genre. Friedrich Schlegel's earlier *Critical Fragments* are specified by their epithet and signature. Novalis had also published fragments in the *Athenaeum* before the publication of the *Fragments*, and his are indicated in a similar manner. More precisely, one can say that between their title (*Grains of Pollen*), their epigraph, and their "conclusion" (the last fragment[5]), they contain a theory of the fragment as seed which aims at an entirely new type of work. It is hardly necessary to mention the other ensemble of fragments (or aphorisms) authored by Novalis; its title, *Faith and Love*, suffices to distinguish it from its predecessors. The second ensemble published in the *Athenaeum* by Friedrich Schlegel, which also contains a theory of its form as part of its conclusion, clearly signals an even more decisive departure, by dint of its title alone, for the title *Ideas* announces something other than pure fragments. Thus, these differences, and especially this last one, must be examined more closely.[6]

We must also hasten to dispel another confusion. It has become customary to cite extracts of the romantics' many posthumous writings (particularly those of Friedrich Schlegel) and to refer to them as "fragments" (sometimes without even qualifying them as "posthumous"), making no attempt to specify whether it is a matter of unfinished drafts or of fragments intended for publication as such.[7] Thus a confusion is maintained, and sometimes exploited, between a piece that is struck by incompletion, let us say, and another that aims at fragmentation for its own sake. A propitious shadow is thus allowed to obscure what this genre essentially implies: the fragment as a determinate and deliberate statement, assuming or transfiguring the accidental and involuntary aspects of fragmentation.

One final condition must be added: The fragment is by no means the romantics' sole form of expression. On the whole, the *Athenaeum* itself included a greater number of continuous texts (essays, reviews, dialogues, and letters) than fragments, to say nothing of the texts published elsewhere by members of the group, or of the numerous lectures and talks the Schlegels delivered. The romantics, that is, in no way restricted themselves to the ostensibly "romantic" statement of theory—the fragment. They, or in any case, the Schlegels, expounded their theory in classical forms of exposition, and their posthumous writings (especially those of Novalis and Friedrich Schlegel) outline projects whose exposition was intended to be complete and entirely articulated. Thus, however different these projects may be from the classical philosophical treatise (from that of Fichte or from the Schelling of the *System of Transcendental Idealism*), they too aimed at the systematic presentation of their theory, its properly theoretical presentation. Although it will soon become necessary to complicate this affirmation, we must nonetheless simply remark that the fragment does not exclude systematic exposition. This is not to say that such exposition is mere surplus or the leftover of academic habits. The co-presence of the fragmentary and the systematic has a double and decisive significance: it implies that both the one and the other are established in Jena within the same horizon, and that this horizon is the very horizon of the System, whose exigency is inherited and revived by romanticism.

The precautions necessary to approach the fragment consist in positing it as a precise and determinate form or genre, concerned with the aim [propos] or general project of the System. But nowhere did any of the romantics propose a definition of the fragment that could, by itself, supply a content for this framework. From the practice of fragments, then, we must begin, in order to try to grasp the nature of the fragment and the stakes it involves.

First of all, we must begin with the use of the term *fragment*. In these texts, this term is almost never confused with the detached piece pure and simple,[8] with the residue of a broken ensemble (what the romantics refer to as a *Bruchstück*, piece, literally: broken piece), or even with the erratic block (like the "several good pieces," here *Massen*, that are redeemed in Jean Paul, in *Athenaeum* fragment 421[9]). If the fragment is indeed a fraction, it emphasizes neither first nor foremost the fracture that produces it. At the very least, it designates the borders of the fracture as an autonomous form as much as the formlessness or deformity of the tearing. But the fragment, a scholarly term, is also a noble term. First of all, it has a philological acceptation, and we will return to the crucial link between the ancient model and the fragmentary state of many of the texts of Antiquity. The philological fragment, especially in the tradition of Diderot, takes on the value of the *ruin*. Ruin and fragment conjoin the functions of the monument and of evocation; what is thereby both remembered as lost and presented in a sort of sketch (or blueprint) is always the living unity of a great individuality, author, or work.

Fragment is also a literary term: "Fragments,"[10] or what, in terms of form, amount to *essays* in the style of Montaigne, were already published in the eighteenth century and in Germany itself. The fragment designates a presentation that does not pretend to be exhaustive and that corresponds to the no doubt properly modern idea that the incomplete can, and even must, be published (or to the idea that what is published is never complete). In this manner the fragment is delimited by a two-fold difference: if it is not simply a pure piece, neither is it any of the genres-terms employed by the moralists: *pensée*, sentence, maxim, opinion, anecdote, remark. These terms are loosely united by their claim to completion in the very turning of the "piece." The fragment, on the contrary, involves an essential incompletion. This is why, in *Athenaeum* fragment 22, it is identical to the *project*, a "fragment of the future," insofar as the constitutive incompletion of the project is its most valuable quality, "the ability to idealize and realize objects immediately and simultaneously."[11] In this sense, every fragment is a project: the fragment-project does not operate as a program or prospectus but as the *immediate* projection of what it nonetheless incompletes.

This is to say that the fragment functions simultaneously as a remainder of individuality *and* as individuality, which also explains why it was never defined, or why attempts at its definition were contradictory. When Friedrich Schlegel notes that "aphorisms are coherent fragments,"[12] he indicates that one property of the fragment is its lack of unity and completion. But the well-known *Athenaeum* fragment 206 states that the fragment "has to be . . . complete in itself like a hedgehog." Its existential obligation [*devoir-être*], if not its existence (is it not understood that its only existence is an existential obligation and that this hedgehog is a Kantian animal?), is indeed formed by the integrity and the wholeness of the organic individual.

But fragment 206 must be read in its entirety: "*A fragment, like a small work of art, has to be entirely isolated from the surrounding world and be complete in itself like a hedgehog.*" Thus, the detachment or isolation of fragmentation is understood to correspond exactly to completion and totality. To borrow a term from a later tradition not unrelated to romanticism, that of Schopenhauer and Nietzsche, one is tempted to say that the essence of the fragment is individuation. As an indicator of a process rather than of a fixed state, this term is in agreement with the important *Athenaeum* fragment 116, where the "particular essence" of romantic poetry is "that it should forever be becoming and never be perfected." And in a certain manner, fragment 116 defines the totality of "romantic poetry," that is, the totality of poetry, as fragment. What we have read thus indicates that the fragment must have the characeristics of the work, and of the work of art.

Yet aside from the fact that a circular definition of the fragment as "progressive universal" poetry, and vice versa, serves only to intensify further the question of the fragment—and temporarily putting aside the fact that fragment 116's "romantic" poetry does not exhaust the romantics' idea or ideal of total, infinite poetry—neither is the fragment simply the work-project of this poetry. It is both more or less. It is more in that it posits the exigency of its total closure, basically in opposition to "progressive" poetry. But it is less in that, in fragment 206 and several others, it is posited only in comparison to the work of art—and to a *small* work of art. The fragmentary work is neither directly nor absolutely the Work. But its own individuality must be grasped, nonetheless, with respect to its relation to the work.

Fragmentary individuality is above all that of the multiplicity inherent to the genre. The romantics did not publish a unique *Fragment;* to write the fragment is to write fragments. But this plural is the specific mode in which the fragment aims at, indicates, and in a certain manner posits the singular of its totality. Up to a certain point, the formula employed by Friedrich Schlegel for the *Ideas* may be applied to all the Fragments: each one "indicates [*deuten*] the center" (*I* 155). Yet neither of the concepts used here belongs to the space of the Fragments themselves, for it is not exactly "indicating" a "center" that is in question in the Fragments. Fragmentary totality, in keeping with what should be called the logic of the hedgehog, cannot be situated in any single point: it is simultaneously in the whole and in each part. Each fragment stands for itself and for that from which it is detached. Totality is the fragment itself in its completed individuality. It is thus identically the plural totality of fragments, which does not make up a whole (in, say, a mathematical mode) but replicates the whole, the fragmentary itself, in each fragment. That the totality should be present as such in each part and that the whole should be not the sum but the co-presence of the parts as the co-presence, ultimately, of the whole with itself (because the whole *is* also the detachment and closure of the part) is the essential necessity [*nécessité d'essence*] that devolves from the individuality of the fragment: the detached whole is the individual, and "for every individual, there are an infinite number of real definitions" (*A* 82). Fragments are definitions of the fragment; this is what installs the totality of the fragment as a plurality and its completion as the incompletion of its infinity.

This might also require an analysis, to which we merely allude here, of the way the fragmentary "genre" may not in fact be limited, for the romantics, to the form of the fragment. *Athenaeum* fragment 77 suggests that dialogue, letters, and "Memorabilia" (another form of monument) belong to the fragmentary; we can see in the following chapters how the romantics' "continuous" texts, those just referred to in the context of "systematic" exposition, are in fact often presented, in their composition, along lines that are indeed fragmentary. This is undoubtedly due, in part, to a sort of ineptitude or incapacity to practice genuinely systematic exposition, in the most ordinary sense of the term. But above all, it bears witness to the fundamental impossibility of such an exposition, whenever an order of principles according to which the order of reasons unfolds is lacking. Such an order is lacking here, but rather by excess, so to speak, than by default. The exposition cannot unfold on the basis of a principle or foundation because the "foundation" that fragmentation presupposes consists precisely in the fragmentary totality in its *organicity*. The fragment thus constitutes the most "mimological"[13] writing of individual organicity. It is in this light that we will read *Critical Fragment* 103's praise, in opposition to "works of beautiful coherence," of a "motley heap of sudden ideas," whose profound, substantial unity rests on the "free and equal fellowship" of its parts. An ideal politics— and consequently, according to the most constant tradition of metaphysical

politics, an organic politics—furnishes the model of fragmentation. Analogous-
ly, if the Bible remains or once more becomes the model of the book, it does so,
as can be seen in several instances, notably in *Ideas* 95, as the plural book (*ta
biblia*), and *as such*, as One.

The principle of the collective writing of fragments, which was put into
practice at least once, obeys the same logic.[14] Anonymity effaces the authors
only in order, through what is referred to as "symphilosophy" or "sympoetry,"
to better assure the universality of the vision of the whole. But here again, it is
not a question of a universality achieved through addition, or simply through the
complementarity of individuals. Rather, it is a matter of the very *method* (our
use of Descartes' master word is intentional) suitable for access to the truth. The
community is part of the definition of philosophy, as is demonstrated by *Athenaeum* fragment 344, because its object, "universal omniscience" [*Allwissen-
heit*], itself possesses the form and nature of the community, in other words, its
organic character. As in Descartes, and because of Descartes, the object of
philosophy is determined here according to the subject, and the anonymity of the
Fragments, like that of the *Discourse*, serves to reinforce the absolute position of
their subject: in this sense, it is hardly an exaggeration to say that the *Fragments*
are simply the collectivization of the *Discourse*.

In another sense, the *Fragments* are a radicalization or exacerbation of the
Discourse. By reason of its subjective foundation (again, see *Athenaeum* fragment 77, which posits the fragmentary, the ideal fragmentary, as the identity of
the objective and subjective), the object—the thought that must think philosophy—must henceforth possess a "physiognomy" (*A* 302). Physiognomy is
what must above all be "characterized with a few strokes of the pen" (*A* 302);
physiognomy summons the sketch or fragment *as* philosophical method. And by
the same token, this philosophy of "mixed thoughts" (*A* 302) implies the plurality of authors. For truth cannot be attained by the solitary path of demonstration
(ridiculed in *Athenaeum* fragment 82), but rather by that of exchange, mixing,
friendship[15]—and love, as we will see. *Symphilosophy* implies the active exchange and confrontation of individuals-philosophers. And thus it implies the
dialogue, that "garland of fragments" (*A* 77), and undoubtedly that perfection
of dialogue which becomes the romantic ideal of drama, a hidden but insistent
motif that should be traced throughout the *Fragments* in order to extract their
particular ideal of natural exchange and its correspondingly *natural* staging.[16]
The completion of the fragment thus emerges in the absolute, absolutely natural
exchange—or change—of thoughts-individuals between individuals-thoughts,
which is also, within each fragment, the production of this same genuine naturalness as a work of art. The truth of the fragment is not, therefore, entirely in the
infinite "progressivity" of "romantic poetry," but in the actual infinity, by means
of the fragmentary apparatus, of the very process of truth. And if from this

perspective the fragment is not exactly the dialogue, this is perhaps because it is already more and because the fragment, in a characteristically romantic fashion, occasions the step from the dialogical to the *dialectical*. That is, if one understands this term, along with Heidegger, in the sense in which, for all of metaphysics, it covers the thinking of identity through the mediation of nonidentity.[17] For this is precisely what forms the basis of fragmentary totality.

It thus becomes necessary, in keeping with Heidegger's analyses, as well as with those of Benjamin,[18] to propose that fragmentation constitutes the properly romantic vision of the system, if by "System" (which we capitalize for this reason) one understands not the so-called systematic ordering of an ensemble, but that by which and as which an ensemble holds together [*tient-ensemble*] and establishes itself for itself in the autonomy of the self-jointure that makes its "systasis," to use Heidegger's term.

But let us make no mistake: we are not maintaining that romantic thought is systematic thought. In many respects, as can be verified in the texts, it posits itself in opposition to this type of thinking. Yet it is even easier to verify that it imposes itself as the thinking of the System, in keeping with a schema that was probably best formulated by Benjamin when he wrote of Friedrich Schlegel: "The absolute . . . in the period of the Athenaeum was in fact the system in the figure [*Gestalt*] of art. But he did not seek this absolute systematically: quite inversely, he sought to grasp the System 'absolutely'" [45].

And for this reason, because *the* System *itself* must be grasped absolutely, the fragment as organic individuality implies the work, the *organon*. "Systasis" necessarily takes place as the organicity of an organon, whether it be a natural creature (a hedgehog), society, or a work of art. Or rather, that it be *all these at once*, as is indicated by the absence of a specific object for the totality of the *Fragments*. Or more precisely yet, that being all these at once (and in keeping with the "at once" of fragmentation and of symphilosophy), it should still exist only as a work of art.

Not that the fragment as such incarnates the work. We have already seen that it is presented only as an analogon of the work, and we will have to return to this point. Nowhere in the texts will we find a theory of the work as fragment, purely and simply, although the signs or tokens of such a theory are everywhere. For the romantics, the work never ceases to imply the fundamental motif of completion. Indeed, they raise this motif to a peak of intensity. The genuine work, the absolute, harmonic, and universal work, is a "life of the Spirit" in which "all individuals live," according to the last of the *Fragments* (A 451), particularly as opposed to "works of isolated," and hence fragmented "poetry and philosophy," whose very completion remains incomplete. The work in this sense is absent from works—and fragmentation is *also* always the sign of this absence. But this sign is at least ambivalent, according to the constant logic of this type of thought, whose model is negative theology. The empty place that a garland of fragments surrounds is a precise drawing of the contours of the Work. It suffices to take one further step—which consists in thinking that the Work as work, as organon and individual, is given, precisely, in its form—to understand simultaneously that the Work is, beyond all "isolated" art, work of art, and that the "system of fragments" (*A 77*) is a precise drawing, using the traits of its fragmentary configuration, of the contours of the Work of art, which are no doubt external but nonetheless its own *contours*, its absolute Physiognomy.

In this manner, the fragment in itself, almost immediately, also sets forth the truth of the work. Beyond or before the work it proposes its very operativity. For the work is individual—every work is individual, every ensemble of works, like Antiquity, is individual, as many fragments attest. What is even more properly individual than the individual, or what determines its radical individuality, is the opening and manifestation of its most intimate life and truth (*Athenaeum* fragment 336, the longest of the fragments, is concerned with this motif). Works need this manifestation, which occurs, in what is both a paradoxical and henceforth foreseeable manner, by means of the fragment. Just as the fragment of Antiquity manifests the essential originality of the ancient work, the modern fragment "characterizes" this originality, and thereby sketches out the "project" of the future work whose individuality will dialectically reunite and sublate (art aside, we are very close to Hegel) the thinking, living, and working [*oeuvrant*] dialogue of ancient and modern fragments.

The relation of fragment to System, or better yet, the absolute fragmentary grasping of the System thus depends on the dialectic concerning the Work taking place within the fragment. The fragment itself is a Work in a certain manner, or is at least "like a small work of art," inasmuch as it is meant to seize upon and "sketch out" its own silhouette in everything—poem, period, science, morals, persons, philosophy—insofar as it has been formed (and has formed itself) into a work. (Hence the constant and crucial motif of *Bildung* throughout the fragments, in its two values of formation as putting-into-form and formation as culture. Man and work of art alike are what they are only insofar as they are *gebildet*, having taken on the form and figure of what they ought to be. The motif of the "education of the human race" is widened and transfigured in Jena, beyond Lessing, Herder, and Schiller, in the motif of the total putting-into-form of an absolutely essential and absolutely individual humanity, in which "every infinite individual is god," and in which "there are as many gods as there are ideas" [*A 406*]. This amounts to saying both that the completion of *Bildung* is the manifestation-in-form of the ideal—which is not the "unattainable" but the reality of the idea [see *A* 412]—or the ideal as work, and that the ideal, like the individual, is as numerous as the fragment—or that ideality is what determines fragmentary plurality.)

Undoubtedly, the fragment is thus a "small work" in that it is a miniature or microcosm of the Work. But also in that, functioning in some sense as the work of work, or as putting into-work of the work, it always operates both as a sub-work and as a super-work. The fragment figures—but to figure, *bilden* and *gestalten*, is here to work and to present, *darstellen*—the outside-the-work [*hors d'oeuvre*] that is essential to the work. It functions as the exergue in the two senses of the Greek verb *exergazōmai;* it is inscribed outside the work, and it completes it. The romantic fragment, far from bringing the dispersion or the shattering of the work into play, inscribes its plurality as the exergue of the total, infinite work.

This is no doubt also because the infinite is presented only through its exergue and because, if the *Darstellung* of the infinite after and despite Kant, constitutes the essential preoccupation of idealism, then romanticism, through literature in the fragment, forms the exergue of philosophical idealism. This is where the romantics, along with Hölderlin, occupy the position we have evoked in their name in the "Overture." Purely theoretical completion is impossible (as stated in *Athenaeum* fragment 451 and several others, notably those calling for the unification of philosophy and poetry) because the theoretical infinite remains asymptotic. The actual infinite is the infinity of the work of art. Yet unlike Hölderlin, and much closer to idealism, the romantics simultaneously postulate the motifs of a present, accomplished [*effectué*] infinite in a work that the logic of the fragment stubbornly summarizes within the contours of its ideal, and as a corollary to this, the potential infinite in itself *as* the actuality of the work. In fact, to return to *Athenaeum* fragment 116, it is in the very "progressivity" and infinity of its movement that "romantic poetry," since Antiquity and for all the future, forms the truth of all poetry. The actuality of romanticism, as is well known, is never *there* (especially during the period of those who do not call themselves romantics, even while writing fragment 116), and likewise, "there is as yet nothing that is fragmentary" (*A* 77). But it is indeed in this not being there, this never yet being there, that romanticism and the fragment *are*, absolutely. *Work in progress* henceforth becomes the infinite truth of the work.

In yet another way, to return to a term already referred to here, the *infinite poetry* of fragment 116, the "Spirit in becoming" of poetry in *Critical Fragment* 93, or "the poetry of infinite value" (*CF* 86) are essentially poetry insofar as their nature is *poietical*. The poetic is not so much the work as that which works, not so much the organon as that which organizes. This is where romanticism aims at the heart and inmost depths—that "most profound intimacy" scattered throughout the texts, which it would be a mistake to reduce to a sentimental interiority—of the individual and the System: always *poiesis* or, to give at least an equivalent, always *production*. What makes an individual, what makes an individual's holding-together, is the "systasis" that produces it. What makes its individuality is its capacity to produce, and to produce itself, first of all, by means of its internal "formative force"—the *bildende Kraft* inherited from the organism of Kant, which romanticism transcribes into a *vis poetica*—by means of which "in the Self all things are formed organically" (*A* 338) and "every man should be a poet" (*A* 430).

It is therefore a matter of determining the System as Poetry, and of apprehending it in the very locus of its production and as production—of exhibiting it as original production. Thus it is also necessary to grasp, in this same inmost depth, the dialectical unity of artificial production (of art) and of natural production: of procreation, germination, and birth. One should never forget, when the term *naive* appears in these texts (especially in connection with the *naive* poetry of the Ancients), that after Schiller[19] this word refers to both naiveté (innocence) and nativity. The motif of the unification of the Ancient and the Modern, as it appears so often in the fragments, always refers to the necessity of bringing about a rebirth of ancient naiveté according to modern poetry. Which leads back to the fragment: the fragment is as yet no more than germinating [*en germe*] because it is not yet fully completed (*A* 77). And according to the last of Novalis' *Grains of Pollen*, the fragment is indeed a germ or seed [*semence*]: "Fragments of this kind are literary seeds: certainly, there may be many sterile grains among them, but this is unimportant if only a few of them take root!" [2: 463] Fragmentation is not, then, a dissemination,[20] but is rather the dispersal that leads to fertilization and future harvests. The genre of the fragment is the genre of generation.

If in this manner the fragment signals its adherence to the order of the organic, this is first of all because the organic itself is engendered from and through the fragment, and because the organic is essentially *auto*-formation, or the genuine form of the subject. In the Self, as we have read, "all things are formed organically." In this sense, the fragment is as much the form of subjectity, to use the Heideggerean term, as is the self-completing speculative discourse in Hegel.

Or more precisely, it forms the double or the reverse of this discourse. For the Hegelian discourse, as earlier for that of Fichte, discursivity itself is ultimately made possible by the original presence of the total *organon*, which is capable of engendering all the rest. Putting aside for the moment the extreme difficulty of the "beginning" in Hegel, and considering him in his opposition to the romantic gesture, it remains true that in philosophical discourse the systematic power must be given, in actuality, from the outset. As soon as one departs ever so slightly from the given of origin—and it is this departure that opens the possibility of romanticism at the heart of idealism, and of the literary genre as such—one encounters, for example, without yet leaving philosophy, the even more obscure difficulty (obscure even to its author) of Schelling's original Indifference. And still, Indifference (which we will again find in the Schlegelian *Witz*) has the status of a concept. But the romantic organon further aggravates its case, so to speak, in that its concept, its very *conception*, in its seminal system, is always given in fragments and therefore always, despite everything, as a sub-work. The organicity of the fragment also designates the fragmentation of the organon and, instead of a pure process of growth, the necessity of reconstituting as well as constituting organic individuality. The model—which perhaps never attains the status of a true model or prototype [*Urbild*]—remains here that of fragmented Antiquity, the landscape of ruins. The individual—Greek, Roman, romantic—must first be reconstructed.

This means, therefore, since "there is as yet nothing that is fragmentary," that the fragment *also* represents the detached piece, the erratic block. And not according to an alternation between the values of the word "fragment" or the functions of different fragments. Rather, in the very same moment and gesture of fragmentation, the fragment both is and is not System. The fragment or the fragment-hedgehog *is* just such a hedgehog in its very proposition, which also, simultaneously, states that the hedgehog *is not*. In a way, the fragment combines completion and incompletion within itself, or one may say, in an even more complex manner, it both completes and incompletes the dialectic of completion and incompletion. In this manner, fragmentation would serve to concentrate or precipitate in a single point the process that allows philosophical discourse, even in Hegel, to designate its own incompletion, to master it, and to introduce it into the element of pure thought that is its completion. The fragment on the hedgehog outlines, and makes all the fragments surrounding it outline, the pure contours of the hedgehog, of the absent Work. This same gesture, which is simply the writing of the fragment, consequently serves to subtract this fragment from the Work, within the continually renewed ambiguity of the *small* work of art, thus serving, in sum, to fragment the fragment. Ultimately, therefore, it effectively dislocates the organic unity of the hedgehog, and presents the fragmentation of the *Fragments* only as an ensemble of *membra disjecta*. In yet another sense, if you like, it suddenly reinvests the fragment's philological value at the very center of its artistic value and grants Modernity its autonomy only on the terms on which Modernity accepts Antiquity, that is, in terms of the definitive loss of great Individuality.

Thus, the romantic origin becomes the always-already-lost of the Organon, or *chaos*, pure and simple. The "motley heap of sudden ideas" in *Critical Fragment* 103 can certainly be taken in its "spirit" as the harmony of a true system. Nevertheless, it presents itelf immediately as a "motley heap," and the romantics' period is indeed that of the chaos of works, or of chaotic works. Even before the *Fragments*, Friedrich Schlegel wrote that "when with equal attention one observes the purposelessness [*Zwecklosigkeit*] and lawlessness [*Gesetzlosigkeit*] of modern poetry as a whole, and the great excellence of its individual parts, the mass of this poetry appears to be a sea of struggling forces in which the particles of dissolved beauty, the pieces of shattered art, clash in a confused and gloomy mixture. It could be called a chaos of everything that is sublime, beautiful, and enticing . . . ."[21] Thus, Jean Paul is considered to be like a "chaos" in the *Fragments* (A 421), the same Jean Paul who is nonetheless described in the *Dialogue on Poetry*[22] as "one of the few romantic products of our quite un-romantic age." Of course it is not only the literary period, but the period as a whole that is chaotic, as is indicated by the French Revolution, among other things (A 424). Chaos is the state of always-already-lost "naiveté" and of always-yet-to-appear absolute art and, in this sense, is also a definition of the human condition. "We are potential, *chaotic* organic beings," as Friedrich Schlegel writes in one of his posthumous fragments (and in this respect it is legitimate to recognize in romanticism's specificity a kind of persistence or resistance, within idealism, of at least an element of the Kantian notion of *finitude*[23]).

Nevertheless, there is chaos and there is chaos, so to speak. *Athenaeum* fragment 389 contrasts the modern "grotesque" of "Chinese pavilions" in literature (and the context makes the grotesque a companion to chaos) with the "skillful chaos" [*Kunstchaos*][24] of ancient philosophies that have been able to "outlast a Gothic church," and "from which one could learn disorganization, or in which confusion is properly constructed, with method and symmetry." Here, in keeping with the precepts of the romantics, the truth must be sought in irony[25]: chaos is also something *constructed*, and thus a supplementary reading of the fragment on the "motley heap of sudden ideas" [*CF* 103] becomes necessary. The properly romantic—poietic—task is not to dissipate or reabsorb chaos, but to construct it or to make a *Work* from disorganization. For "potential organic beings," organization and generation can and must occur in the midst of disorganization, both as a parody of themselves and in keeping with the true "method and symmetry" of the System. The fragment, in this case, is the genre of the parody of the putting-into-work, or of the parodic putting-into-work, which inevitably refers back to "chaos" *also* as an exemplary Work, particularly in Roman satire and, above all, in Shakespeare (see A 383, for example). By also affirming itself as a dramatization, fragmentation would thus refer, both parodically and seriously, to itself, to its own chaos as the genre of the Work.

Of course, through the well-known duplicity of parody, another value of chaos has been present from the start. The text on the chaos of modern poetry cited above continues as follows: "It could be called a chaos of all that is sublime, beautiful, and enticing, a chaos that, like the ancient Chaos out of which, according to legend, the world was ordered, awaits a love and a hatred to separate the parts that are different, but to unite those that are similar." Chaos is also the locus of possible generations, of potential production; and since Descartes it is in reconstructing the world from a primitive chaos that the subject measures its knowledge and power or, quite simply, constitutes itself *as* subject.

We will have to return to the development of the motif of chaos, a development that takes place by no mere chance in the *Ideas*, outside the fragments properly speaking. But for the moment let us recall that fragmentation as chaos is also the material available to the creator of a world, and thus that the romantic Fragment conclusively confirms and installs the figure of the artist as Author and Creator.

This creator, however, is not the subject of a *cogito*, either in the sense of immediate self-knowledge or in that of the positing of a substance of the subject.[26] In light of Kant's decisive critique of the subject, it is the subject of judgment, the subject of the *critical* operation or, in other words, of the operation that distinguishes incompatibles and constructs the objective unity of compatibles. In sum, the modern poetic chaos awaits nothing other than the subject of the operation of "love and hatred," according to Friedrich Schlegel; or, better yet, nothing other than the subject *considered as* this operation. To the aims of the Work corresponds the decidedly *operative* status of the subject.

This operative status is indicated by one of the most familiar of romantic motifs, the motif of *Witz*, which is very closely related to fragmentation.[27] With *Witz*, we arrive at what is undoubtedly the final and most specific element of fragmentation. By the same token, if one takes *Witz* as a measure of romanticism, one is led to circumscribe it more strictly than usual (with reference only, or almost only, to Friedrich Schlegel, Jean Paul, and later Solger, along with one and only one aspect of certain texts by Novalis), and it is not by chance that the Hegelian criticism of romantic art will concentrate on this circumscription.

Witz is concerned with the fragment, first of all, in that both of these "genres" (insofar as they can be given such a name) imply the "sudden idea" (*Einfall*, the idea that suddenly "falls" upon you, so that the find is less found than received). The "motley heap of sudden ideas" implies something of *Witz*, just as, because "many witty sudden ideas" [*witzige Einfälle*] are like the sudden meeting of two friendly thoughts after a long separation," *Witz* seems to imply within itself the entire fragmentary, dialogical, and dialectical structure that we have outlined. The essence of the "sudden idea" consists in its being a synthesis of thoughts. As a result of a tradition that goes back to the seventeenth century, *Witz* is basically qualified as a unification of heterogeneous elements; that is, both as a substitute for true *conception* (which occurs in and by the homogeneous) and as the double of judgment (which links together the heterogeneous only under the control of the homogeneous). It is as if, on the basis of its semantic origin (*Witz* is a doublet of *Wissen*, knowledge) and throughout its history as the French *esprit* and as the English *wit*, *Witz* constituted the other name and the other "concept" of knowledge, or rather the name and "concept" of knowledge that is other: of knowledge that is other than the knowledge of analytic and predicative discursivity. What this means is that *Witz*, as the romantics inherit and ennoble it, is constituted in the greatest proximity to what Hegel will call "Absolute Knowledge," which is absolute less because it is limitless knowledge than because it is knowledge that knows itself even as it knows what it knows, and which thereby forms the actual infinity of knowledge, and its *System*.[28] *Witz* very precisely represents an *a priori* synthesis in the Kantian sense, but one that is removed from Kant's limiting conditions and critical procedures and that involves the synthesis not only of an object but of a subject as well (or at least the synthesis of the power of the producer-subject). In this respect, *Witz*, in short, is the solution of the enigma of transcendental schematism, as discussed in the "Overture."

Witz, then, is not merely a "form" or a "genre" (although it is indeed, as can be seen in the *Fragments*, the preferred genre of conversation, of *sociality* [see *CF* 9], the genre of a literature that would be the living and free exchange of opinions, thoughts, and hearts in a society of artists, in a group like that of the authors of the *Fragments*.) Simultaneously, and in keeping with a plurality of values that can be traced through the texts, *Witz* is also a quality attributable to every type of genre or work, a spiritual faculty, and a type of spirit. Or perhaps it is the spirit-type, which in a single glance and with lightning speed (the assonance *Blitz-Witz* was often used, although it does not appear in the *Fragments*), in the confusion of a heterogeneous chaos, can seize upon and bring to light new, unforeseen and, in short, creative relations. "Witz is creative, it produces resemblances," Novalis writes in *Grains of Pollen*. *Witz* is an immediate, absolute knowing-seeing [*savoir-voir*]; it is sight [*vue*] regained at the blindspot of schematism and, consequently, sight gaining direct access to the productive capacity of works. Romantic *Witz* produces the assumption of what we have taken the liberty of calling *eidaesthetics:* it gathers, concentrates, and brings to a climax the metaphysics of the *Idea*, of the Idea's self-knowledge in its auto-manifestation. In no way is it reserved for a certain category of productions, which would be grotesque, piquant, unusual, or generally "bizarre," to adopt one of the terms used in *Athenaeum* fragment 429. On the contrary, a reading of this fragment will suggest that "the infinitely bizarre" is compatible with all genres and with the "highest *Bildung*" or, in other words, that, if the bizarre can be infinite, it is because the infinite cannot but be bizarre in its manifestation, if not in its essence. Indeed, by means of its bizarre combinations of heterogeneous elements, *Witz* plays the role of speculative knowledge itself (and thus may be referred to as an "end in itself" in *Critical Fragment* 49; see also *CF* 16 and 126).

In his *Theory of Language*, Bernhardi, an author close to the romantics, wrote in 1805 (and August Schlegel cites the passage in his review of the work) that "the essence of the truth is to be a *Witz*, because all science is the *Witz* of intelligence, all art is the *Witz* of fantasy, and any witticism [*pointe*] is *witzig* only insofar as it calls upon the *Witz* of truth." Nowhere in the network of fragments on *Witz*—and for reasons that will soon appear—will we discover an absolutely identical formula, but we will often come quite close. In this manner, *Witz* ultimately provides the essence of the fragment, as *Critical Fragment* 9 points out: "*Witz* is absolute social spirit, or fragmentary geniality." Which must first of all be understood as the geniality of the fragment, the poietic geniality of instantaneous production, in the lightning flash, in the completed form of the System at the heart of the incompletion of Chaos. Fragmentary speculation, the dialectical identity of System and Chaos, *operates* [*s'opère*] in the conflagration of *Witz* (see *CF* 34 and 90).

Yet at the very same instant, *Witz* reproduces or manifests fragmentary dislocation. Within the network of *Witz*, a series of fragments warns against the low, equivocal, or dangerous *Witz*. This gesture of suspicion toward *Witz* on the part of the very partisans of *Witz* is as old as its entire tradition. It was never really possible to assimilate *Witz* to a genre or a work. Its absolute combinative quality is always threatened from below by its inferior, fleeting, almost formless character. Thus, *Witz* itself needs to be *poeticized*, as *Athenaeum* fragment 116 says. The absolute idea of the Work, it is also the not-even-work [*même-pas-oeuvre*] that must still be made to work [*mettre en oeuvre*]. The motif of *Witz* is consequently almost continually divided in two: on one hand, one must retain or contain the "chaotic," "telluric" *Witz* that provokes "fright and coagulation," in the terms of several of Friedrich Schlegel's posthumous fragments; yet on the other hand, and this is in fact the major exigency with regard to *Witz*, one must abandon oneself to its fundamentally involuntary character (see *A* 32 and 106). To want to have *Witz* is to fall into *Witzelei* (*A* 32), the forced, artificial *Witz*, the "Chinese pavilion" rather than Shakespearean drama. The solution, paradoxically—if one can call it a solution—appears in *Athenaeum* fragment 394: "genuine *Witz* is still conceivable only in written form." It must be torn from its too-immediately explosive and dangerous existence in the salon. In other words, it must be put to work in the work.[29] The writing of the fragment thus constitutes the dialectical *Aufhebung* of the internal antinomy of *Witz*. "Fragmentary geniality" preserves *Witz* as work and suppresses it as non-work, sub-work, or anti-work. Which implies, it seems, that geniality also forms the *Aufhebung* of the voluntary and the involuntary.

Writing and geniality thus seem to provide keys to the fragment. Writing as the passage into form, into the formal legality of the work, one could say, exploiting without exaggeration the comparison found in *Athenaeum* fragment 394: "Genuine *Witz* is still conceivable only in written form, like laws"; and geniality as the auto-assumption of *Witz*, of the spirit in *Witz*, according to *Athenaeum* fragment 366: "Understanding is mechanical spirit; *Witz* is chemical spirit; genius is organic spirit" (cf. *A* 426).

That the truth of the *organon* becomes accessible in geniality should not be surprising: romanticism is less romantic at this point than it is the inheritor of the eighteenth century and of Kant. What belongs more properly to romanticism is rather the way that genius—which is finally no more clearly defined than the fragment or *Witz*—becomes associated in the Fragments with the entire problematic of the fragmentary. First of all in the following way: if "*Witz* is fragmentary geniality," but also if the work beyond *Witz*, the truly poetic work, is swept away in infinite romantic "progressivity," one wonders whether the "organic" genius is able to present itself in the era of chaos. It undoubtedly cannot if "Antiquity is the only genius that, without exaggeration, can be called absolutely great, unique and unequal" (*A* 248). Like the individual, and because it *is* the Individual, genius is always already lost, and like Antiquity, exists only in fragments.

Thus it becomes apparent that in more than one text the term "genius" refers, in fact, alternatively, to the unique Genius, the individual-Antiquity, and to a type who, despite being the type of the creator, nonetheless remains inferior or secondary to that other type, or rather ideal, of the cultivated (*gebildet*) man. The cultivated man, as the romantic absolutization of the "*honnête homme*" and of the "*Aufklärer*," is the subject of a superior reason that has been completed in its total form. This is the well-known "complete" celebrated in *Athenaeum* fragment 419, a "serene divinity that lacks the crushing power of the hero and the creative [*bildende*] activity of the artist." *Bildung* as completion designates something that is removed from becoming and from the effort of *bilden* itself. In a sense, it constitutes the System as a pure conjunction of form with itself: the *Bild*—or Idea—present at last, and above all present to itself. Genius on the other hand, like *Witz*, implies a relative absence of form—if not deformity—as the power of putting-into-form. It implies the disparity between *sight* and *work* of which *Athenaeum* fragment 432 speaks ("the leap from the most intuitive knowledge, from the clear sight of what ought to be produced, to its accomplishment always remains infinite"), an infinite disparity that genius overcomes, but only through a blind and formless leap, as it were. The production of works is not yet, nor is it ever what it essentially is and ought to be: the self-adequate auto-production of the Work-Subject, of the Work-Self-knowledge [*l'oeuvre-savoir-de-soi*]. And yet what the fragmentary apparatus aims at, as has by now become sufficiently clear, is this same auto-production. But this goal implies at least three specific exigencies that form the very limits of the fragment (the limits that define it, and that cut each fragment off from absolute fragmentation):

— A poiesy capable of losing itself in what it presents (see *A* 116);

— irony as the sublime assumption of *Witz*, the positing of the absolute identity of the creative self and of the nothingness of works, "transcendental buffoonery" (*CF* 42, see also *CF* 108);

— an absolute "combinatory art" that permits philosophy to "no longer wait for genial sudden ideas" (*A* 220), and thus to escape the accidental quality of *Witz* and genius.

As one can see, these three exigencies precisely outline the form required for the ideal of the fragment-hedgehog. The Work must be nothing other than the absolutely necessary auto-production in which all individualities and all works are annihilated. Not altogether in artistic geniality, but rather, more rigorously, in its ideal (in the romantic sense of the word), in the necessary auto-production and the auto-production of necessity, does one henceforth find the structure of the System-Subject, the *Bild* beyond all *Bild* of the fragment, *or in other words of the absolute*, because it is indeed this *ab-solutum*, detached from everything, that the hedgehog represents.

On the path toward the absolute, toward absolute fragmentary absolution, romanticism will now follow two distinct and continually crossing paths. The first, that of Novalis, redefines *Witz* as simultaneous combination and dissolution: "*Witz*, as a principle of affinity, is at the same time *menstruum universale*" (*Grains of Pollen*) [*Blüthenstaub* fragment 57]. The universal dissolvent undoes the systematic, undoes the identity of the poet and sweeps it toward the "dissolution in song" evoked by a posthumous fragment intended for *Heinrich von Ofterdinger*, a dissolution that includes the sacrifice, in all its ambiguity, of the poet ("he will be sacrificed by savage peoples"). The ambiguity of sacrifice (sanctification), however, corresponds to the ambiguity of the motif of dissolution, which leads the chemistry of the *Witz* back to the alchemy of the *menstruum*, and therefore to the Great Work, while at the same time leading back to *Auflösung* (dissolution) in the sense, found notably in Kant, of organic assimilation, of "intussusception."[30]

The second, Schlegelian path might be indicated by *Athenaeum* fragment 375 as the path leading toward "energy" or toward "the energetic man," defined by the "infinitely flexible . . . universal power through which the whole man shapes himself," well beyond the "genius" who "shapes a work." Energy extends to the limit of the work and of the system; its "infinite flexibility," linked to "an incalculable number of projects," effects an infinite fragmentation of work and system. But what is this flexibility, if not an infinite capacity for form, for the absolute of form; and what is energy, *en-ergeia*, if not the putting-into-work itself, the completed *organon*, whose works (of genius) are mere potentialities? (The Aristotelian *act* is *energeia* as opposed to *dynamis*, potentiality.[31])

Dissolution and energy, then, the ultimate forms of the fragment, would inevitably lead back to the work-subject.

The fragment on energy, however, is unique, a single element lost in the ensemble of the *Fragments*. And if Novalis never wrote his text on the "dissolution of the poet," it is not only because he died, but because this work, like all of his larger projects, was continually getting lost in the multiplication of its own productive germs [*semences*]. Which may mean, at least in the fragment, that romanticism's most specific gesture, the gesture that distinguishes it infinitesimally but all the more decisively from metaphysical idealism, is one by which, discreetly and without really wanting to, and at the very heart of the quest for or theory of the Work, it abandons or excises the work itself—and thus is transformed in an almost imperceptible manner into the "work of the absence of work," as Blanchot has put it.[32] It is the minimal but incisive particularity of this mutation that the motif (and not the form, genre, or idea) of the fragment has continually led us to perceive, without ever placing it before our eyes. Rather than a mutation coming from elsewhere, what is involved here is a minute displacement or interval that is undoubtedly the most romantic aspect—or most modern, beyond all modernity—of romanticism, but that at the same time is what romanticism itself continually obscures behind the very Idea of romanticism, and of modernity.

Let us say that what the fragment continually portends—to speak romantically, and not without irony—while never ceasing to annul it, is—in Blanchot's words—"the search for a new form of fulfillment that mobilizes—renders mobile—the whole, even while interrupting it in various ways." On this count, "the fragmentary exigency does not exclude totality, but rather goes beyond it." Also on this count, Novalis' seminal dispersion exceeds or extenuates the generation within it, and disseminates it. Within the romantic work, there is interruption and dissemination of the romantic work, and this in fact is not readable in the work itself, even and especially not when the fragment, *Witz*, and chaos are privileged. Rather, according to another term of Blanchot, it is readable in the *unworking* [*désoeuvrement*], never named and still less thought, that insinuates itself throughout the interstices of the romantic work. Unworking is not incompletion, for as we have seen incompletion completes itself and is the fragment as such; unworking is nothing, only the interruption of the fragment. The fragment closes and interrupts itself at the same point: it is not a point, a punctuation or a fractured piece, despite everything, of the fragmentary Work. This is said in *Athenaeum* fragment 383, which perhaps we can just begin to reread in spite of what it says; "There is a kind of *Witz* that, because of its purity, its thoroughness, and its symmetry, one is tempted to call the architectonic *Witz*. Expressed satirically, it produces the only true sarcasms. It must be properly systematic, and yet also not systematic; with all its completeness, something must still appear to be missing, as if torn away . . . ."

2   The Idea: Religion within the Limits of Art

> Is there then a finer symbol of the paradox of
> the philosophical life than these sinuous lines
> which, with visible constancy and regularity,
> can appear only furtively and in pieces, be-
> cause their center is located in infinity?
>
> —*Friedrich Schlegel,* Über Lessing

In a certain manner, fragmentation never ceased to preoccupy romanticism. Romanticism, in other words, could never have protected, defended, or preserved itself from its "unworking"—its incalculable and uncontrollable incompletion: its incompletable incompletion. It could never, in other words, have avoided the most simple and derisory form of incompletion, the most accidental, as it were, or "empirical": that incompletion provoked by both character and circumstance (or persons and history), even though the exact degree of their respective agencies can never be known. In the case of Jena, they became quite jumbled: the fluctuations in intellectual moods and appetites, internal group rivalries, a certain laziness (or a virtuosity that came too easily), incertitude and the inability to dominate or "finish," permanent instability (outings, invitations, meetings, an impossible amount of activities), precipitation (and at times confusion), the overabundance of projects, the startling rapidity—all around them— of History itself, energy heedlessly wasted, death. . . . Where, in the thousands of pages left behind by Jena (*Hymns to the Night,* perhaps, excepted) can anything be found that can be considered, without reservation, as a *work*?

But this does not mean that all of the texts left behind by Jena belong to the genre of the "fragment," or that they could be grouped under that heading. Far from it. Fragmentation, or a certain "tendency" toward fragmentation finally dislocates and "unworks" texts, as we will have occasion to verify, that should have been sheltered from such an accident by their genre (the letter or novel, for example, particularly in the case of *Lucinde*). Yet the fragment itself—which, by this name at least, no longer appears after the second issue of the *Athenaeum* in 1798—in the very brevity of this adventure, also delimits, quite precisely circumscribes, a kind of abbreviated era. Thus it is certainly inadequate to speak of a history or evolution of the Jena movement without taking into account, and relating it to, a history of fragmentation itself.

What, first of all, does this history consist of?

Of an ensemble of reasons which, in keeping with all that we have said, must obviously be characterized as anecdotal. But only on condition of suspecting (as soon as the existence of the group, for example, comes into play, thus becoming one of the principle modalities of the "fragmentary system") that the anecdote harbors something other, on the very level of minor events [*la petite histoire*], than minor events: the absolutely empirical essentiality of the empirical.

It is impossible to go into particulars here.[1] But it is necessary to at least recall that the question of the fragment provokes the first serious divergence between August and Friedrich, and thus, since all of this is interconnected, the first real (i.e., open) threat of dissension within the group (whose unity was perhaps never anything but Friedrich's own utopia). Behind August, who preferred that the journal publish no more fragments in the future, is Caroline, with her overt hostility toward any attempt to "collectivize" writing and with her distrust of Friedrich's projects (always countless and often confused or cumbersome); and behind Friedrich not only do all the others appear, here and there, but the shadow of Goethe stands out as well—Weimar, the literary *establishment*, the authority over matters of taste and propriety, over publishing, over university appointments. Aside from the survival of the entire enterprise, up to a certain point, nothing of what makes up romanticism depends on it. In sum, it would hardly be an exaggeration to say that the history of fragmentation hinges on the mute resistance that "they" manifest toward Friedrich; and consequently, on the (stubborn, complex, and cunning) resistance to this resistance, which in large part determines Friedrich's "strategy": his renunciation of all collective projects (at least as they had been conceived up to that point), his abandonment of the very term "fragment," his seemingly docile shift to the practice of other genres (the novel, the letter, the dialogue—even the poem[2]). As might be expected, this does not prevent him from being somewhat obstinate, in a slightly lowered tone, or from going ahead with the publication of the *Ideas*, which we will now have to examine. Its kinship with the fragment (although the "ideas" are shorter and more succinct) is hard to deny.

In effect, this is to say that the history of fragmentation is linked, in the most intimate manner, to Friedrich's individual itinerary—which in this case (the destiny of Novalis aside) happens to mean the itinerary of romanticism itself. For while it has been said many times, it is no less true that Friedrich alone, throughout those four years, holds to the initial course of romanticism; he alone maintains the romantic exigency (which is in fact nothing but exigency) when the others, for various reasons and with various results, have already begun to grab hold of the thing in order to *deal in it* and to subject it, as if its history were complete and its doctrine fully constituted, to academic exploitation.[3]

That fragmentation does not cease but on the contrary persists and traverses all of romanticism (even at the expense of a transformation or reorientation) is thus the result of a stubborn determination—and, virtually, the stubborn determination of a single person. Beneath this history, it is not difficult to recognize the obscure workings of that *dissatisfaction* that always appears, a bit externally, as a dominant trait of romanticism. Nevertheless, it remains true that, far from contenting himself with the potential for "profiteering" on the already-established, Friedrich never ceases, whether forced to do so or not, to bring *everything* into question—moving in a sort of "retreat forward," which certainly cannot be attributed solely to an obsession with originality or a supercilious desire to be different. It is also true, for such is the law of dissatisfaction, that this movement always implies a deepening of the question. Of course, this does not exclude the possibility that setbacks may occur or that the movement itself may sometimes appear, superficially, as a regression. In general, this period, in other words the publication of the *Ideas*, is said to mark the "turning" that makes possible the conversion of 1808 or the dubious political compromise of 1815. But aside from the fact that such a trajectory, for anyone who can read, is already entirely inscribed in the *Fragments*,[4] nothing guarantees without further ado that an accentuation of the religious motif merely represents a "regressive" gesture and would be incapable of leading to or authorizing a radicalization of the earlier attitude. On the contrary, the "transition to religion"—approached for our purposes from the perspective of the question of the work—most likely coincides with a general putting-into-question and, let us retain the word, a deepening.

What sort of deepening?

Actually, it is a matter of a twofold deepening. On the one hand, the group's reserve with regard to the fragment prescribes a reconsideration, with new stakes, of the problem of *form*. And prescribes it all the more because, as we have seen, no concept, theory, or even delimited or fixed form of the fragment ever existed. This return to the formal problematic is not, however, a simple one (Friedrich's "strategy" must be taken into account), and the gesture, in this case, is at least equivocal. For everything goes on as if Friedrich were both endorsing the condemnation of the fragment (and going so far as to warn of the threat or danger concealed in its "absence of form"[5]) and at the same time surreptitiously taking advantage of this condemnation in order to get back not at the fragment itself, but at its "wild" or overimmediate exploitation—that is, the type of exploitation that, precisely because it presupposes an implicit theory of the fragment and makes the fragment into a "form without form" (form without the exterior, calculated, artificial element of form), permitted all the subjective complacency that had to such a great extent compromised the rigor of the fragmentary experiment. Everything goes on, therefore, as if, in a certain abuse of the fragment, the effacement of the entire formal problematic were being silently incriminated, or what amounts to the same thing, as if the deepening of the question of form were taking aim, in the fragment, at a utopia of formal transparency, finally guilty of having authorized a somewhat oversimplified presentation of the fragment as the form adequate to the expression of the subject. The subject of subjectivity, it should be understood, and not—for this is where the entire problem lies—of "subjectity."

For on the other hand, precisely, and in an indissociable manner—since for Friedrich fragmentation has been "the form, properly speaking, of universal philosophy"—the deepening that begins in 1798 is *philosophical*: it is the deepening of the fundamental question contained in the fragmentary exigency, which is none other, as we now know, than that of auto-production. Or the question of the Subject itself, but this time in a far more radical sense. In such a way, and this will be our hypothesis, that what might be called the *fragmentary obstinacy* represents a crucial step toward the enigmatic joining [*jointure*] where, at the very locus of the interminable (if not impossible) auto-conception of the Subject, literature and philosophy continue in spite of everything to act as a "system."

This is why we have chosen to examine here two texts by Friedrich Schlegel whose object—to specify it at least externally—is philosophical, and both of which, in different ways, renew the problematic of fragmentation. This obliges us to invert their chronological order and to give first place, for reasons that should henceforth become evident, to the *Ideas*, which constituted the last fragmentary ensemble published by the romantics. The *Ideas* appeared in 1800, in the fifth (penultimate) issue of the *Athenaeum*—or, to be precise, in the first fascicle of the third volume—and consequently just before the dissolution of the group and at the moment when, except for an imminent theory of the novel,[6] the adventure is all but finished (and its theory, all but exhausted).

We are relying as well on an earlier text (which appeared in 1799 in the third issue of the *Athenaeum*) whose appearance suggests nothing fragmentary: the celebrated letter *On Philosophy* (modelled after August's earlier *Letters to Amalia*[7]) addressed to Dorothea (Brendel Veit), who at the time, of course, was living "freely" with Friedrich, and who sometime later was to become his legitimate (and converted[8]) spouse.

But we have also found it necessary to refer to a third text here, a text not by one of the Schlegels, but by Schelling—although it was nowhere printed under his own name, save posthumously. It is a rather surprising text. We will return to the reasons that have led us to consider it here but, for the moment, it suffices to be aware that *Heinz Widerporst's Epicurean Confession of Faith* (such is its title) is a poem—violently antireligious, as usual for the young Schelling—that Friedrich wanted to publish in the journal to counterbalance Novalis's *Europe, or Christianity,* but that August, acting on the advice of a slightly shocked and very prudent Goethe, and despite the provisions for rigorous anonymity insisted upon by Schelling, would not allow to appear. Schelling, nevertheless, found the text sufficiently important to publish a long excerpt two years later (i.e., in 1801), still anonymously, in his *Journal of Speculative Physics.*[9]

The history of fragmentation, then, passes from the *Fragments* to the *Ideas.* But what is an "idea?"

Of course, as in the case of the fragment, no definition exists. While the history of fragmentation undeniably moves toward a certain deepening, it is not at all certain that it proceeds in the sense of a clarification. In fact, besides a very vague (but very "profound") proposition near the beginning of the collection ("Ideas are infinite, autonomous, continuously moving in themselves, divine thoughts," *I* 10), and a reminder, *in extremis,* of the function of the "idea," no formal determination whatsoever of the thing ever appears. And in addition, we know that as part of his careful "placation" of August, Friedrich vacillated between the titles "Thoughts" and "Views," before settling, at the very moment of publication, on "Ideas." Certainly, it was no small task to locate a suitable substitute for "Fragment."

But this hesitation, as might be expected, is not without interest. The path leading from the *thought* to the *idea* at least reveals that the fragmentary obstinacy is not without a precise relationship with idealism itself. In any case, it goes without saying that around 1800, the master term of idealism cannot be used with impunity as the title of an ensemble of "fragments" (or something very close to them). To call this the master term of idealism is to say, strictly speaking, that it is the speculative word *par excellence,* the word that all of idealism—from Schelling to the greater *Logic*—endeavors to tear away from the analogical and simply regulative status it has in Kant. Yet, that Schlegel should make this word (and thus, at least in part, this concept) into a title is in no way a clear indication that, after a few deviations, he returned to the fold of idealism. In reality, the relation he maintained with the philosophy of the period, no less than his own conception of philosophy, are far more complex.

First of all because, in his own way, Schlegel maintains a certain fidelity to Kant. In this connection, the two titles initially considered are quite revealing, especially the first, if one thinks about the precise definition of *thoughts,* which is given in the letter *On Philosophy,* and which appears in the context of an assuredly paradoxical praise of understanding (and not of reason): "A thought is a representation that is perfected for itself, fully formed [*ausgebildet*], total, and infinite within its limits. It is the most divine element in the human spirit."[10] The obvious proximity of this definition to that of the future "ideas" (cited above) serves here as one more indication that if the "thought" is the infinitization of representation (in the Kantian sense), this infinitization operates within a philosophy of understanding, that is, intentionally or not, within the limits of a philosophy of finitude. The idealistic "step" has been effected (in the motif of infinitization), but not without a kind of obscure resistance to idealism itself, or more precisely, not without a sort of (quite unexpected) folding back of idealism into Kant, and of the transgression of finitude into the finite itself. Here is something that, once more, seems to double the movement of Hegelian dialectics—but that is nonetheless separated from it by an abyss. This, perhaps, is what lies behind the constant use of the plural (always ideas, never the Idea), or if you will, the strangely labile status of the idea. As well as the relativization of its function and its "subjectivization." The *Ideas* closes on this disabused declaration: "I have expressed a few ideas pointing toward the center, and have greeted the dawn in my own way [literally: *nach meiner Ansicht*, according to my views, using the word that Schlegel had considered as a title], from my own point of view. Let anyone who knows the road do likewise in his own way, from his own point of view" (*I* 155). And the final dedication to Novalis, using what was certainly an unexpected parallel, even speaks of "these images of incomprehensible [*unbegriffenen*] truth."

The "idea" is thus quite far from the speculative Idea, and the *Ideas* are no more successful than the *Fragments* in constructing or reconstructing the "systematic" totality that nonetheless remains their horizon. In point of fact, they are far less successful. This is because the philosophical connotation is actually far from exhausting what, as title, they signify.

As Schlegel's hesitation, once more, with regard to the title suggests, the *Ideas* (and *a fortiori* the "thoughts" or "views") cannot fail to evoke the kind of privilege attributed to the "classical" aspect or form of the fragment considered as *maxim* or *aphorism*. If only as opposed to the fragment considered as a piece of an essay. In a certain manner, in other words, the *Ideas* seem to turn back toward what can be called the properly *moral* genre of the fragment. This is fairly evident (on condition, it is true, of effecting a slight cut in the text, to which we shall return later) right from the beginning of the collection, in the first "idea," where not only the "moral theme," but also the style of injunction, the voluntarism of truth, and even the distant reminder of the oracular aphorism, are quite unambiguous signs: "The calls for and the traces of a morality that might be more than the practical part of philosophy are becoming increasingly obvious. . . . It is time to tear away the veil of Isis and reveal the mystery. Whoever cannot endure the sight of the goddess, let him flee or perish" (*I* 1).

It remains to be seen, however, what should be understood by "the moral genre of the fragment." For this understanding, as might be suspected, will determine the very meaning of that *return* which the *Ideas* are almost unanimously held to represent.

The moral genre of the fragment is no doubt nothing other, in the last analysis, than the specifically *Latin* model of philosophy. In other words, the model of an essentially oral philosophy of facts, without the least trace of an original "first philosophy," but simply anchored in Stoic, Epicurean, or Cynical (which is far from indifferent in relation to the formal problematic[11]) post-Platonism, and intersecting on various registers and at the same time with the edifying historiography of Rome, quasiphilosophical doxologies, and the genre of exemplary biography as summarized or fixed in Plutarch. That Rome is much more than a simple historical moment here is evident. The *Fragments* had already multiplied their references to it, in a provocative way, in the midst of the resurgence of Hellenism *à la* Winckelmann (doing so, moreover, in a journal entitled *Athenaeum*), sketching out the contours of a sort of "perverse" neoclassicism essentially founded on the very values of the *Aufklärung*: urbanity and sociality, "spirit" (the irony of Socratic posterity or *Witz*, which the Romans, of course, called the "nose"), or even the Republican ideal (see *I* 56 and 114, among others). And, not surprisingly, the *Ideas* will contain echoes (certainly distant and deformed, but quite perceptible nonetheless) of Epictetus' *Manual*, or of Marcus Aurelius' *Meditations* [*Pensées*]. Formally, in any case, the kinship is beyond dispute. Actually, as its name *also* indicates, romanticism fulfills the tradition of Rome in "modernity." Hegel, who makes no mistake about it, will include both in a single condemnation.[12]

Closer to home, however, and yet without breaking the thread of the Latin tradition, the moral genre of the fragment points toward the genre of the Moralists themselves—toward that genre of hortatory discourse that Rome had, in fact, illustrated, but that henceforth develops in terms of subjective utterance, i.e., in the specifically "modern" mode of the statement [*parole*] of authority, through which social and literary authority relay the authority of thought itself (the authority included in the very definition of the *maxima sententia*, the highest thought). The difference in utterance that makes all the difference, for example, between Gracian's *Oraculo manual* and Epictetus's *Manual* (or between La Rochefoucauld and Marcus Aurelius), is indeed also constitutive of those *Ideas* in which, as Ayrault notes (3: 136), Schlegel introduces the "I" of subjective utterance into the fragment for the first time. But if this modification of sententious utterance and this transfer of authority indeed signify that the truth is henceforth constructed (and no longer simply gathered and transmitted), one consequence at least becomes clear: the subject of sententious utterance itself must now coincide with the function of exemplarity traditionally fulfilled by the aphorism or maxim. Here again one recognizes the discursive position of the Cartesian subject or, to select an example closer to the problematic of the fragment, that which founds the posthumous authority of Pascal and establishes the *Pensées* as the great model of the modern tradition of the maxim. In its modern version, in sum, the moral genre of the fragment assumes that the paradigmatic and the exemplary have entered the sphere of Subjectity. The model, the absolute model, is one that gives itself the right to say, "Me (the truth), I am speaking. . . ."

On condition, of course, that someone is listening, which is never dependent on the strength of its voice (the *"Ego vox in deserto clamans"* has never ceased to be a truism), nor even, as in ancient rhetoric, on its power of persuasion—but rather on its skill [*adresse*], if you will excuse the bad *Witz*, in *addressing itself*, that is, in orienting or directing utterance itself. Hence its recourse to what we have called the style of injunction (of discourse "in the imperative," if not imperative discourse as such); hence also its recourse to a surreptitiously "dialogical" form like the letter—in short, to what formally but not superficially authorizes the articulation of the *Ideas* to the letter *On Philosophy* to Dorothea (or the reverse). For the conditions have now been assembled that will allow the interlocutor of sententious discourse to reproduce in his or her own self this coincidence of the aphorism's subject with the exemplary value of what it utters. The conditions have been assembled, in other words, that will allow for the establishment of a relation of imitation between the uttering subject and the interlocuter—if one takes into account, however, the inflection that ancient imitation has undergone in modernity, or to speak like August, in one of his *Lectures on Art and Literature*, "if one takes . . . the expression "imitation" in the noble sense in which it means not the aping of a man's exterior characteristics but the appropriation of the very maxims of his action" [2: 91]. If, consequently, one grants the concept of imitation the very sense that the romantics will convey upon that of *artistic creation*.[13]

This "moralization" of the fragment or, if one prefers, this return to the moral tradition of the fragment, therefore supposes a certain relation between *imitation* (also, in other words, *exemplarity*) and *creation*.

And, as it happens, the question of this relation is continually present in the *Ideas*.

Not in these terms, obviously, but in those of the invasive and tenacious motif of the *artist*. This motif seems to constitute one of the most visible guiding threads of the collection, thereby acquiring a far greater importance than it had in the preceding fragments. Not because it is quantitatively more frequent (this would be true only in relation to the *Fragments*), but precisely because it is capable of serving as a guiding thread (nothing of the sort is to be found in the *Fragments*), or in other words, because the artist, with the *Ideas*, achieves the status of a genuine *figure*.

But what, in fact, is the artist's relation to imitation?

This question, contrary to what one might think, does not bear directly on the artist, but rather on imitation itself. Or in other words on the subject. If the *Ideas* tend toward a deepening, to repeat once again, this deepening primarily affects the problem that has continually appeared *as* romanticism itself and that is nothing other than the problem of the constitution or formation of the subject.

When he writes, "*No one can be the direct mediator [Mittler] for even his own spirit*" (*I* 44), Friedrich Schlegel is not merely "appropriating" in his own manner a theme or concept that he may have found in Novalis (who had in turn probably borrowed it from Lessing[14]); nor is he postulating, in what was for him a new register, the question of the recognition of the subject. Rather, he is once again, and more radically, confirming the rupture of the Cartesian subject—and thus the impossibility of auto-constitution, i.e., the absolutization or infinitization of the subject. Here again, the difference that separates Schlegel from the speculative properly speaking (and particularly from Fichte[15]) becomes evident. There is nothing in philosophy, then, that can provide the subject with access to itself. But on the other hand, there is this (traditional) religious figure of the mediator that Friedrich, following Spinoza, had already secularized and "pantheized" (or dissolved in the totality of things[16]) in the *Fragments*, and which, in the *Ideas*, is on the contrary incarnated in the artist.

But why the artist?

The reason is given in the very next "idea" (*I* 45): "*An artist is someone who has his center in himself.*" This amounts to saying that an artist is someone who needs no mediator, but who can, on his own, fulfill the function of a mediator—because, as the rest of the same "idea" informs us, whoever lacks such a center in himself "has to choose some particular leader and mediator outside of himself," if only on a provisional basis. Mediation (in an active or passive sense) is therefore a matter of a center or lack of center: "to have or not to have" is generally the way humanity is divided—a division that, as one can already see, distinguishes between the artists on the one hand (that is, the "models"), and everyone else on the other. And the relation that such a division establishes (which is *the* relation, absolutely speaking, the relation *par excellence*: "To mediate and to be mediated are the whole higher life of man" [*I* 44]) is fundamentally *mimetic* in nature. Or rather, since precision is necessary here, even at the risk of getting ahead of ourselves: mediation is mimetic in nature when it is passive, and initiatory when active. "Idea" 45 adds: ". . . a man cannot exist without a living center, and if he does not yet have one within himself, then he can only seek it in another man, and only a man and a man's center can stimulate and awaken his own."

Let us for the moment put aside the content of mediation and concentrate on its function alone. As we will see, this function is more or less pedagogical, or more exactly, since it is essentially concerned with the subject, "psychagogical." At least, it would be a function of this kind (and we will see that the motif of an "education of the human race," derived from Lessing, persists throughout the *Ideas*) if, for Schlegel, there could be a pedagogy that was simply and unproblematically *moral*. But this is what Schlegel protests most resolutely: "I consider all moral education to be foolish and illicit," he says in the letter *On Philosophy* and adds, basing his remarks as if by chance on all the "ambivalence" associated with mimesis: "But as for educating someone in order to make him *into a man*, this strikes me much as if I heard someone talking about giving lessons in resemblance to the deity" [*DA* 448]. "Humanity," then, cannot be learned; it "does not allow itself to be inoculated," as Schlegel puts it. This is why mediation, which takes the place of an impossible moral pedagogy, actually means *exemplarity*. But exemplarity, as should be apparent by now, cannot in turn signify simple imitation—the exterior reproduction of a type or model. On the contrary, it is "appropriation," as August puts it, an appropriation of the very intimacy or interiority of the subject: a reproduction, therefore, a repetition of the very movement of the production or constitution of the subject. A mimesis, in sum, of auto-production—which is moreover the extreme limit of mimesis (or its most secret core), a bit like Kant's statement on the education of the genius, explaining that one genius does not imitate another but goes to his sources. This is also why Schlegelian "mimetics," in keeping with a very old tradition, is actually based on an erotics and is linked with the esoteric theme of initiation. The proscription of all moral pedagogy does not, as we shall see, rule out the possibility of a mystical psychagogy. The letter *On Philosophy* to Dorothea, which in this respect doubles an earlier commentary on the *Symposium*,[17] states this unequivocally: "Humanity cannot be inoculated, nor can virtue be either taught or learned, except through friendship or love of genuine and capable men, and through familiarity with ourselves, with the gods within us" [*DA* 448].

The possibility of auto-formation or of auto-production that thus opens up here needs to be examined: it is clearly one of the artist's privileges. But one must first see that it is on the basis of such a "mimetics" that Schlegel, who is faithful in this respect to the general program of the period,[18] gives the artist the role of "educator" of humanity. An educator who does not actually teach, but rather serves as a "model" (with the restrictions mentioned earlier), an initiator whose sole vocation is nonetheless to "cultivate" [*bilden*] (*I* 54), and ultimately, although this is rather crudely to combine Lessing and Schiller, to ensure the aesthetic education of the human race. For this is indeed the central concern of the *Ideas*, this *Bildung* through which, alone, "a human being, who is wholly that, becomes altogether human and permeated by humanity" (*I* 65), and which is defined by "idea" 37 as "the highest good and the only useful thing."

It is also necessary to note that this *Bildung* is not, rigorously speaking, "aesthetic" (this term is always given a pejorative coloring in the *Ideas*; see *I* 72, for example). The "fullness of *Bildung*" can of course be found only in the "highest poetry." But to find "the profundity of humanity," one must nevertheless still seek "among the philosophers" (*I* 57). This is because the artist fulfills the function of mediator (or of "educator") only to the unique extent that, in him, poetry and philosophy find a way to reconcile themselves or to "fuse." To the extent, therefore, that he is a *religious* man.

But let us not get ahead of ourselves. The question is still to understand how the process of *Bildung* can function or be organized.

"Idea" 54, to which we referred a moment ago, reads as follows in its complete form: "The artist should have as little desire to rule as to serve. He can only cultivate [*bilden*], do nothing but cultivate, and so help the State only by cultivating masters and servants, only by exalting politicians and managers into artists." Politically, nothing could be more clear. And for good reason. For, in fact, the model of the functioning of *Bildung* is *also* political (which certainly does not mean exclusively political). It is political in that the goal of *Bildung* is "republican" (a theme that was already frequent in the *Fragments*), and in that this goal, according to the logic of the example, must therefore be presented or represented (*dargestellt*), at least in "microcosmic" form. Hence the artist's independence with respect to the State (i.e., vis-a-vis all social relations reduced to the division between mastery and servitude), but hence also the constitution of artists into a "nation of Kings" comparable to the assembly of Roman senators (*I* 114)—or a sort of egalitarian, absolutely "democratic" republic of artists in which no "citizen" could make himself director or, as "idea" 114 says, no artist could be "the sole artist among artists, the central artist, the director of all the others."

The "elitist," so to speak, aspect of such a "society of artists" obviously contradicts the "republican" ideal it claims for itself. But also, in contrast to what takes place in the *Fragments* (where *Bildung* is understood as an immediate "putting-into-form"), *Bildung* is conceived as a *process*. *Bildung* is not yet completed, according to the "system" established by the *Ideas*: "As yet," says "idea" 96, "there exist no wholly cultivated human beings." The "society of artists" is thus nothing other than the utopia of completed *Bildung*. And doubly so, since as yet it does not actually exist as such but simply forms the object of a vow or of a call—a call that is no longer, as in the time of the *Lyceum*, a mere project for a journal but, on the very eve of the group's dislocation, a sort of Manifesto for future use (and what are the *Ideas*, at bottom, if not the text of such a Manifesto?). This is actually why the model sketched out here of an exemplary society—artist is not only "elitist" but also "mystical" (which is also to say "mysterious," secret, esoteric)—and why the mediation that such a society must perform is more "initiatory," strictly speaking, than exemplary.

Hence the motif, which appears continually throughout the *Ideas*, of the necessity of constituting a secret "alliance" of artists, a League like the medieval Hansa (*I* 142) or, better yet, a sort of "Masonic" *Bund*, wherein each member would be joined to the others by an oath (*I* 32),[19] and where the very possibility of the auto-constitution of the subject—i.e., the possibility for each artist to be a "mediator for all the others," as "idea" 44 puts it—would be collectively felt. The *Bund*, in other words, would present (in the sense of *Darstellung*) the very thing that Kant, speaking of the Sage, declared unpresentable, that is, by means of the auto-mediation of each individual through himself and of all individuals through one another, the efficacity of the subject's access to itself.

From this it becomes clear why the "initiatory" artist (for whom, and we shall return to this, Schlegel reserved the name "cleric" [*Geistliche*]) could be held up, in the formation of the human race, as absolute example or, more accurately, as absolute *figure*—that is, as example and figure at the very limit of exemplarity and figuration. He *is* the Subject itself, in the possibility of its own infinitization or absolutization. The subject, as we shall see, insofar as it is equated with the divine. Thus, the artist is not only the one who is among men "what men are among the other creatures [*Bildungen*] of the earth" (*I* 43); nor is he only the one who "makes humanity an individual," a "higher organ of the soul where the vital spirits of all external humanity join together, and where inner humanity has its primary sphere of action" (*I* 64). Rather, he is that absolute mediator who "perceives the divinity within himself"—who perceives himself as divine or as "the God within us"—and who is charged with "revealing," "communicating," and "presenting this divinity to all mankind in his conduct and actions, in his words and works" (*I* 44). Which in fact presupposes, and we will have to speak of this again, that mediation as such *operates*, literally, puts itself to work in the absolute (or absolutely productive) because annihilating form (or "figure") of auto-sacrifice.

It also becomes clear why, if the "model" or "example" is this both auto-centered and pluri-centered society-artist, the *Ideas* themselves, in their own "organization" are its perfectly adequate Manifesto, i.e., its *Darstellung*. In this sense, and according to what Schlegel himself calls the "esoteric concept" of the book, the *Ideas* achieve the status of the book. They at the very least prefigure that "Bible" that will be, in the politico-artistic project sketched out here, "the new, eternal gospel that Lessing prophesied" (*I* 95). The Bible: the plural book, "system of books," "infinite book," "eternally developing book"—and not the "isolated" or "particular" book. As "idea" 95 says, "no idea is isolated, but is what it is only in combination with all other ideas." But then, too, each of the "ideas" that in their fragmentation make up the *Ideas* "points toward the center" (*I* 155)—that center which each artist incarnates or carries within himself and which is unique only in its very dispersion.

But what is striking in this project is the place it reserves for love.

First of all, the motif is relatively new. The "symphilosophy" of the *Fragments* presupposed friendship—which one rediscovers here in the same place (or nearly), and with a comparable function. But the model of the creative relation, in an altogether classical fashion—and despite (or because of?) Friedrich's fascination with the Diotima of the *Symposium*—remained the Platonizing model of the homosexual relation. In the *Ideas*, however, the "pedagogical" aim, which presupposes the letter *On Philosophy* to Dorothea, takes the difference between the sexes into account and assigns heterosexuality a more precise role: the education of women is *also* in the program, and even plays a determinant part in the sort of "cultural revolution" that is being announced (if not prepared for). "If you want to achieve great things," says "idea" 115, "then inflame and educate [*bilde*] women and young men. Here, if anywhere, fresh strength and health are still to be found, and this is the way that the most important reformations have been accomplished." In sum, what could be called the moment or period of the "idea" marks the taking into account of "femininity." Why?

To remain solely with the text of the *Ideas*, the reason is very simple: woman, being the very essence of the "mystical," is the *figure* of initiation. Twice Schlegel states: "Mysteries are feminine" (*I* 128 and 137), adding, in order to make himself clear, "They like to veil themselves, but still want to be seen and solved" (*I* 128). And this is why the *Ideas* (from the first entry) are placed under the sign, already invoked by Novalis in *The Disciples at Saïs*, of the goddess Isis, that is, of mystical eroticism and esoteric (or "Masonic") initiation—in accordance with all the constraining power of this metaphor of the truth continually falling back on the truth of the metaphorical in general, which connects the quest for truth to the desire for nakedness and makes revelation an unveiling: "It is time to tear away the veil of Isis and reveal the mystery." The old story of the truth-woman. . . .

But also, and perhaps above all, *Bildung*, if it must be the formation of the "completed human" (of the "total man"), cannot ignore the sexual division of humanity: another old story about a division—about nostalgia for unity[20] and the desire for fusion.[21]

In this case, however, the division is precise: it is a division of faculties, or of suitabilities, for the "sublation" that clearly supports the entire unitary and totalizing aim of *Bildung*. If one intends to dissolve or resolve this division, one is thus obliged to analyze it beforehand. This is, moreover, why the letter *On Philosophy* constantly must be assumed behind the *Ideas*.

In its initial intention at least, the letter *On Philosophy* can be understood to propose a commentary that is meant to explicate the "pedagogical" consequences of two of the Fragments, which very schematically and almost presciently contain both a representation [*tableau*] of the division and an indication of its possible solution or resolution. "'Women,'" states *Athenaeum* fragment 102, "have absolutely no sense for art, but for poetry they do; no talent for science, but for philosophy. They certainly don't lack a capacity for speculation, for inward intuition of the infinite—but they have no sense for abstraction, something that can be learned much more easily." And *Athenaeum* fragment 420 states, as part of a discussion of the possibility of a criterion for determining the morality of a "cultivated woman" [*gebildete Frau*]: "if she knows of something greater than greatness, . . . if she is capable of enthusiasm, then she is innocent in the moral sense. In this respect, one can say that all feminine virtue is religion."[22] In amplified form (and nourished, it must be noted, by an attentive reading of the Kant of *Observations on the Feeling of the Beautiful and Sublime*[23]), such in fact is the "system" of the letter *On Philosophy*.

This division in fact corresponds to the distinction drawn in the letter *On Philosophy* between "nature" and "destination" [*Bestimmung*]. By nature, woman is a domestic being (hence the ordinary "misery" of her condition, against which Schlegel protests with all his energy); her destination, on the other hand, or her virtue, is religion. Indeed, as we know, this is not "religious" religion (which we would do better, says Schlegel, to call something else), but the "sense" or the (speculative) intuition of the divine, and of the divine "within us." Or in other words the height of "humanity." By the same token, from the viewpoint of what Schlegel calls "organization," the maternal finality that determines the feminine figure, the union between body and soul that she manifests, the "tender sympathy" that is proper to her (and that gives her all her power to gather together and embellish life)—in short, everything that makes up her beauty (as opposed to the "sublime" that characterizes the masculine figure) is indissociably humanity and religion. But as we know, humanity, in its very absoluteness (it is "indisputably" superior to the divine) cannot be learned; at the very most, it can fulfill or complete itself or, in other words, "form" itself. The discrepancy between nature and destination makes the fulfillment of woman (her feminization, if you will), which is the fulfillment of her destination, presuppose her "acculturation" or formation, her *Bildung*—which passes through both the amorous relation (since man is the formative power *par excellence*) and the free apprenticeship of an element of *Bildung* in general. This, then, is why women need to initiate themselves into philosophy (thus the letter *On Philosophy*'s directive: "philosophy is indispensable to women"). Or, if you prefer, this is the origin of that "disposition to philosophy" that women manifest, obviously not as a result of their nature (of which the cultural analogon is poetry[24]), but because philosophy is nothing other than the *instrument* of religion. As "idea" 34 says: "Whoever has religion will speak in poetry. But to seek and find religion, you need the instrument [*Werkzeug*] of philosophy."

On this basis, the entire "pedagogical" program of the letter *On Philosophy* to Dorothea, that of an amorous initiation to philosophy, can be organized. But this initiation is actually double, for such is the law of amorous reciprocity. That man should initiate woman to philosophy, thereby providing her with access to fulfilled religion, supposes in return that woman should be capable of satisfying man's need for poetry. Without an exchange, in other words, between one and the other sex, without the simultaneous intersection of their natures and destinations, no completed "humanity" and no effective religion is possible. This is also why sexual difference is relatively secondary: it is the human in general alone that is divine—according to the harmony of that "Golden Age," in which genius and love were combined (*I* 19). "Only a gentle masculinity," states the letter *On Philosophy* to Dorothea, "only an autonomous femininity are right, true, and beautiful. And if this is so, one must not further exaggerate the character of the sex in any way . . . but rather seek to soften it by means of powerful counter-measures, so that everyone, in what is proper to him or her, is able to find a space as boundless as possible in which to move freely, according to pleasure and love, in the entire sphere of humanity" [*DA* 449]. Which amounts to saying that initiation becomes complete only with the reciprocal co-penetration of poetry and philosophy. It should be noted that this is also one of the great themes of the *Ideas*: "Depending on one's point of view, poetry and philosophy are different spheres, different forms, or simply factors of religion. For only try to combine the two and you will find yourself with nothing but religion" (*I* 46). And this explains the adoption of the very genre of the letter or, more precisely, the necessary mediation of such a genre in the general project of romantic writing.

The fragmentary obstinacy, in effect, with all that it carries along with it or accentuates (i.e., in general, the *religious* motif), presupposes a passage through the letter. In fact, to be even more precise, and because it is radically indissociable from the problematic that Schlegel envisaged under the name of religion, it assumes the simultaneous disparity and intersection of the letter and the fragment—of the love letter and the Manifesto, of the "pedagogical" project and the "political" project. What is inscribed within their disparity or separation—is already in the process of inscribing itself—is the "work" in yet another genre (the novel, as we shall see, and we are thinking of *Lucinde*), a work that is at once part and whole, in keeping with the fragmentary logic itself, of that "perfected literature" that never ceases to assemble and disperse itself in the "eternally developing" book of which "idea" 95 speaks. What is involved in their intersection, on the other hand (if it can be isolated in this manner), just as it was, albeit differently, in fragmentation—is what we have called the moral genre of the fragment. Schlegel would no doubt have called it a "religious" genre, or would at least have conceived of it as a variant of the religious "propaedeutic"—although that does not prevent him, and we will soon see why, from calling it "moral." In any case, this is what Schlegel was concerned with as the question of the popular.

As the letter *On Philosophy* to Dorothea does not fail to re-mark,[25] the genre of the letter is a popular genre. In the order of the written (and for the initiator— man—who claims it[26]), it is at least the equivalent of that conversation or dialogue through which the (amorous) apprenticeship to philosophy could also, and more easily, take place. And consequently, it corresponds, on the level of the "social spirit" or "sociality" that ultimately delimits the sphere of activity of the popular (the salon[27]), to the sort of popularizing works, intended for "ladies," typified by Algarotti's *Newtonism* or Fontenelle's *Entretiens*.[28] In short, the letter (in other words, the letter *On Philosophy* as well) is something like the "philosophy lesson in a park"—or rather, see *Lucinde*, in a bedroom.

It would be, that is, if the letter *On Philosophy* did not, instead of immediately giving such a lesson, undertake to demonstrate its necessity and examine its conditions of possibility. This is why the letter *On Philosophy* remains "programmatic" and applies itself to defining, precisely in the name of popularity, that union between philosophy and poetry which alone is capable of providing the transition to religion, or in other words, of presenting what Schlegel calls a "philosophy for man." It is also why, after having inventoried the different philosophies available (recognizing the necessity of "rewriting" Kant,[29] extolling the philosopher of philosophy in Spinoza, erecting Fichte as a model, and dreaming of an ideal introduction to Plato), the letter *On Philosophy* nevertheless comes to the conclusion that such a popular philosophy is still to be written.

Its model would be . . . the letter *On Philosophy* itself. At least provisionally, in a "preparatory" sense, as the sketch of a more complete *Darstellung* whose vastness overwhelms Schlegel. And it is certainly not by chance that Schlegel in the end resigns himself to calling this more modest "genre," for which he admitted having no name, "moral." "Imagine," he said,

> conversations with oneself on objects concerning man as a whole, or at least taken from that single perspective alone; without more analyses than are permitted in a friendly letter, or in the tone of a flowing conversation, like this letter I am writing you. I would prefer to call it *morals* rather than philosophy, although it is different from what is commonly understood by this word. In order to produce what I am thinking of in this genre, one must above all be a man: and then, of course, a philosopher as well [*DA* 468].

This sounds like Montaigne. But that is because, *mutatis mutandis*, it is Montaigne. In other words, because it defines, as *moral*, the "genre" (if it is one) of the "essay" itself that, as we know, is a mixture of conversation with oneself, free conversation, the letter or the address, and, as we have seen, the sentence and the maxim. The moral genre: the unassignable and plural genre, between essays and fragments, of the subject itself; or, if one prefers, the genre of the *Darstellung* of man (of the human condition). And consequently, the genre of exemplarity—and of the reciprocal initiation. But from Montaigne to Schlegel (as from the classical Moralists, whose tradition is founded by Montaigne, to Schlegel), exemplarity has been transformed into "characterization" (a characterization of the philosopher is the only thing lacking in Fichte, and thus the "only piece of work" that remains[30]), and the amorous relation begins to be privileged over friendship. Above all, because we have entered the age of Subjectity and, within it, the period of the speculative and of the auto-constitution of the absolute Subject, the Ancients are no longer the only "authority" (the only authors), nor is Plutarch or Diogenes Laertius the only reservoir of maxims, examples, or citations. Rather, it is a matter of "sublating" the opposition of the ancient and modern, and of striking, for the subject being born, the first "maxims" in whose mirror he will be able to recognize himself, and which will form the cornerstones of the future *Darstellung*—of the work in which and as which he will come to himself.[31]

Nevertheless, the fact remains that this moral genre, as we have said, is altogether inscribed under the sign of religion. And that, despite everything (despite Schlegel's multiple precautions[32]), we still do not know exactly what this word refers to. More specifically, we must be wary of the confusion to which it lends itself.

Schlegel himself, returning several years later to the experience of the *Athenaeum*, tried to explain it:

> In their beginnings (in the earliest issues of the *Athenaeum*), criticism and universality are the predominant goal; in the following issues, the spirit of mysticism is the most essential. One should not be upset by the word: it indicates the announcement of the Mysteries of art and science, which, without such Mysteries, would not deserve their names. But above all, it indicates the most vigourous defense of symbolic forms and their necessity, against profane meaning.[33]

One should make no mistake about it, even though the misunderstanding, clearly, is ultimately simultaneous with the thing itself: religion, here the religion of the *Ideas* or of the letter *On Philosophy*, is not religion, and especially not

Christianity. More precisely, if it has anything to do with religion in the ordinary sense of the word (or better: in the *historic* sense of the word[34]), it is only in the context of a complex relation, a relation that cannot be construed as a relation of identity or even of analogy. As a result, this in no way amounts to saying that it is simply a matter, as in the later or final "lapses" of romanticism, of a religion of art, or even of an "aesthetic" religion. No, what is in question here is something altogether different: it is strictly speaking *art as religion*.

If, in effect, all the threads drawn out up until this point (the question of the subject and of the work, *Bildung* and the relation between the sexes, the role of the artist and sociality, etc.) intertwine in the motif of religion, this is because it is their common motif or, what amounts to the same thing, because it does not transfer the question of the subject's production of the work of art elsewhere, nor does it submit it to any exterior agency; on the contrary, it reveals its logic and formulates its law. It is totally unrelated to religion, as we will see. This is so true that the irreligion, or rather the antireligion of *Widerporst*, far from discouraging Schlegel, struck him, on the contrary, as quite useful in combatting the growing "theologism" or "clericalism"[35] of Schleiermacher and especially the specifically Christian mysticism that, after the composition of *Europe*, became Novalis' great temptation.[36] It also explains how Schlegel could place (or take a mischievous pleasure in placing) all of the *Ideas* under the preliminary invocation of Isis that figured in Novalis' earliest texts, as if to clarify from the outset what was at stake in that religion of which "there is already talk" (*I* 1). And, in fact, the allusion is very clear. Just as "idea" 106 discreetly advises the author of *Faith and Love* not to dream of the ancient (i.e., medieval) political incarnation of religion but to stick with art and culture, so too, the adoption of the "mystical" theme of the *Disciples at Saïs* signifies unequivocally that religion is a matter of the unveiling of truth (in other words, of the subject[37]). And not of a re(veiling), as is suggested by this or that cryptic (or veiled, as long as we are on the subject) homage to Schleiermacher, the veil-maker, in Novalis' *Europe*.[38] *Widerporst*, incidentally, did not fail to play on this allusion in turn.[39]

The paradox, here, seems to consist in seeing the artistic protest against religion carried out in the name of the unveiling of the goddess—truth—that unveiling which philosophy, precisely, from Kant to Hegel, will continually and stubbornly hold up *against* the aesthetic, against the "philosophy of art," and (at least in Hegel's case) against romanticism itself.

But this paradox, as it turns out, is enlightening.

It suggests first of all that the religion that Schelling and Schlegel conjointly attacked is nothing other than that religion which completes itself in aestheticism, or, in other words, in the (ultimately pietist) religion of an inaccessible deity, whose relation with man, consequently, implies the necessity of passing through representation and moral modesty. Conversely, what Schelling and Schlegel claim as their own—and which is *also* presented as religion—is nothing other, in keeping with the same paradox, than what speculative metaphysics itself is aiming at. But in *art*—and in *form*. Religion, in other words, is art itself, but art henceforth thought as the (absolute, remainderless) *Darstellung* of truth. As the motif has reminded us several times since the "Overture," truth, to which theoretical access is pushed back to infinity, in the work and as the work (that is to say also in the artist and as the artist, and therefore in what should be referred to as the "subject-work"), is immediately and infinitely accessible— immediately accessible in its very infinity. In sum, and at the risk of a slight exaggeration, one could say that art, the work, and the artist, are in this perspective what the System, the Concept, and the philosopher himself (the one who for example speaks "for us" in the *Phenomenology of Spirit*) are in the Hegelian perspective. Which suggests that the figure (the *Gestalt*) in the Hegelian sense has no place here. Or again, one could say, changing the reference—but the result would be exactly the same—that the religion in question here is not religion "within the limits of reason alone," but rather *religion within the limits of art*—that is, the illimitation that art confers on the "subject-work" existing within its limits. For this reason, the great question in religion understood in this manner is that of the *formation of form*. Which is not representative form, but rather, as we can see for example in the letter *On Philosophy's* statements on masculine form and feminine form, the fusion of everything that composes the absolute. This status, however, does not prevent the incompletion of form, or what Schlegel—with reference to an ancient Pallas—called roughness[40] or, in short, that *schematization* which alone is capable of drawing out the essential.

Schlegel had a word for that. He spoke of the *symbol*—or of "symbolic forms," whose symbolism consisted, he said, in "that by which, everywhere, the appearance of the finite is placed in relation with the truth of the eternal and, in this manner, precisely dissolved therein."[41] But he also speaks in analogous terms of man himself. Thus, in the *Ideas*: "Think of the finite formed [*gebildet*] into the infinite, and you will think of a man" (*I* 98). Therefore, what was at stake in the question of the formation of form—in the "religious" question *par excellence*—was indeed the possibility of thinking the "subject-work," in other words the becoming-artist of the work or absolute auto-production itself: man as the work of art creating itself, art henceforth identified with the being-artist.

It thus becomes understandable that the "religious" motif of the mediator plays such an important role in the *Ideas*. In the order of *Bildung* in general, it is the motif of the subject-work, of the possibility of a presentation of the infinite as the auto-production of the subject. This is why "idea" 44 makes the mediator "the one who perceives the divine within himself" and who, in a gesture comparable to (although the inverse of) the movement that animates the Hegelian

Absolute, sacrifices himself in order to "present [*darzustellen*] this divinity to all mankind." Fundamentally, the exemplarity of the absolute Subject (of the artist), absolute exemplarity, is auto-sacrifice. Although it is certainly one of the great "romantic" themes, only "religion," in other words, artistic speculation, allows it to be envisaged without stupidity. For sacrifice, the "hidden meaning of sacrifice," is "the annihilation of the finite because it is finite" (*I* 131): it is infinitization itself. This, moreover, is the reason for human sacrifices: "to demonstrate that this is its only justification," continues "idea" 131, "one must choose to sacrifice whatever is most noble and most beautiful; and especially man, the flower of the earth. Human sacrifices are the most natural sacrifices." But "natural" is not to be equated here with "human": "man is more than the flower of the earth; he is reasonable, and reason is free and in itself nothing but an eternal auto-determination into the infinite." Thus, the true sacrifice, the properly "human" sacrifice is the self-sacrifice of the artist: "All artists are Decians,[42] and to become an artist means nothing other than to consecrate oneself to the gods of the underworld. In the enthusiasm of annihilation, the meaning of divine creation is revealed for the first time. Only in the midst of death does the lightning bolt [*Blitz*] of eternal life explode." We might also remark that this scheme is precisely that of *irony*, as Kierkegaard will understand perfectly.[43] It is the scheme of irony, if one recalls that irony, insofar as it addresses the poet himself, reveals to the poet that his truth—from the point of view of the infinite—is his own limitation, or in other words, his finitude.[44] This is also the scheme of irony with respect to the problematic of form, if irony, as Benjamin notes,[45] is that destruction of form that makes every work into the work absolutely speaking.

And perhaps at bottom it is a "stroke" of irony to refer to such a metaphysics of art as "religion." Unless irony itself, by a supplementary turn (by an imperceptible movement of reflection), were the mockery of what should be understood by "religion." Or again, unless there were no *Witz* in these denominations. "No occupation," says "idea" 53, "is so human as one that simply completes, joins, fosters." And what if "religion" should be understood in the proper meaning of the word? As *re-ligion*, the possibility of "linking together"? Or as a means, like (and in the "same" position as) the future Hegelian *Aufhebung*, of linking the indefinite series of oppositions—of art and religion, paganism and Christianity, man and woman, work and artist, philosophy and poetry, etc.—as parts of the Same in general? *Athenaeum* fragment 121 clearly "programmed" this eventuality and, at the same time, anticipated the true reason for the title: "An idea is a concept completed to the point of irony, an absolute synthesis of absolute antitheses, the continual self-engendering exchange of two thoughts in strife."

Appendix:
Note on Heinz Widerporst's
Epicurean Confession of Faith

Schelling proposed this poem to Friedrich Schlegel in 1799 for the *Athenaeum*. As we have already suggested, it represented a reaction—which Caroline and Friedrich shared—to Schleiermacher's *Discourses on Religion* as well as to Novalis's religious direction in *Europe, or Christianity* and, generally, to the climate of religiosity that had become dominant within the Jena group. The name *Widerporst*, coined by Schelling from the adjective *widerborstig*, means "recalcitrant." Friedrich, who somewhat maliciously wrote to Schleiermacher that he himself had encouraged Schelling to reawaken his "old enthusiasm for irreligion," hoped to publish the texts of Novalis and *Widerporst* (because Schelling's name was to remain undisclosed) side by side. His brother, August, opposed to this project, appealed to Goethe, whose intervention obliged Friedrich to renounce this textual *Witz.*[1]

We have indicated above (in "The Idea: Religion within the Limits of Art") the way this text's "irreligion" is, in fact, in perfect agreement with the "religion" of Friedrich's *Ideas* and letter *On Philosophy* to Dorothea. We must still, however, mark the place that this poem occupies in Schelling's development, which is to say, in the development of "philosophical romanticism." Between the "Earliest System-Programme" and *The Philosophy of Art*, it constitutes what might be called Schelling's (roundabout) attempt to realize the *"speculative epic"* that he regarded as the true fulfillment of philosophy, as its poetic *Darstellung,* its presentation of its auto-poiesy in a *Dichtung* comparable to the one frequently alluded to in *Widerporst* (see lines 46, 59, 122, 128, and 299). In fact, the extract of the poem that Schelling published in his *Journal of Speculative Physics* in 1801—the epic of the "giant spirit" that comes to consciousness within man—is nothing other than a sort of abridgment of his system, which was published, after all, under the title: *Several Words More on the Relation of the Philosophy of Nature to Idealism*. Nothing other, therefore, than the "great heroic poem" whose preparation was mentioned in *The Ages of the World*, and apparently nothing other than the living *Darstellung* of that philosophy, which the posthumous dialogue *Clara* puts into question. And yet, it is something

79

altogether different, since it is a satire—in the modern sense of the word, first of all, but also in the old sense (the poem is written in a popular meter that originated with Hans Sachs and is mixed with more recent meters, in the manner of Goethe's *Faust*)—and is thus also the mockery or reverse of an epic. Because *The Night Watches of Bonaventura*, romanticism's other "satiric" text, is also quite possibly attributable to Schelling (who in 1802 had signed poems with the pseudonym Bonaventura[2]), it is undoubtedly not too much to say that the romantic desire for the speculative poem, for the auto-presentation of the *opus philosophicum*, could only lead—with reference at least to what was published—to the carnavalesque genre, which seems to contradict its properly philosophical intention. Unless this intention is ultimately confirmed when the carnavalesque turns out to be philosophy's own criticism of the retrospective putting-into-form of a given system, a putting-into-form that has been substituted for the auto-poiesy through which it ought rigorously to produce itself *as its own form*. Hans Sachs would then be the critical model here of the incompletion of the poem, whose ideal example was the *Divine Comedy*, to which Friedrich had exposed Schelling.

It hardly needs to be said that Friedrich, too, returns to the carnavalesque—albeit in the novelistic "genre"—with *Lucinde*, to which *Widerporst* makes a reference that is at once complicitous and ironic.[3] In other words—and to recall Benjamin's formulation, which was mentioned above in "The Fragment: The Fragmentary Exigency"—the systematic vision of the absolute and the absolute vision of the system face each other, stare at each other, and in a certain sense disfigure each other in the same satire of the work, in what amounts to a double parody of theory—or of religion—in the Work.

3   The Poem: A Nameless Art

> Spirit is like a music of thoughts: where soul
> is, there feelings too have outline and form,
> noble proportions, and charming coloration.
> Temperament [*Gemüt*] is the poetry of sub-
> lime reason and, united with philosophy and
> moral experience, it gives rise to that nameless
> art which seizes the confused transitoriness of
> life and shapes it into an eternal unity.
>
> —*Athenaeum fragment 339.*

We will refer in this chapter to two texts. First, Friedrich Schlegel's
Dialogue on Poetry [*Gespräch über die Poesie*], which is one of the last major
texts of the *Athenaeum*.[1] It appeared in 1800, divided between the two final
issues of the journal and, along with the *Fragments*, has remained the best-
known text of the entire enterprise—its second "monument," as it were.

We will also refer to August Schlegel's *Lectures on Art and Literature* [*Die
Kunstlehre*]—which are not a simple "complement" to the *Dialogue*. Here, of
course, we are no longer dealing with a "text" properly speaking, or even with a
"document" that might be unproblematically included in the output of the
Athenaeum: the approximately thirty lectures that August Schlegel announced
under this title were delivered at the University of Berlin during 1801 and
1802—immediately following the discontinuation of the journal and the breakup
of the group. And the manuscript that survives, as is almost always the case in
such a situation, does not consist of a continuous text, but rather of a series of
more or less elaborated developments, interspersed with notes, outlines, and
various sketches or frameworks meant to serve as guides for improvisation. As it
stands, however, this course (along with Schelling's *Philosophy of Art*, which
was composed soon afterward[2]) represents one of the rare attempts at systematization (after the fact, no doubt, but after only a very short delay) that the Jena
romantics succeeded in bringing to completion. And the fact that it is a lecture
course is far from insignificant here. As we have already noted, the question of

81

academic exploitation must surely be taken into account—and in fact, certain of these lectures will rigorously and precisely recapitulate, reassemble, order, or reformulate that which the *Dialogue* "fictions" or "sets to work" in an entirely different way; but the *Dialogue,* too, leaves behind it only rough sketches, approximations, or bits (not to speak of "fragments") of a decidedly improbable or, at least for Friedrich, decidedly unrealizable system. This in no way prevents the lecture course, as we will learn from the *Dialogue* (and in more ways than one), from relating to what is essentially in question in the name of romanticism—from relating, in other words, to what we can call, without anticipating ourselves, *literature*—in a manner that is more complex than one might suspect. Especially today. For its "academic" style of exposition raises more than the questions concerning, for example, the didactic genre (or "didascalic," as the *Dialogue's* philologist says);[3] concerning what romanticism refounds, in order to definitively found, in the name of "criticism";[4] or concerning, in short, everything that is indicated, as we have seen, in the general problematic of the *Darstellung* of the theoretical. For it remains to be understood why romanticism should have been the first literary movement to demand entry into the University—into universality—in order to complete itself and lose itself there at the same time and in the same movement, thereby inaugurating the entire modern history of literature in the University (or of the University in literature). As everyone knows, if only by denying it, this history is far from finished. And this is truly the least one can say.

What is in question in these two texts?

Quite simply, what we have just referred to, and what the *Lectures,* if only by their title, unambiguously designate as *literature.*

It is true that in the announcement of the lecture series, as was perfectly normal in light of academic imperatives and the inherent demands of an exoteric presentation, August Schlegel used the term "fine literature" [*schöne Litteratur*]. But besides the fact that the word itself—without the qualifier—had already appeared in the *Athenaeum,* taken in the modern sense that the romantics were, precisely, attempting to delimit and conceptualize,[5] the addition of the qualifying adjective in the *Lectures's* title also marks that moment (almost exactly contemporary with the appearance of Madame de Staël's *De la littérature*) when "literature" ceases to refer, within the totality of written things, to the ensemble of lettered (or "classical") culture that should form the basis of every completed education (the equivalent of the future "humanities" of our academic systems), and begins to name the art of writing in general. It marks the moment, in other words, when "literature" is raised to an art. *Lectures on Art and Fine Literature* should thus be understood as: Lectures on literature considered as art—and as a specific art.

However, as we will soon see, it can also be understood thus: Lectures on art considered as literature. Or, if you prefer: Lectures on literature considered as the essence of art.

In this ever-possible reversal of the title, there is the—probably insolvable—entire question of literature.

What then is in question?

Quite simply the question itself: what is literature?

In romanticism's own terms—and in those particular to the well-known *Athenaeum* fragment 116 (of which it would seem, in the end, that the *Lectures* and the *Dialogue* are no more than the commentary)—the question is: what is "romantic poetry?" Or more precisely: what is the "romantic genre?" Consequently, the question is nothing other than what we have referred to in a condensed manner as the question of the "literary genre."

The important thing, however, is that it be a matter of this question as such. In other words, the important thing is first that the question should persist and insist, and that its answer, obviously, should be awaited. This does not simply mean that romanticism, strictly thought, is the place where this question appeared, or if you prefer, that romanticism opens the very epoch of literature. Nor does it simply mean that romanticism consequently can be defined only as the perpetual auto-referring of the question: What is romanticism?—or: What is literature? Rather, it means that literature, as its own infinite questioning and as the perpetual positing of its own question, dates from romanticism and as romanticism. And therefore that the romantic question, the question of romanticism, does not and cannot have an answer. Or, at least that its answer can only be interminably deferred, continually deceiving, endlessly recalling the question (if only by denying that it still needs to be posed). This is why romanticism, which is actually a moment (the moment of its question) will always have been more than a mere "epoch," or else will never cease, right up to the present, to incomplete the epoch it inaugurated. It was well aware of this, moreover: "The romantic kind of poetry [*Dichtart*] is still becoming; that is its real essence: that it should forever be becoming and never be perfected" (*A* 116).

This impossibility of romanticism's answering the very question with which it is confounded, or in which all of it is brought together, this *native impossibility* of romanticism, of course, explains why this question should in reality be quite empty and why, in the name of "romanticism" or "literature" (no less than "poetry," "*Dichtung*," "art," "religion," etc.), it should bear only upon an indistinct, indeterminable *thing*, indefinitely retreating as it is approached, open to (almost) any name and suffering none: a thing that is unnameable, shapeless, faceless [*sans figure*]—in the last instance, "nothing." Romanticism (literature) is that which has no essence, not even in its inessentiality. This is perhaps why the question itself, ultimately, is never posed, or else is posed an incalculable number of times; and why the romantic texts, in their fragmentation or very dispersion, are only the interminable (forever approximate, somnambulant) answer to this question which is by right unformulatable or again, in other words, always too hastily formulated, or too facilely and thoughtlessly formulated, as if the "thing" always simply goes without saying.

Neither the *Fragments* (by their "form") nor, for example, religion (by its "content"), unless this should be the reverse, was capable of answering for, or putting-into-question, literature (romanticism). Both, after all, were mere effects of the withdrawal of what they sought to delimit. If you prefer, both were merely the *Darstellung* of what in itself, and in exact proportion to its will to appearance, refused all presentation. "Literature" has always been devoted to the withdrawal of truth; and if, as we have seen, the term "mystical" designated the speculative itself for Schlegel,[6] we noted nonetheless that it also refers, as one might expect, to negative theology and Jacob Böhme. Consequently, an additional "turn of the screw," so to speak, was, as it always will be, necessary. In many ways, this is what the *Dialogue* represents here.

There are two reasons for this. The first, of course, is that the *Dialogue* seems—once more—to approach the question head on. It deals explicitly with "poetry" (literature) and indeed, of all the texts that appeared in the *Athenaeum*, it is the only text of any length to be devoted to this question. And certainly the most ambitious.

Above all, however, it makes itself known by its very mode of exposition, its *Darstellung*: it is a *dialogue*. This alone is sufficient for the question of literature to arise within it, to the point of demonstrating its impossibility. This question can never take place, as is well known, except through this "formalist" wrinkle [*repli*]—through this indissociably specular and speculative *mise-en-abyme*, where it is not so certain that this question could avoid missing the very thing (what?) it wanted to be the question of.

Here it becomes necessary to decompose.

First, in order to indicate that the dialogue, like the letter or the aphorism, is no stranger to fragmentation. As you will recall, this is what *Athenaeum* fragment 77 states quite clearly: "A dialogue is a chain or garland of fragments. An exchange of letters is a dialogue on a larger scale, and memorabilia constitute a system of fragments." We spoke earlier, in reference to the *Ideas* and the letter *On Philosophy*, of the "fragmentary obstinacy"; in this case, too, the phrase is entirely appropriate. Friedrich, in sum, never renounced this earliest exigency of romanticism. He even "overdid" it to some extent (considering, for example, that the *Dialogue* in turn contains—a letter) and, no doubt, as we will see shortly, this is what explains the quite peculiar nature of his conception and practice of the dialogue—which is in no way comparable to what we find in

August (who had urged Friedrich to take up this genre[7]) or even in Novalis (whom Friedrich, in turn, in keeping with his customary strategy, had encouraged along the same path[8]).

This fragmentary essence of the dialogue has at least one consequence (among several others that we cannot explore here), namely that the dialogue, similar in this to the fragment, does not properly constitute a genre. This is why the dialogue, like the fragment, turns out to be one of the privileged sites for taking up the question of genre as such. We should not rush things, however.

That the dialogue is not a genre means first of all—in keeping with an equation that is familiar by now—not that dialogue is somehow inadequate with respect to genre, but rather that it is by definition capable of gathering all genres within itself. Dialogue is the "non-genre," or the "genre" of the mixture of genres. Consequently, even more than to its own origin (which for Schlegel is Platonic), the dialogue leads directly back to Roman satire and, in general, to all of the late (and fundamentally "critical") "literature" of the Alexandrian Period, in which the totality of ancient poetry—including philosophy, of course—is assembled, reflected, and completed. Hence, the intimate relations that the dialogue (like the fragment, but in a more immediate manner) maintains with the social spirit (urbanity or sociality), *Witz*, High Culture, the popular, the lively exercise of intellectuality, virtuosity, and so forth—or, in short, with all of those values and qualities that romanticism, as we have seen, inherits from the *Aufklärung* and from (English or French) "moral philosophy" (both of which, moreover, granted a privileged place to dialogue).[9]

Thus far, we are on well-charted ground. But this is also what explains why dialogue, while it perpetuates the fragmentary exigency, also opens up the possibility of overcoming [*lever*] a certain number of antinomies that none of the genres (or "genres") practised in the *Athenaeum* by Schlegel up to that time had been capable of overcoming [*lever*]. Indeed, as opposed in particular to the "letter," which was grounded in—and also intensified—the opposition between writing and speech (i.e., between masculinity and femininity as well, as we recall), thereby bringing the problematic of the popular to its highest pitch,[10] it is no exaggeration to say that dialogue is properly in a position of "sublation" [*relève*]. At least insofar as the *Dialogue* explicitly presents dialogue as the (more or less exact—we must return to this point) transcription of real conversation. Moreover, the fact that it is the women here, precisely, who object to the spontaneous practice of mere conversation (even if brilliant) and demand discourses, i.e., the reading of written texts, is not the least paradoxical aspect of this text. But this exchange of roles is highly revealing, for we shall soon see that in the meticulous "fictioning" [*fictionnement*] of the *Dialogue* the masculine protagonists' obedience to this feminine injunction allows the dialogue's author to fulfill the vow he had formerly made in the letter *On Philosophy*. By mixing styles and genres (including that of the "letter" itself), the author is able to write the multiplicity of short essays he envisaged without any longer fearing a proliferation of "projects," since rapid changes of subject in a lively conversation are, after all, perfectly normal, and can be seen as a necessary stage on the way to the genuinely popular. In this sense, dialogue represents the fulfillment of what we have called the "moral genre of the fragment," and if it does not fulfill it absolutely (and we shall see why), it certainly comes very close. Thus it should not come as a surprise if one of the discourses in question makes a point of insisting, in the name of the "didascalic genre"—or, what amounts to the same thing, in the name of "reciprocal transfers between poetry and philosophy"—on gnomic aphorisms (and philosophical dialogues[11]) or if one of its substitutes (the "letter," in this case) refers, by way of Rousseau, to the tradition of confession and of "subjective literature" in general.[12] Dialogue is the "genre" of the Subject *par excellence*.

And this, paradoxically, brings us to its origin; in other words, Plato. All of the intersecting motifs we have rapidly surveyed here are gathered and tied together in what *Critical Fragment* 42 calls "the sublime urbanity of the Socratic muse"—demonstrating once again that, for the modern age of metaphysics, Socrates (the figure and the person) has always represented the anticipatory incarnation or prototype of the Subject itself. The reason for this, in Schlegel's case at least, is that Socrates—i.e., the Socrates of Plato, Socrates in Plato— by a sort of absolute privilege, is what could be called the subject of irony; Socrates, in other words, becomes the locus of the very exchange that, as both a figure and a work, defines irony (or "logical beauty," as *Critical Fragment* 42 puts it), which is the exchange of form and truth or, and this is strictly identical, of poetry and philosophy. This amounts to making Socrates the subject-"genre" through whom—and as whom—*literature* is inaugurated (and inaugurates itself, with all the force of the reflexive, since irony is also precisely this: the very power of reflection or infinite reflexivity—the other name of speculation). To be entirely rigorous, one must therefore say: Socrates, the Subject in its form or its figure (the exemplary Subject), is the eponymous "genre" of literature as— indissociably—the work and reflection of the work, poetry and criticism, art and philosophy. And consequently a "genre" beyond all genres and containing the theory of this "beyond" within itself—or in other words, at once a general theory of genres and its own theory.

It is precisely at this point that the *novel* comes into play.

But it is still necessary to proceed patiently in order to unfold matters in a methodical fashion.

Assuming, of course, that these matters as such are unfoldable. As things stand, three elements are involved here. For the sake of convenience, let us call them the name, the author, and the reflection. From these elements, three questions arise: the question of genre, the question of the subject and, finally, the question of theory. These three questions, however, enter into an inextricable relation with one another. As always in romanticism, no position is provided from which one might enjoy a commanding overview of the ensemble; no fixed point is offered on the basis of which a system might be securely set into place (and thus ordered, if not organized). This is why *Critical Fragment* 42, still in the name of irony, pointedly presents dialogue as a pure and simple substitute for the system: ". . . wherever one philosophizes in oral or written dialogues, and not in an entirely systematic mode, irony should be demanded and provided."

Nevertheless, in order to gain a clearer view of the matter, ironically or not, one must start from this platitude: the *Dialogue* is deliberately modelled after the Platonic dialogue, which it re-marks at least twice. And not after any sort of dialogue whatever, but after one which, by its agonistic nature, connotes sociality more than any other—namely, the *Symposium*. This does not mean that the *Dialogue* assumes the fiction of a banquet. Unlike Hemsterhuis, for example, who pushes the cult of the genre (or of "genre") to the point of pretending to retranscribe miraculously "rediscovered" Platonic dialogues, Schlegel imitates only the structure of the model (that of a dialogue interspersed with talks or conventionally constructed "discourses"). To be precise, he is interested, for reasons that will soon appear, only in structural complexity of the "Symposium" type. He is not concerned with a "dialogue," in other words, but with a *narrative* [*récit*] containing (or recalling) a dialogue, interspersed, in turn, with discourses.

As we know, this type of structure, from antiquity on, constituted the true originality of Platonic writing. In greater and lesser degrees of complexity, this sort of structure is found in most of Plato's major dialogues, from the *Republic* to the *Sophist* by way of *Theatatus*. Yet this same structure, as we also know, was not only "reflected" and condemned (as epic structure and under the name, if it is one, of "mixed diegesis," i.e., a *mixture* of pure narrative and of "mimetic" or dramatic form[13]) by Plato in the *Republic*, but also obstructed the taxonomic effort of the Aristotelian *Poetics* to such a degree that it had to be abandoned, thus leaving blank—or "'anonymous' (*anōnumos*), for we can find no 'common term' (*koinon ónoma*)"[14]—the missing concept of a single genre that would have made it possible to classify together (between poetry and prose, as Diogenes Laertius reminds us) the mimes of Sophron and Xenarchus, the *Sōkratoi logoi*, and didactic poems like those of Empedocles.[15] If one adds to this—rendering justice to the inventor of this "nameless art"—that the Platonic condemnation of this "genre" (or Plato's "auto-critique") was part of a general indictment of *mimesis*—or, in relation to writing, an indictment of "apocrypty," the dissimulation or dispersion of the author (or the subject of discourse) behind the figures (characters or mouthpieces) of dialogical narration—and that for

Schlegel this mimetic power had always represented the privilege of genius (and particularly of the great writer[16]), then one can see how Platonic dialogue, in the context of romanticism's attempt to be a kind of "return" [*"après-coup"*] of the Greeks, could appear to be the very model of the union of poetry and philosophy, and thus the originary matrix of the *novel*, or in other words, the matrix of that for which the Moderns will at last have discovered a name.

Critical Fragment 26: "Novels are the Socratic dialogues of our time."
Athenaeum fragment 252:

> . . . a philosophy of poetry in general . . . would hover between the union and the division of philosophy and poetry, of praxis and poetry, of poetry in general and genres and types; and it would conclude with their complete union. . . . The keystone would be a philosophy of the novel, the rough outlines of which are contained in Plato's political theory.

This is the thesis of the *Dialogue*.

Or, at least, it is what accounts for its particular *Darstellung*, or if you will, its particular mode of fictioning.

Irony, of course, is its rule and principle.

The ironic in the *Dialogue* is, first of all, even on the level of detail, what belongs to the order of "putting-into-fiction" [*"mise en fiction"*] in the narrow sense (and not of staging [*mise en scène*], an inappropriate term in this case). Ideally, one ought to take time at this point to dismantle carefully the entire "fabrication" of the text. Short of that, however, we must content ourselves with a discussion of two major and virtually indissociable aspects of the text.

The first, of course—for we must not forget that we are still concerned here with the "fragmentary exigency"—is the mirror-like representation of the group itself. The group is, not by chance, represented in its most "critical" phase, the phase inaugurated in the autumn of 1799 by the last large meeting at Jena, which gathers together all members of the "alliance" except Schleiermacher.[17] Say what you will, it is not very difficult to identify the protagonists of the *Dialogue*. The entire *Athenaeum* is in place, each of its members with his or her own preoccupations (from the "new mythology" to the "character sketch [*caractéristic*] of Goethe"),[18] his or her tics of language and thought (especially notable in the "talks," where Friedrich's virtuosity and talent for pastiche are given free rein), the salient aspects of each participant's character or personality (from humor to reserve, and from playfulness to rivalry or repartee)—and each of them with his or her complex relations with all the others, in which the seeds of the group's coming dissolution are plain to see. No doubt it is correct to say that, fundamentally (and regardless of the *Dialogue's* "realism"), it is the text's signatory alone who is speaking or professing his theoretical views;[19] this is indeed the second major aspect of this "putting-into-fiction," and we will return to it shortly. But it goes without saying that the two possibilities are not incompatible. On the contrary, the logic of mimicry [*mimétisme*] is such that the more the differences (i.e., the dissimilation) are accentuated, the more the identity is reinforced and vice versa. Schlegel was, of course, well aware of this, having made virtuosity a vocation and having taken this principle (which, considered from a certain angle, is nothing but the principle of the auto-constitution of the Subject) as the foundation of novelistic power and, as we shall see, of "characterization."[20] This is why there is no point in refusing to recognize Caroline and Dorothea, respectively, in the *Dialogue's* two female roles, Amalia and Camilla.[21] Or in refusing to see that, as for the male roles, Ludovico, the group's philosopher and the author of the "Talk on Mythology," corresponds to Schelling; Lothario, whose pseudonym is borrowed from Goethe[22] and who here represents the poet, always promising a work that never appears, corresponds to Novalis; Marcus, the Goethe "specialist" who is preoccupied with problems of the theatre, corresponds to Tieck; Andrea, the philologist who opens the series of talks with a recapitulation of the history of literature (the "Epochs of Poetry"), corresponds to August; and finally, last but not least, Antonio (the pseudonym of Schleiermacher, the one who knows all about veils, in *Lucinde*) corresponds to Friedrich himself, or "himself," whose performance (i.e., the "Letter on the Novel," which is precisely not a talk and was not even intended for public consumption, and which re-marks, in a "literary" mode, all the stakes of the letter *On Philosophy*[23]) occupies the center of the *Dialogue* and, as the proposal for a "theory of the novel," constitutes the "keystone" of the "philosophy of poetry" that thoroughly delimits it. But the "Letter on the Novel" is not situated exactly at the text's center. For this to be the case—at least if one's calculation is based on the series of talks—Marcus' essay on the styles of Goethe would have to be followed by Lothario's reading of the *work* that he has promised—from the beginning—to produce, and merely promises once more at the end.

The "theory of the novel" would, therefore, form the center of the *Dialogue*, if only the work—the "poem," the *Dichtung* (its particular genre is beside the point here)—were not missing. In which case, and by a new effect of irony, the re-mark would be faultless—doubly faultless. It would be the re-mark of the author, first of all, or of the "novelist," insofar as he projects or disperses himself (the better to ensure his power, of course) into the multiplicity of personages or "characters" that he constructs: and this would be the second aspect of the "putting-into-fiction" of which we spoke earlier. But it would also be the re-mark (this time marking a new step or a new degree of complexity in *Darstellung*, taken in the widest sense) of this "putting-into-fiction" itself, or in other words, the quite Platonizing (if not truly Platonic) re-mark of the infinite capacity for self-reference [*repli sur soi*] of "literary" mimicry.

Yet this is not the case. Of course, there is no shortage of allusions in which the "fabrication" of the *Dialogue* is subtly "reflected" (Schlegel is a master of this sort of trickery, and the Platonic model is law here in any case). Thus, the first pages contain a brief development on the division, within this transcription of real conversations that the *Dialogue* claims to represent, between fiction and truth; likewise, the initial discussion—during which the regulations of this modern "Symposium" are adopted—deals, not surprisingly, with the theatre. But precisely with the theatre (Plato's purely mimetic genre), and not the novel. It is as if Lothario's missing work, which unbalances—or more precisely, *de-centers*—the *Dialogue*, ought to be a tragedy. The power of irony, here, is found wanting.

But this also means that it is reinforced. For nothing, in all this, is left to chance or to the hazards of improvisation. Above all, one should not be deceived by appearances.

That nothing is left to chance means, more precisely, that the "Letter on the Novel" cannot occupy the center of the *Dialogue*, for the *Dialogue* itself *is not a novel*. Or, formulated differently, according to a formulation borrowed from the "Letter on the Novel" itself and modified by a simple inversion of terms: Only a novel is capable of containing its own reflection and of comprehending the theory of its "genre" (or the law of its own engendering, which amounts to the same thing). Or again, but this time reestablishing the order of the terms: there can be no theory of the novel that is not itself a novel. Which is not the case with the *Dialogue* or with its "Letter on the Novel." *Lucinde*,[24] on the other hand, would seem to qualify. Unless of course, within all this falsely abyssal play, and as a final turn of irony, it were precisely the incompletion of *Lucinde* (of which the "Letter on the Novel" is in many respects the commentary) that was aimed at and reflected. Unless the dialogue, therefore, were the form of renunciation here, the *Darstellung* of impossible auto-constitution, and the parody of Plato (or the multiple pastiche, already, of the romantic "style"), the admission of the failure and insufficiency of the work, if not the index—perhaps—of its "un-working." In which case, beyond (or short of) the question of literature, something like the ghost of writing would be secretly at work on (and in) this structure. But in that case, what would become of the difference—and would irony still have the power to master such indistinction [*démarquage*]?

This, perhaps, is fundamentally why the *Dialogue* ultimately cannot define or delimit the romantic genre. In other words, the literary genre. Especially not in (or as) the novel, regardless of traditional ideas on this subject.[25] This does not mean that the novel is not the "genre" that romantic theory so stubbornly sought;

indeed, the contrary is true. Rather, it means that the inability to be defined or delimited probably belongs to the very essence of genre. Genre is undoubtedly the completed, differentiated, identifiable product of an engenderment or of a generation; even in German, where the word's etymological filiation is entirely different,[26] *Gattung* is not unrelated to assemblage in general, or to union and even marriage. But the process of generation, or the process of assemblage, obviously supposes interpenetration and confusion. Or in other words, *mixture* (*gattieren* means "to mix"). It could be said that this is precisely what the romantics envisage as the very essence of literature: the union, in satire (another name for mixture) or in the novel (or even in Platonic dialogue), of poetry and philosophy, the confusion of all the genres arbitrarily delimited by ancient poetics, the interpenetration of the ancient and the modern, etc. But would this be sufficient to define the essence of mixture? What, in fact, is the nature, here, of fusion or union? And what, finally, is a genre? Or, more precisely, Genre?

The answer is simple, and we know it already. Simple and abyssal: Genre is "more than a genre" (*A* 116). It is an Individual, an organic Whole capable of engendering itself (*A* 426), a World, the absolute *Organon*. Or in other words, generation is dissolution, *Auflösung*—in the sense, as we have seen, of Kantian "intussusception,"[27] i.e., once the idealist step is taken, in the properly speculative sense of the word. Not only dissolution as decomposition or resolution but, beyond simple chemism (*A* 426 once again), organicity itself or the process of auto-formation. Actually, this is far from able to delimit a genre, but it equates Genre with totality (with the absolute) in the dissolution of all limits and the absolutization of all particularity. The literary Genre is Literature itself, the *Literary Absolute*—"true literature," as Schlegel will say a few years later, which is not "this or that genre, content to attain some formation [*Bildung*] or other by chance, but rather literature itself that would be a great, thoroughly connected and organized Whole, comprehending many worlds of art in its unity, and being at the same time a unitary work of art."[28] But reread *Athenaeum* fragment 116, or refer to "On the Essence of Criticism," which follows "On the Combinatory Spirit" in Schlegel's *Lessing's Spirit in His Writings*. It says the same thing about poetry—that is, about Poiesy:

> —Romantic poetry . . . is not destined merely to reunite all the separate genres of poetry and to put poetry in touch with philosophy and rhetoric. It wants to and should sometimes mix and sometimes fuse poetry and prose, geniality and criticism, the poetry of art [*Kunstpoesie*] and the poetry of nature [*Naturpoesie*]; make poetry lively and sociable, and life and society poetical; poeticize *Witz*, and fill and saturate the forms of art with every kind of genuine cultural material [*Bildungsstoff*], and animate them with flashes of humor. It embraces everything that is purely poetic, from the greatest systems of art containing within themselves still other

systems, to the sigh, the Kiss that the poeticizing child breathes forth in an artless song. . . . It is capable of the highest and most comprehensive formation [*Bildung*] . . . ; for each whole that its products should form, it adopts a similar organization of its parts, and thus opens up a perspective on an endlessly increasing classicity. . . . Other kinds of poetry [*Dichtart*] are finished and are now capable of being fully analyzed. . . . It alone is infinite, just as it alone is free. . . . The romantic kind of poetry [*Dichtart*] is the only one that is more than just a kind [*Art*], the only one that is poetry [*Dichtkunst*] itself; for in a certain sense all poetry is or should be romantic [A 116].

—Just as the common source and the origin of all the genres of human poetry and culture [*Bildung*] are to be sought in mythology, so too . . . poetry is the highest goal of the whole, in whose flower the spirit of all art and science is finally resolved [*sich auflöst*] when it attains its perfection [*sich vollendet*] [KS 394].

Under these conditions it is understandable that Literature (or Poetry), the "romantic genre," inasmuch as the thing exists, is always envisaged as a sort of beyond of literature itself. And this is what condemns the *Dialogue* to an inability to produce the concept that it promises. The process of absolutization or infinitization, the Process as such, *exceeds*—in every way—the general theoretical (or philosophical) power of which it is nonetheless the completion. The "auto" movement, so to speak—auto-formation, auto-organization, auto-dissolution, and so on—is perpetually in excess in relation to itself. And this, too, in a certain sense, was noted in *Athenaeum* fragment 116: "the romantic kind of poetry is still becoming; that is its real essence, that it should forever be becoming and never be perfected. No theory can exhaust it, and only a divinatory criticism would dare to characterize its ideal."

This hyperbolic movement is clearly discernable in the *Dialogue* as well as in August's *Lectures*—or in Schelling's *Philosophy of Art* [*Philosophie der Kunst*]. It is Schelling who lies behind the *Dialogue*'s introduction on poetry in general and who constrains Schlegel, by explicit submission to the very principle of excess ("The spirit that knows the orgies of the true Muse . . . will never be able to quench a longing that, even at the height of gratification, is eternally regenerated"), to dissolve the concept of poetry in the idea of a "natural poetry," which is nothing other than nature itself, or the earth:

the world of poetry is as boundless and inexhaustible as the riches of animating nature with her plants, animals, and formations [*Bildungen*] of every type, shape, and color. Nor are the artificial works or the natural products that bear the form and name of poems easily included under the most inclusive term. And what are they, compared with the unformed and unconscious poetry that stirs in the plant and shines in the light, smiles in a child, gleams in the flower of youth, and glows in the loving bosom of women? Yet this poetry is the first, original poetry without which there would be no poetry of the word. Indeed, for we humans, there is not and never has been any other object or source of activity and joy but that one poem of the Godhead of which we too are part and flower—the earth [*Dialogue* 53–54].

The hyperbole here, that is, the hyperbolization of poetry, proceeds from nothing other than the literalization of the organic metaphor. Or more precisely—since the organicity of the work of art or of the general poem is far more (or far less) than a metaphor—the hyperbolization of poetry, the poetic dissolution, is the very effectuation of the idea of *organon*—or of the *organon* as Idea. This is why we read, even in the first lines of Schelling's course, that artistic organicity is, in fact, superior to natural organicity—and is something like its truth:

> If we are interested in observing as closely as possible the structure, the internal disposition, the relations and intricacies of a plant or of an organic being in general, how much more must we be tempted to acquaint ourselves with the same intricacies and relations in this more highly organized and complexly interwoven plant called the work of art [*Philosophie der Kunst* 378].

Fundamentally, all of this amounts to what Benjamin had already said very well, in a concise formula: what is missing in Schlegel (in both of them, and even in Schelling—what is missing therefore in "Schlegel") is the *content of art*.[29] This is why the *Dialogue*'s "Talk on Mythology" (which is virtually a pure distillate of Schelling, and can be read as a commentary on the "Earliest System-Programme") describes the "new mythology," which "must be developed [*herausgebildet*] from the deepest depths of the spirit" (it is the work-subject *par excellence*) as "the infinite poem . . . concealing the seeds of all other poems," or what amounts to the same thing, as the "artwork of nature"—i.e., an "allegory" of being or of the divine itself (of what is highest). And it is also why August's *Lectures* make language itself the original Poiesy. Thus, we can understand how, in their own manner (which occupies a sort of middle between that of Friedrich[30] and that which Schelling attempts a year later), the *Lectures*, given their general premises (nature as "hieroglyphic poem,"[31] beauty as the finite presentation of the infinite, poetry as absolute work, etc.) and by way of a reformulation of the concept of *mimesis* (henceforth equated with *poiesis*[32]), ultimately lead to a general linguistics, the first to be properly modern in that it overcomes or annuls the classical difficulty of the origin of languages and adopts a rigorous symbolics.[33]

But one sees precisely that what menaces such a conception of Poetry or Literature is not so much the loss of "content" as the loss of *form* itself, i.e., the resolution or dissolution of all form in the process of symbolization, which is the very process of the infinitization of the finite, or conversely, of the passage (of the presentation) of the infinite into the finite. And Schelling, for example, suddenly quite close to Hegel (to the absorption of form and the sublation of art), closes his *Philosophy of Art* with the herald of a purely "interior" or "ideal" work of art, which would effectuate (but how? and as *what?*) the dissolution of all the separate and particular arts and would be capable of completing the fusion of form and spirit, of art and philosophy (but from which side, if not from that of the Spirit?).

"Schlegel," however, was well aware of such a menace. For example, if we carefully read the discussions that follow each discourse of the *Dialogue* (excepting the "Letter on the Novel," of course), we discover throughout the text the continuous thread of a sort of warning, which Friedrich naturally attributes to Amalia-Caroline: "If it goes on like this, before too long one thing after another will be transformed into poetry. Is everything poetry then?" [75]. This interruption of the perpetual temptation of infinitization requires that one return (laboriously, Amalia nevertheless thinks) to "theory," or in other words, in this case, to the problematic of genres. In a general manner, this movement, which is contrary to that of hyperbolization, is found wherever hyperbolization itself occurs—in keeping, for that matter, with the "perennial alternation" ["*ewigen Wechsel*"] (exit from self/return to self) that, according to the "Talk on Mythology," defines the very movement of the Spirit as idealism understands it. Such a return to theory, in the introduction to the *Dialogue*, for example, makes possible the very idea of a Poetry identified with the divine work or with the world: "We are able to perceive the music of the infinite instrument [*Spielwerk*] and to understand the beauty of this poem because a part of the poet, a spark of his creative spirit, lives in us and never ceases to glow with secret force deep under the ashes of our self-induced unreason" [54]. We observe such a return again when, in the *Lectures*, from the moment Poiesy is conceived as language (or in the second stage, as mythology), it becomes necessary to divide *Naturpoesie* from *Kunstpoesie* and, within the latter category, to practice less a "construction" of genres (in the sense Friedrich will envisage in "On the Essence of Criticism") than a deduction or a genetic (and thus historic) explication of the genres, comparable, in fact, to the one Andrea outlines in the *Dialogue*.[34] And this does not solely depend, as the introduction to the *Dialogue* would have one believe, on the power of auto-theorization, which is necessarily the privilege of the Subject-work. For there is also the related necessity of the formation of form (and this, as we now know, marks the unbridgeable distance from Hegel) or of the conceptualization of genre—a necessity inscribed in the very essence of organicity, such that each genre effectively becomes a member or such that the Whole is not exposed to a kind of death (however Orphic) by dismemberment and dispersal of the *membra disjecta*.

Hence, once more, the necessity for a poetics—in other words, because it amounts to the same thing in the logic of reflection and irony that governs the *Dialogue*, for a "poetry of poetry" or a "transcendental poetry" (*A* 238).[35] As the discussions in the *Dialogue* continually point out, this poetics is assigned a double purpose: not only, as Marcus wishes, to reassume and rearrange the classic division of the genres (which need not be respected as such, as Goethe did, for example,[36] but whose principle nonetheless must be maintained, once one is forced to recognize, or else lose the essence of poetry, that "the genres," as Lothario says, "are actually poetry itself"), but also to *operate* this very division, to found and organize it, to resolve it by giving it, as we have seen, its *telos*— that is, by directing it toward the production of a genre capable of "embracing everything" and of sublating, in the strict sense, generic difference itself.

Yet a double obstacle continually interferes with this process.

First of all, there seems to be no principle of classification. As is indicated by the exchange that follows the reading of "Epochs of Poetry," in which its author Andrea is opposed to the philosopher Ludovico, such a principle would require the conjugation of a historical type of classification (that is, one which is derived from the "natural" division of ancient poetry) with a "theoretical" (that is, systematic) classification that would offer its truth. Which immediately refers one back to the—perhaps "insoluble"—problem of the relation between "Ancients" and "Moderns," or classicism and romanticism. Clearly, such a relation, in keeping with the logic of *Auflösung,* cannot be reduced to a simple transposition or modernization of the ancient, or to the ("chemical") decomposition of the ancient "organization" of poetry or art. Rather, it should fundamentally be a *reorganization,* which assumes that the very principle of this reorganization has been determined or, similarly, that the question of the "romantic genre" has already been answered; or, at least, in other words, that a decision has been made as to what part of ancient poetry is still alive enough to be simultaneously killed and conserved, as Hegel would say—or resuscitated.

And as for the second obstacle, not only is one faced with a total absence of living members of the ancient organization (Antiquity itself, in its late Alexandrian or Roman period, decomposed its art[37] and, as we know, "all the classical poetical genres have now become ridiculous in their rigid purity" [*CF* 60]), but even supposing that one or another of the members, or even (*a fortiori*) all of them, were still alive, it would still be necessary to determine which one in itself possessed vitality as such and could therefore serve as a principle of reorganization. Crudely reformulated, this amounts to posing the elementary question: which is the originary genre—epic or drama?

In an approximate manner, we know the answer: it is the epic; it is Homer. It is, in Schiller's categories, the naive. Or, in those of Schelling, it is the *Darstellung* of mythology itself, the natural or "unconscious" epos. It is "Homer," then, or in other words, *Naturpoesie,* or else, it is the ultimately ahistorical monument forever bearing witness to the pure point of the origin or emergence of art and unveiling the Mystery of the articulation of the subjective and the objective, necessity, and freedom, the instinctive and the intentional, etc.[38] And if it were possible to produce its concept or idea, it would, in fact, be the matrix-like genre whose assumption and sublation would be the novel—at the end of history, at the moment of the completion of the Subject and of the Spirit's return to itself, in the "sentimental" mode.

This, in fact, is the *ordinary* interpretation of romanticism. But besides the fact that it is difficult to see what separates this from an obsession that properly belonged to classicism (to bring off a modern epic), it is also quite clearly the interpretation that romanticism will never be able to halt at or become attached to. Perhaps for the very simple reason that the epic, according to all poetic taxonomies (beginning with the Platonic), is not a pure genre. It occupies the middle, as Plato says, between *diegesis* and *mimesis*, between dithyramb and tragedy; as the romantics will say, it is neither purely subjective nor purely objective, but subjective-objective.[39] This, assuredly, could be the advantage of epic: it would already represent the dreamt-of union or fusion, it would itself be in a position of resolution or sublation. But it is also its greatest drawback: for if sublation has already taken place, is there anything left to do? But is this not because resolution has always already taken place, has always already "come to pass"—and is lost? The same difficulty—and the same hesitation, whether one admits it or not—can be found, and not at all by chance, in Hegel.[40] And just as in Hegel, or in Schelling's *Philosophy of Art,* the difficulty is doubled in that ancient art is to modern art what the objective (or real) is to the subjective (or ideal): one could say that epic had operated the "synthesis" on the objective side and, consequently, that it remains to be brought about on the subjective side. But in that case, is it not necessary, as Plato demanded for the City (or for philosophy) to place the most subjective genre (pure diegesis) in a dominant position? And henceforth to seek (re)solution in pure lyricism (which would have been Hölderlin's path, had he only thought the relation between ancient and modern in dialectical terms[41]) or in pure discourse—but this would be Descartes's path, or else the path that both the romantics (in "criticism"[42]) and the Hegel of the *Phenomenology of the Spirit* will follow, in keeping with the divergence we have so often emphasized.

Nevertheless, these are the difficulties—linked to the movement of hyperbolization that carry all efforts at classification beyond themselves—that continually undermine from within the well-known theory of the novel, with which romanticism attempted to confound—and (re)possess—itself. This is demonstrated quite graphically by the "Letter on the Novel," which not by chance disrupts the *Dialogue* at the very moment when the discussion is once again faltering on the question of the comparative merits of epic and tragedy (nor does chance explain why the "Letter" should be followed by a meager discussion, composed in a "mixed" style, no less, which has no relation whatsoever to the problems of the novel[43]).

Actually, we already know everything (or practically everything) it has to say. The "Letter" contents itself with transposing to the novel what *Athenaeum* fragment 116 says of poetry. Hence its definition of the novel—as "a romantic book"—which clearly advances us no farther than fragment 116's "all poetry is romantic." It would certainly seem excessive to reduce the "Letter" to this (celebrated) formula, which the "Letter" itself after all recognizes as a "meaningless tautology," if only the "Letter" were not engaged in explicating it. But, the fact remains that this so-called explication, precisely, fails to make matters very explicit.

The different motifs of the "Letter" may be ordered as follows:

(1) A "romantic book" means first of all a *book*, that is, not only a work[44], but also a "subjective" work, a work destined to be read (and not viewed, like drama). Still,

(2) nothing prevents drama, in turn, from being declared "romanticizable"—"like all poetry [*Dichtkunst*]." Granted, it will never become anything other than an "applied novel," but this will immediately serve to affirm that "there is so little opposition between the drama and the novel that it is rather the drama—conceived and treated fundamentally and historically, as for instance by Shakespeare— that is the true foundation of the novel." Which brings us, then,

(3) to the question of "mixture": certainly one can emphasize that the novel is primarily related to the epic genre (to the "narrative genre") but it must immediately be recalled that, on the other hand, a *Lied* can also be "romantic" and that it is scarcely possible to "conceive of a novel but as a mixture of storytelling, song, and other forms." Here, Cervantes and Boccaccio are invoked as evidence.[45] The reason for this is

(4) that the novel, as opposed to the epic, is the "genre" of subjective freedom itself—of fantasy—which demonstrates, in a perfectly coherent manner, that it is equal to romanticism. And romanticism, as the "Letter" says a bit earlier, is "not so much a genre as an element of poetry, which may more or less rule or retire, but must never be entirely absent." Which therefore leads us back to our point of departure ("It must be clear to you why, according to my views, I insist that all poetry should be romantic and why I detest the novel insofar as it wants to be a separate genre"), unless

(5)   such a "romanticism" is itself actually—already—"a thing of the past," if it is truly in Shakespeare that one must find "the actual center" or "the core of romantic fantasy" or if it is in the "older moderns"—from Dante to Cervantes, but also "in that age of knights, love, and fairy tales, in which the thing itself and the word for it originated"—that one must look for the model of what ought to be produced.

Hegel's attitude toward this formidable equivocity is well known—Hegel who, as Blanchot points out,

> draws disastrous conclusions from this [romantic] tendency toward histori-
> cal universalization when he decides to call the art of the entire Christian era
> *romantic* and yet, on the other hand, recognizes in romanticism proper
> nothing but the dissolution of the movement, its mortal triumph, the moment
> of decline in which art, turning the principle of destruction that is its center
> against itself, coincides with its interminable and pitiable end.

It is true, adds Blanchot, that "romanticism from its beginning and well before Hegel's *Aesthetics* was perfectly aware—and this is its greatest merit—that this is its truth" (168). And in his own manner, Schlegel had clearly said as much: "Whoever desires something infinite does not know what he desires. But the converse is not true" (*CF* 47). This does not prevent it, however, from introducing an insurmountable contradiction into what must be called the romantic "programmation."

And this contradiction, as one would say today, is the contradiction between the drama and the novel.

From the moment that the novel, in the romantic sense, is always more than the novel, what happens to the novel itself, in the restricted sense? It becomes execrable. At the very most—but reading the texts carefully, one sees that it is always "at the very most"—one can recognize in the modern equivalent of satire, in Sterne or Diderot, in the grotesque epic *à la* Jean Paul or the *Bildungsroman à la* Goethe (who is a perpetual counter-model to Jean Paul, or vice versa)—or in short, in all that connects modern narrative prose to mixture, irony, arabesque, auto-critique, and so on—a tentative outline of what ultimately ought to be realized, at least if one wants to inaugurate a literature that would not be inferior to the great "transcendental poetry" of the Moderns (the dead: Dante, Shakespeare, Cervantes). But this recognition always occurs within the larger context of a general depreciation of the novel (reread "idea" 11, for example) which, basically, is corrupted by the redhibitory defect of not being able to achieve organicity. The novel is dissolution in its chemical form, it is—as is said in the *Dialogue*—too "French" (reread *A* 426, as well). Yet this depreciation has less to do with the novel's inability to reunify, beyond mixture, what ought to be unified (the genres, prose and poetry[46]) than with the absence, within it, of a possible effective presentation of the unifying principle—that is, of the "subject." The novel, because it originates in the epic, is still too mimetic. And this, incidentally, is why autobiography—in the form of Rousseau's *Confessions*—is help up as a model at the end of the "Letter."[47] The novel cannot or will not become the "romantic genre" until it becomes equal to the "subject-work."

But we know quite well that this exigency assumes its reversal, and that the realization of the subject-work means nothing without the prior realization of the work-subject. The "auto" motif is absolutely constraining here. Hence the position, in the *Dialogue*, of a Lothario—whose search for a "mystical" tragedy based on ancient mythology's rejuvenation through physics perhaps takes up the idea of a "philosophical tragedy" (earlier advanced by Friedrich at the time of his *On the Study of Greek Poetry* and apparently abandoned ever since). Hence perhaps also—and especially—the final lines of Schelling's *Philosophy of Art*, where it is not surprising to find the foreshadowings of Wagnerian drama,[48] lines with a very odd ring:

> I will content myself with adding one further remark, that the most perfect-
> ed connection of all the arts, the reunion of poetry and music in song, of
> poetry and painting in dance, each in its turn synthesized, constitutes
> dramatic manifestation at the summit of its composition, as was the drama
> of Antiquity, of which no more than a caricature is left to us—the *opera*
> which, given a more elevated and noble style of poetry and of the other arts
> collaborating with it, could bring us at best to the execution of ancient
> drama tied to music and song.

Only the theatre, in other words, could authorize "the total work of art," that is, the *organon* as such. And this is precisely what Lothario says at the moment Antonio is about to begin reading the "Letter on the Novel": "The tragic and comic works of the ancients . . . are only variations, different expressions of one and the same ideal. As far as systematic structure [*Gliederbau*], construction, and organization are concerned, they remain the best models and are, if I may say so, the works among works."

What is commonly called the *lack of lyricism* in (Jena) romanticism should probably be attributed to this oscillation between the two poles of the poetics (not to say the aesthetics) of the Subject. But between drama and the novel, epic and the mimetic—or even between autobiography and musical drama, the pure subjective and the pure objective—yet without being of the order of mixture and no doubt really escaping all these categories, there may actually have been, as Hölderlin suspected; a "pure lyricism"; and not merely "poetry," which no doubt allowed too facile a success to someone like Novalis, in whom "mysticism" never completely hides an obvious penchant for subjective effusions (which of course have assured Novalis, through surrealism and beyond, the international reputation he has today and which have done so much harm to romanticism). But rather something far more primitive and inaccessible—something other, in any case, than what comes together under the concept (however difficult to locate) of "literature." Schlegel seems to have glimpsed it. His *On the Study of Greek Poetry* suggests this: he thought of Sappho, of a lost lyric—or of a lyric still more fragmentary than fragmented Antiquity. He wrote: Homer's poems are the source of all Greek art; they are even the foundation of Greek culture in general, the most complete and most beautiful flower of the most sensual age of art. One must not however forget that Greek poetry achieved higher degrees of art and taste. If we could supplement that which nothing can supplement, Horace could to some degree console us for the loss of the greatest lyrics . . ." [*KS* 216–217]. Or again, in *Critical Fragment* 119:

> Sapphic poems must grow and be discovered. They can neither be pro-
> duced at will, nor published without desecration. Whoever does so lacks
> both pride and modesty. Pride: because he tears his inmost essence out of
> the holy stillness of his heart and throws it into the crowd. . . . And it will
> always be immodest to set oneself up as a standard [*Urbild*]. And if lyrical
> poems are not completely personal, free, and true, then, as lyrical poems,
> they are worthless. Petrarch does not belong here: for the cool lover utters
> nothing but elegant generalities; and thus he is romantic, and not lyrical. [49]

And thus he is romantic, and not lyrical. . . . Perhaps this was Schlegel's deepest obsession. A second part of *Lucinde* was supposed to appear—and would have consisted of poems. But it was never written. In its place, and in order to forget that *Lucinde,* therefore, remained a mere novel, Schlegel set about a great tragedy—his *Alarcos,* which even he declined to defend.

And what, then, is the relation between lyricism and "unworking"—or writing?

4   Criticism: The Formation
of Character

Transcendental Idealism is a tautology: *critical*
Idealism, if one thereby envisages art criticism, including polemics, is better.

—*F. Schlegel, note from the posthumous "philosophical fragments" (1796–1806)*
                              [*KA* 65, Frag. 453]

The characters in the *Dialogue* were able to fulfill their roles because, as
the text points out, they had all in one way or another devoted themselves to
poetic composition. Once invoked, however, the authority of this practice, as we
have seen, turns out to be nonexistent. Only one of them, toward the end, refers
to several of the poems that he has written; as if by chance, this is Lothario,[1]
who has not kept his promise to prepare and deliver a text. Far more than
authors caught up in the movement of their practice, the protagonists are
characters waiting for the work [*en attente d'oeuvre*]. They are, perhaps, so
many figures of this waiting for the work.

But insofar as they are nonetheless poets, the "narrator," in his preamble, has
carefully assigned them a task that overflows, so to speak, poetic creation,
thereby providing the motif and motive force for the dialogue as such: because
"the poet cannot be satisfied with leaving behind . . . the expression of his
particular poetry," he must "continually strive to expand his poetry as well as his
view of poetry." "Elaborating a work" [*oeuvrer*], therefore, can no longer be
sufficient: it is also necessary to attain a view of the work. The characters of the
Dialogue are waiting for the work and waiting for a view of the work. It may be
that the two motifs are inseparable.

For the moment, let us content ourselves with saying that these two motifs
lead us to a banal observation—to the most banal observation that can be made
about the Jena romantics, that is, that apart from a few rare and minor
exceptions, they produced only critical works.[2] Or, if one prefers, they pro-

101

duced only "theoretical" works, to use the currently fashionable term—which, as we will have occasion to note, merely recalls and elaborates in the contemporary context everything that was at stake in the romantic idea of *criticism*.

As the promise or putting-to-work (but up to what point?) of a *view* of the work, romantic criticism is situated in the place, or time, of waiting for the work; and since romanticism, as is by now only too clear, finally consists in the infinitization of this waiting, criticism occupies the place of the absence of the work (in the ordinary sense of this expression, at least initially, and not in the sense Blanchot gives it). Thus, the final question that must be raised in the context we are exploring here is: what is at stake, then, in that which takes the place of the work. Or better yet: what is at stake in the absolute *literary genre* inasmuch as the place of its inevitable absence is occupied by "criticism"?

We will basically refer to two texts:

—The introduction to Schelling's lectures on the *Philosophy of Art*, delivered in Jena during the winter of 1802–1803. (This lecture course was published in 1859 by Schelling's son and was based on his father's lecture notes.)

—A text by Friedrich Schlegel that is also an introduction. "On the Essence of Criticism" was written as the preface to a collection of Lessing's texts that Schlegel published in 1804 (*The Spirit of Lessing in His Writings*). This general introduction was extended in the introductions to each of the collection's three parts, and we will refer to them in the lines that follow.

It may seem somewhat arbitrary to set these two texts in relation to one another. Therefore, let us at least briefly indicate the initial reasons for such a gesture: Schelling's "Introduction" not only postulates a philosophy of art as the object of the course, but also postulates, as the object of this philosophy, the formation of the judgment on art, a formation that is itself posited as an essential part of "social culture" [*gesellschaftlichen Bildung*].[3] In other words, his objective is at least *also* "critical," even though this word is never used—and no doubt for good reason, as we shall see. Conversely, the "criticism" of which Friedrich Schlegel speaks cannot be defined outside its essential relation to philosophy. And furthermore, the dates of these two texts relate them in yet another way: in 1802, the Jena group's dissolution had been brought to a conclusion. Schelling's lectures on art in this same city, at a moment when Friedrich Schlegel is living in Paris and giving his own lectures there, symbolize, if you will, the aftermath of the *Athenaeum*, of "symphilosophy," and of the staging of the *Dialogue*. The waiting for the work has found an outlet in the University, and in a rivalry no longer characterized by irony (a sign of which, for instance, may be seen in the references in Schelling's lectures to the mere "bits" [*Bruchstücke*] of art theory produced in the recent past).

Thus, it is understandable that the authority of the anecdote is more "essential" here, if that is possible, than anywhere else in this story: the dispersion of the Jena group is *truly* the suspension of the romantic project, the effective fragmentation of its "fragment of the future," the confirmation, by the "romantics" themselves, of their epoch's "lack of romanticism"—and thus, as we now know, in a roundabout and ineluctable manner, the (paradoxical? ironic? critical?) confirmation of "romanticism" itself.

This is, indeed, what is revealed by the juxtaposition of Schelling's and Schlegel's texts. The object that they delimit together, despite themselves, that is, criticism or the theoretical construction of art, arises in the aftermath of Jena (and as this aftermath, as the henceforth resolutely theoretical exposition of the very problem of theory) only because it has preoccupied and to a certain point constituted romanticism right from the start.[4]

Thus it becomes necessary to begin again from the actual origins. If we have frequently emphasized, on the one hand, that the birthplace of romanticism is situated in philosophy—in the philosophical question of art and poetry—we must now indicate, on the other, that this birth resulted above all from the meeting of philosophy and literary criticism. The Schlegel brothers were destined for critical careers by family tradition;[5] they are first of all philologists and theoreticians, not poets.

Thus, in these two texts, both Schelling and Schlegel legitimate their statements by referring to the history of critical theory—or to use the term that both of them vilify, to the history of aesthetics. If *Critical Fragment* 40 condemned the use of this term,[6] this is because in Greek it designates only a science of sensation. This assumes that, without hesitating at Kantian aesthetics, one is directly denouncing the theoretical apparatus that, in the eighteenth century, had almost exclusively[7] provided the ground (how is it possible, even today, to avoid using the same criteria as the romantics in this respect?) for theoretical discourse on art and the judgment of taste. In other words, and to schematize what both of these texts indicate, it is a matter of denouncing the empiricism of a psychology of aesthetic faculties (in the "artistic" sense of the word this time, which is, however, inseparable from the preceding sense) as developed by Wolff (to whom Schlegel refers) and his disciple Baumgarten, the "inventor" of Aesthetics (whom Schelling mentions). But it is also a matter—and to a certain degree, with the same intention as this psychology—of denouncing a theory of art (in the tradition, say, of Shaftesbury and Diderot) built on pure geniality and the hazards of its enthusiasm. Fundamentally, then, it is a matter of denouncing, with regard to the production of the work (but also with regard to its appreciation, for they are inseparable), the anthropological decompositions or degradations of the *cogito* (be they of a "natural" or "supernatural" order). To recall a motif that we have more than simply alluded to, it becomes necessary to restore to the Subject of subjectity, beyond subjectivity, the creative and critical power of the work of art—of art as work. And it is likewise necessary to remove this work from any and all exterior finality—whether it, in turn, be "natural" or "supernatural," of the order of pleasure or morality—in order to restore it, precisely, to the *operation* of such a Subject. Therefore, this time in keeping with idealism's fidelity to Kant, it is a matter of retrieving *for itself* what might be called the auto-operative power, including the "free play of the faculties" and the "finality apart from an end" [*Zweckmässigkeit ohne Zweck*] of the Subject, a Subject that must henceforth be qualified as subject-of-art.

This implicates art—*die Kunst, ars:* at once the technique and the order of fine works—in two ways. On the one hand, insofar as the Subject is envisaged as operator, or as operation itself (beginning with idealism and regardless of contrary opinions, it effectively became useless to distinguish and oppose subject and process), it must come to itself as *artifex*, or even as *ars*, or more specifically as the very artificiality of the process of the work's production. In this manner, and contrary to what the customary banalizing imagery might lead one to believe, romanticism effectuates the Subject's decisive break with all "naturality";[8] even if the production of the work is always thought according to the archetype of natural organic engendering, what now begins to specify subjectity is pro-duction as such, the *pro-ducere*, outside any natural given, of that (the one) which pro-duces itself by itself. And this production is always the institution and constitution of its form, its putting-into-form, its *Bildung* or *Gestaltung*.

On the other hand—but always in the direct line of this logic—the essence of pro-duction cannot simply be the positing of forms (as it is in nature). If, from the beginning of his course, Schelling elevates "the work of art" above "organized being in general," because the former is "more highly organized and complexly interwoven," it is ultimately for the very reason that makes a philosophy of art necessary; namely, that pro-duction is "more" than the engendering of form. It must be the putting-into-form of form—that "formation of form" which seemed earlier to constitute all that was at stake in the "religion" of the *Ideas*. The formation of form is its access to *beauty:* "All beauty is a *self-illuminating* [*Selbsterleuchtetes*], completed individual," says one of Novalis's fragments.[9] Thus, in the epoch of romanticism, the Subject passes from art to the *fine arts* (*die schöne Kunst*, as Kant still said), and from the fine arts to *art* taken absolutely and in all senses.

In its critique of aesthetic criticism, then, romanticism sought less to correct or perfect art criticism than to institute the true concept of art (of the Subject).

But now one can understand how this concept in turn implies the true concept of criticism. And it implies it in two ways: first because the formation of form demands, if one can venture such an expression, the putting-into-form of this formation; the operation of forming must be seen for itself ("eidaesthetics," once again), and thus take on form. *Theory*—the "spiritual intuition of the object," as the word was translated in the *Dialogue*, in reference to the theory of the novel—is consubstantial and coextensive with the operation. At the same time, nevertheless, and here again in keeping with that "theory of the novel" whose abyssal complexity we shall not unfold here, criticism is implied in a second way: the necessity of giving form to form actually indicates the absence of Form in all form, and demands that Form be restored, completed, or supplemented in any given form.

Thus, this double determination [*assignation*] situates criticism simultaneously in the space of the "auto-illumination" of the beautiful work and in the space, in every work, of the absence of the Work.

In this manner, ultimately, the motif (if not the concept) of the Kantian *critique* was taken up and *sublated* in romanticism. Kant's critical "system" had implicated art at the point where the critical power of reason needed to apply itself to critical (or formative: they are the same) activity taken in its own right: the *Critique of Judgment* constitutes after all the ultimate assembling [*montage*] of the subjectity of reason. There, reason comes to itself as the pro-ducer of its own ideality. But as is well known, this ideality remains merely "reflected" or "analogical" in Kant. Idealism consists precisely in *positing* it, and consequently in raising judgment itself to the level of the Idea. This is why the philosophical "science" of art, in Schelling's course, is destined to form—in a juxtaposition that poorly distinguishes them yet nonetheless coordinates them—both "the intellectual intuition of works of art" and the "judgment of time."[10] And intellectual intuition is nothing other than the Subject's reflection—in a sense that is no longer limiting, as it was in Kant—of the primordial Identity that is present as such in each form, or in each "power" [*Potenz*], as Schelling says. [11]

Romantic criticism proceeds directly from idealist *reflection*.[12] Indeed, in a certain manner, it constitues *the* poetic reflection *par excellence*; for if, as the preceding analysis suggests, the judgment on the work must be identified with the production of Form in the work, then it comes as no surprise that *Critical Fragment* 117 had already stated: "Poetry can only be criticized through poetry. A judgment on art that is not itself a work of art, either in its substance, as the presentation of a necessary impression in the state of becoming, or through a beautiful form and liberal tone in the spirit of ancient Roman satire, has no civil rights in the realm of art."

In this respect, the definition of criticism could easily be extended, formally at least, to include that of "transcendental poetry" itself, which is defined as the "poetry of poetry." To present "the productive element along with the product," or "to present itself in each of its presentations," in the terms of *Athenaeum* fragment 238, is to identify criticism with poetry. Or more precisely, this implies that the definition and function of poetry's criticism has been included or absorbed in advance in a definition of poetry. Thus, one might soon be forced to consider "criticism" a redundant element of "poetry"—and indeed, this is what a certain aspect of romantic thought tends toward asymptotically. And this asymptote indicates that the complete absorption of criticism into poetry, or the absence of criticism, is nothing other than the original state of poetry, "the age of great poets" full of the "sense of poetry," described at the beginning of "On the Essence of Criticism." In consequence, insofar as the critical motif nevertheless continues to subsist in its own right, and insofar as the origin has been lost (we will return to this shortly), the essential task is still that of determining a concept of criticism that would not simply be the concept of poetry. This is what we will need to apply ourselves to—but the fact remains that the point of departure must still be the one we have just established: criticism can be comprehended only from the vanishing point at which, in principle, pure poetry begins.

In other words, the point of departure must still be the *philosophical* concept of criticism, as *Athenaeum* fragment 281 (adopting it from Kant, and raising it to a higher power) understands it: "The essence of critical method consists in this, that the theory of the determining faculty and the system of determinate effects of the mind [*Gemütswirkungen*] should be united therein in the most intimate manner, like things and thoughts, in preestablished harmony." Of course, the strange intrusion of Leibniz into such a context is a good indication, from a philosophical perspective, of what could be called a "precritical" regression in all senses of the word. In another way, nevertheless, this fragment— which, incidentally, is meant to demonstrate, in a rather forced manner and as if for the good of the cause, that Fichte is more critical than he appears to be— also indicates a fidelity to Kant, however hidden and roundabout it may be (and by the same token, an unacknowledged departure from Fichte). For this "most intimate" union remains one that cannot be posited and presented as such. As we have suggested with Benjamin, since the "Overture," it is a reservation or retreat in relation to the *position* of the Fichtean Self, and represents the first properly romantic incursion into idealism. Properly speaking, therefore, this gesture would appear to be a resurgence or return of the *critical*.[13] The union sought here is that of a "mind" that can be given only under the aegis of *two* distinct authorities: determinant and determined, producer and product, presenting and presented, etc. To aim at a reduction of this duality, one must follow the full course of the detour it imposes, a detour, in a way, it never completely annuls. In Kantian terms, this detour consists in the necessity of presenting, with the object, the conditions of possibility of the object's production. In romantic terms, it concerns the entire logic of the formation of form, which has no doubt been sufficiently outlined by now.

These two vocabularies are certainly not equivalent. At this point, a more detailed analysis must show us how the critical gesture of romanticism behaves in an ambivalent manner in relation to that of Kant: on the one hand, it operates a "precritical" return toward the goal of a pure auto-presentation (and such a return is also equivalent to Hegelian *Aufhebung*, to say it rapidly); on the other, it draws this entire set of questions into a kind of aggravation of the critical motif.

In many ways, Schelling's course represents the first of these two poles. The *force majeur*, if you will pardon the expression, with which idealism seizes upon art in this text is so powerfully exercised that criticism quite simply becomes superfluous and, thus, never appears. The philosophy of art—regardless of its effusive praise of art's grandeur—is never more than one of the reproductions, specific to a particular "power," of *the* system of philosophy. In this manner, the sketch of this system contained in the "Introduction" places art on the same level as other possible "qualifiers" of the word "philosophy," which are so many "accidental aspects" of philosophy itself [*Philosophie der Kunst 385*]. For philosophy "immediately leads always and only to the Absolute" [*Philosophie der Kunst 387*]: art is finally short-circuited in the very "science" that has operated its "construction." And to such an extent that not only the concept of criticism, but also the properly romantic underpinnings of this concept (as they appear in "On the Essence of Criticism"), that is, the *history* of art, find themselves dismissed here. Because temporal determinations are "inessential and formal," the gesture of construction consists explicitly in their "negation or suppression"—their *Aufhebung* [*Philosophie der Kunst 392*] (almost nothing is lacking here, perhaps precisely nothing, to arrive at the Hegelian concept). At this point, one has reached what we would like to call, to parody Schelling, romanticism's "point of indifference," the point at which it dissolves into the auto-speculative unity of the Idea.

But things are not this simple. And their complexity may yet prove—if only for the elegance of the demonstration—to be situated at this same point, where the "suppression" of the history of art occurs. For with regard to this history that in principle or in tendency has been suppressed—or with regard to history in general—Schelling earlier made this statement: The Homeric epos is identity itself, as it resides in the absolute in the ground of history [*wie sie der Geschichte in Absoluten zu Grunde liegt (Philosophie der Kunst 389)*]. Such a proposition is incompatible with the simple suppression of history for two reasons. First, the negating identity of history, here, gives *itself* in a historical product situated on one side of the historical difference (of the ancient and the modern); second, the absolute gives itself here in a form. These two reasons would nonetheless be inconsequential, were it sufficient to note that the absoluteness of the Absolute consists precisely in occupying, in identical fashion, all forms in general, as well as in returning to its own pure identity. But this does not suffice here, where it would be necessary for all forms to be indifferent vis-a-vis one another in their relation to the Absolute. For such is not the case. The Homeric epos serves as an illustration of the case of forms of art. Unlike all the others (that is, unlike the "effective things" [*wirklichen Dinge*] of nature and history), these forms are not "imperfect reproductions": they are the objectivity of archetypes [*Urbilder*] presented in the world of "effective things." Art is the presence of the Idea in the "reflected world"; it is indeed its presence as a "copy," but this "copy" is identical with the "perfection" of the archetype [*Philosophie der Kunst* 389]. Reading this passage closely, a passage that properly constitutes the gesture of the philosophical "construction" of art, the following observation must be made: the traditional pair of model and copy, of *Urbild* and *Gegenbild*, is employed here in a rather singular operation, whereby the *Ur* is made to pass into the *Gegen* and vice versa. Or rather, everything happens as if the prefixes—with their traditional value and hierarchy—were actually less important than the *Bild* common to both. In other words, if the absoluteness of the Absolute consists in its capacity to give itself in every form, then it is *Bildung*, or putting-into-form that is essential to this Absolute. Thereafter, it is sufficient to observe that, as opposed to this *Bildung*, which constitutes the specificity of art, the *philosophical* presentation of the absolute, its ideal *Darstellung*, is not only nowhere specified in relation to *Bildung*, and presented in its own right even less, but further—if one follows the concepts closely—is never granted the *objectivity* that gives art its value and raises it "to the same height" as philosophy. What is missing here, if you like, is what Hegel will attempt to present as "the element of pure thought," or the purely speculative *Darstellung*. The conclusion is obvious—and radically opposite to that which results from the same problematic in Hegel: the presentation of presentation, here, is the putting-into-form of and in the work of art.

In the end, this is where one finds the true ground [*raison*] of a philosophy of art, which is a "repetition" of philosophy in general only insofar as it passes, or ought to pass, into the element of its true presentation. It is imperative that this articulation be grasped in as precise a manner as possible, for in it the entire possibility of romanticism, its very principle, is at stake. Let us put it this way: it should be pointed out that the process that has just been reconstructed also constitutes an *Aufhebung* of art; this observation, however, is correct only up to the point where what will be present in Hegel is *lacking* here, that is, the attempt at least to determine [*assigner*], outside all form, the very presentation of this *Aufhebung*. With respect to this point, on the contrary, it is here artistic (and especially poetic) *Bildung* that *takes over* [*prend le relai*], you might say, although this takeover is not exactly the sublation [*relève*] of the task of the presentation of the Idea. Certainly, this is because, in its principle, the Idea or the Absolute, here, is revealed within a problematic of *form* (and thus of the work), which is never entirely identical to the Hegelian problematic of *figure* (as a living incarnation moving throughout a history).

The difference between the two is, of course, infinitesimal. Yet it is large enough to be responsible for the *effective* reintroduction into Schelling's treatise of the apparently banished motif of criticism. This motif is reintroduced in what seems to be the most modest of manners, but for the most imperious of reasons: it is clear that "construction" cannot remain merely "general," for it would thus lack the necessary individuality of form. Therefore, says Schelling, it will extend "even to those individuals who stand for an entire genre; I will construct both these individuals and the world of their poetry." Which translates: I will poieticize their poetry, and I will make *criticism* of it, in keeping with this concept's ultimate value. Schelling adds, as if this were not sufficient: "In the doctrine of poetry and of poetic genres [*Dichtarten*], I will even descend to character sketches [*Charakteristik*] of particular works of the most eminent poets, such as Shakespeare, Cervantes, and Goethe, in order to supplement the inadequate vision we have of them today" [*Philosophie der Kunst* 384]. This we will translate, with only a hint of malice, as: I will singlehandedly remake the *Dialogue on Poetry*. The *character sketch* is the most proper concern of criticism—and must now be examined. Because, to repeat ourselves yet again, the philosophy of art cannot complete itself as a "speculative epos," it can effectuate itself only in the function and virtually in the guise [*en les espèces*] of criticism.

. . . to continue to animate the picture a bit, the time has come to picture Friedrich Schlegel, at the end of "On the Essence of Criticism," addressing the philosopher (the scene takes place one year later, and the philosopher, at Würzburg this time, is repeating his course on the philosophy of art) and telling him that the essence of criticism consists in characterizing the philosopher, and that the character sketch "in philosophy is . . . by far the most difficult, either because its *Darstellung* is as yet less complete than that of poets, or because of the very essence of the genre" [*KS* 400].

But it is no accident that this *dialogue* never took place. The critical point at which Schelling and Schlegel intersect is also the point that irrevocably separates—or blurs—"philosophical genre" and "literary genre."

Thus, it is necessary to begin again with that from which "the essence of criticism" takes its primordial support: with history, precisely. And with history conceived, against the grain of its philosophical *Aufhebung*—and with recourse to a term and a theme already mentioned here several times—as a succession of *epochs* (as it is in the title of the first discourse of the *Dialogue*, where the word used is indeed *Epochen*): that is, of suspended moments, or suspensions of the historical continuum. The history Schlegel draws upon here is entirely made up of such suspensions: two epochs of poetry (the Greek and the romantic), as dazzling as they are quickly interrupted, and two long periods of criticism, during which the "meaning of poetry" or the poietic capacity is (up to a certain point) suspended. —And finally, the present epoch—the epoch *par excellence* because, to recall quickly some of the *Fragments'* obsessive themes, it is the epoch of dismemberment [*morcellement*] and pure "tendency," the "chemical" (and not organic) epoch, the fragmentary or fragmented epoch *par excellence*. Schlegel undoubtedly indicates the ultimate feature of this epoch, the"romantic" epoch, in "On the Combinatory Spirit," one of his partial introductions to the work on Lessing: "(for the Moderns, or at least for us, Germans) criticism and literature are born at the same time; and the first, in fact, almost a little earlier."

An epoch that begins with criticism—that *almost* begins with criticism, so unthinkable is such a beginning (although Friedrich Schlegel had ironically regretted the absence of the "almost" or the "nearly" among the categories of Kant, see *CF* 80)—is an epoch that founds itself, so to speak, on a loss of origin: always on the loss of a great poetry (the Greek, the romantic), or in other words, of *poetry* itself, by which is meant not so much works as the creative capacity of works (and in this regard, one should track down the indices in Schlegel's text of the superiority of romantic poetry: its spontaneous, un-"lettered" character, its connection with the *Heimat*, or in short, its free and generous, profuse and mixed charm—characteristics that are never stressed in the same manner, here or elsewhere, with regard to Greek poetry).

This theme of lost origin would, however, be no more than extremely *classical*, as we know, had it been restricted to its proper thematic (in other words, to begin with, had it not occasioned, as it does here, a doubling of the lost origin and the "romantic" as a sort of belated origin). But if the loss of original poiesy can go so far as to become the (*almost*) original nature of criticism, this is because its stakes are a bit different. Criticism at the origin is also the *construction* of the work at the origin, for art itself must always be—how could it be otherwise?— the construction of its work: "it would be premature to call poetry or prose art before they have reached the point of completely constructing their works (*A* 432). Construction (criticism) is art—or more precisely, the *entire* construction is the critical complement or supplement that the work requires in order to be a work (of art).[14] An epoch that begins with criticism is perhaps an epoch that begins (without beginning, for it is in suspense) with the supplement or with the *perfection* [*parachèvement*] of the work of art rather than with the completed [*achevée*] work of art.

Such is undoubtedly the profound duplicity that constitutes the romantic concept of criticism. In a first sense, criticism is nothing but the reflux of "*Dichtung.*" It preserves its meaning and its monuments, it establishes a classicism by applying the meaning to the monuments—but it does not produce works, it is never anything more than a substitute: "Criticism is the sole surrogate for the moral mathematics and science of propriety that so many philosophers have sought in vain and that is impossible to find" (*A* 89). "Propriety" here translates *das Schickliche,* that which is fitting or appropriate, in conformity with a destination or a destiny. After the analyses undertaken above, in the chapter entitled "The Idea: Religion within the Limits of Art," the designation of this propriety as moral can no longer be misinterpreted. In "On the Essence of Criticism," the entanglement of the moral and the aesthetic occurs both in the social or "national" function attributed to great poetries and in the "popular" destination of criticism, or again in the reminder that "since Kant . . . it is in referring each particular aesthetic sentiment to the sentiment of the infinite or to the recollection [*Erinnerung*] of freedom that the dignity of poetry has at least been redeemed" [*KS* 396]. *Das Schickliche* is the conformity of the work to itself, in the sense of the work's propriety vis-a-vis the moral destiny of humanity. To declare that a "mathematics" of this propriety is impossible and to offer criticism as its surrogate is precisely to reproduce the Kantian situation *par excellence:* the mathematical mode of "presentation," that is, the mode that presents the intuition along with its a priori concept—the mode that Kant's first *Critique* calls "cognition by the construction of concepts"—is inaccessible to . philosophy. All of critical philosophy is the substitute for an impossible *mathesis.*

But in a second sense, criticism perhaps returns to the interior of that for which it is the surrogate—and even, to speak romantically, to the innermost part of this interior. By assuming the task of construction (that "reconstruction" or "after-the-fact construction"—*nachkonstruieren*—referred to at the end of "On the Essence of Criticism"), criticism returns to this concept, which idealism, as Schelling's text indicates, had (against the Kantians) restored to philosophical function and dignity. Construction attains the heart of what it constructs or reconstructs; it seizes, articulates, and presents its concept and its intuition as one. It returns to the core of the superior organism that is the work and, in sum, reconstitutes its engenderment: this is the final motif of Friedrich Schlegel's text.

In this manner, if the properly idealistic direction of Schelling's philosophy of art leads, beyond all *Bildung* and indeed beyond all *Darstellung,* toward a pure *revelation* of the Absolute absent from all form, criticism's inverse direction leads toward a penetration to the heart of the formative process, and toward the reconstitution of its efficacity. One can easily see that this direction is no less idealistic than the first. One could say that it opposes to—or imposes upon—an idealism of manifestation another idealism, the idealism that is always at work in our modernity, even and especially where a "materialism," a "structuralism," or a "machinism" seems uppermost: the idealism of production, of the conditions of production and of the exhibition of the conditions of production. Romantic criticism thus decidedly opens the entire history that leads to the present; its *critique* of imitation[15] (of simple and second reproduction) inaugurates criticism as re-production, second and first, or twice the first production of the work, so to speak. From this point on, the genuine identity of art (of the work, of the artist) no longer depends on the relation of resemblance to another given identity (or on veri-similitude), but on the construction of *critical identity*. If, from now on, the author can no longer be an author without also being a critic, theoretician, or poetician (Baudelaire, Mallarmé, Valéry), if the critic himself and as such must be an author (Benjamin, Barthes, Genette), if the work cannot operate itself without its auto-construction (or deconstruction) (Mallarmé, Proust, Joyce), it is always in the name of this critical identity—that is, ultimately in the name of the very identity of the "romantic poetry" in *Athenaeum* fragment 116, which "wants to and should sometimes mix and sometimes fuse poetry and prose, geniality and criticism," etc.

The poetic *perfection* [*parachèvement*] of poetry is its attainment to the status of critical identity: it is at once the height of its completion [*achèvement*] and—in keeping with the entire logic of the Work-Subject—a supplement of completion that always remains infinitely reproducible in its ideality. The modest task of ancient criticism (the determination of a corpus and of a classical canon), a task whose essence consists in knowing how to judge that which is "excellent, complete, and worthy of being eternally reproduced" [*KS* 392] (and thus presupposes a *judgment* that is itself sublated into *Witz*, geniality, or even intellectual intuition), is now transformed in order to satisfy what from this point of view defines the *romantic* project: the institution of *modern classicism*, or of modernity as classicity—or in other words, according to the social origin of the term, of the institution of the *classicum*, of art of superior rank. This is clearly the value implied in *Critical Fragment 20*: "A classical text must never be entirely comprehensible. But those who are cultivated and who cultivate themselves must always seem to learn more from it." And it is clearly the project of romantic classicity— the critical project *par excellence*—that Friedrich Schlegel, citing this fragment, invokes in his text "On Incomprehensibility," published in the final issue of the *Athenaeum*; although the texts of the journal, August's didactic elegies, and Friedrich's own *Lucinde* are incomprehensible today, they will nevertheless become classics "in the nineteenth century." Romantic criticism—and indeed criticism and poetics since romanticism—conceives of itself as the construction of the classical work to come. This is also why, with regard to romantic poetry "itself," criticism in turn possesses its own superior and as yet unactualized status: that of this "divinatory criticism," which alone (again in *Athenaeum* fragment 116) "would dare to characterize" the ideal of such a "poetry."

This is not however to say that romantic criticism can be uniformly and simply traced back to the idealism from which it proceeds. Rather, it complicates idealism, as we have already said, by one additional turn [*tour*] of the screw; and one additional turn is hardly enough to frighten metaphysics in general or idealism in particular; for idealism always turns these matters to infinite advantage, and romanticism capitalizes on that advantage just as much as we other "moderns" do. And yet, this turn nonetheless disturbs or displaces it.

It consists, if one will approach it with some irony, first of all in the trick that is turned on the philosopher—the idealist—at the end of "On the Essence of Criticism." If one follows the sinuosities of its last paragraph—which sketches out a "more scientific concept" of criticism—one discovers that criticism, which must appeal to both philosophy and history in order to carry out its task, must also "reunite the two in order to form a third and new agency." This is as yet only the first part of a turn that turns out to be a turn of *Aufhebung*, a further idealistic turn within idealism. But farther on it will become apparent that such an operation requires that criticism characterize philosophy. Philosophy cannot therefore be set to work by criticism without beforehand (unless this beforehand, as the text can be understood to indicate, forms the "proper task and inner essence" of criticism . . .) being characterized by this same criticism. Consequently, the operation of characterization—presented in Schelling's course as a necessary but nonetheless secondary or at least subordinate aspect of the task of the philosophy of art (and yet an operation that, as we have seen, acts as an insurmountable obstacle for idealist intentions—must first be applied to the characterizing philosopher.

And this is because, let us remember, "its presentation is as yet less complete than that of the poets," unless of course it is "because of the very essence of the genre" [*KS* 400]. Whatever the hypothesis, the conclusion is the same: philosophy must be poeticized, and criticism must accomplish this task. In other words, philosophy—and here this means *the very science of the Ideal*—is not *formed*. Criticism must form its character.

(And first off, thinks Friedrich, it ought to form the character of Schelling, whose courses in Jena were too much competition for my own!)[16]

The science of the Absolute must be perfected [*parachevée*]. Everything depends on this; (romantic) *poetry* itself depends on it. And consequently, everything depends on the double logic of perfection, which is simultaneously the absolutization of the Absolute, a fulfillment of every work in its Work, and the disparity, the surplus, the almost unaccountable excess of one more completion, of a singular remainder of completion.

This occurs, then, in characteristics.[17] The object of *construction* is character (and we will recall from now on that the essence of character, or the characteristic character, is apparently the philosopher). Character covers two things at once: it both forms the "designation of concepts by the aid of accompanying sensible signs,"[18] as Kant defined it, in contrast to schemata or symbols considered as direct presentations, and constitutes the distinctive mark, the proper imprint—and thus the *criterion*—of an essence or nature. Characteristics is the essence of criticism because it wants to be the science of the criterion in a sense of the term that, were it necessary here, would lead us back to the common origin of the entire history of semiotics, of judgment, and of criticism (and of the genre of moral exemplarity as well): namely, to the Stoic theory of the sign, and of the *kritérion* as the adequate relation of the representation to the thing represented. The *kritérion* furnishes the *idioma*, propriety, and distinguishes it from the *phantasma* or vain illusion. Convert representation into presentation, make the phantasm into an idiom, and you have the criteriology of romanticism. Apply it to the Platonic exigency of philosophical poiesy, and you have the *literary genre*, at least if you prefer superficial views and forget for the moment that the literary genre can never be *seen*.

As the proper mark of a nature, character, in Schlegel's text, announces itself through the exigency of a "physical" knowledge about "the nature of the soul," which soon becomes a demand for a "science" of poetry that would be analogous to a "physics of the eye and ear" for painting and music (this is the insufficiency that privileges literature: lacking a physics, going beyond all physics, literature is metaphysical). This science specifies its project as that of a "pathetics": "an accurate insight into the essence of anger, voluptuousness," etc. [*KS* 396]. A science, therefore, of character as *pathos*—or, in other words, if Friedrich had bothered to be coherent in his use of the Greek language, an *aesthetics* of profound sensibility. Which is to say, yet another science of those *passions* which, since Plato, have been held in check by philosophical reason, and which, since Aristotle's *catharsis* and up until Schlegel, by way of the history of the "pathetic" in the seventeenth and eighteenth centuries), have aroused the clearest or most obscure aspects of the desire of literature, giving it, for better or worse, the essence of its "genre."

A *science* of pathetic character is of course the aim of a philosophical will to mastery. But Schlegelian criticism cannot content itself with this: "it would be of little help to the poet in his practice" [*KS* 396]. Criticism itself must be, is expected to be, practical and productive, if not of works then at least of capacities to make work; it must be formative, not in the pedagogical sense of the term[19] (this is another break with traditional criticism, and one that will be reproduced in the context of our century) but in the specific sense of the formation of putting-into-form.

This is why criticism must become a characteristics, must perfect itself, as it were, through a *formation* of character. But it is through this "formation of character" that, in more ways than one, it returns to itself in literature, and becomes—at least in Schlegel's ideal—what its own desire and a healthy irony might call a *literary criticism*, according to the double value, subjective and objective, of the epithet.

The *character*, first of all, constitutes a genre by itself. With his characteristics—whose earliest example, within the tradition that was authoritative for the romantics, would be Shaftesbury's *charakteristics*—La Bruyere "immortalizes" the modern version (for La Bruyère as we know imitates the *Characters* of Theophrastus, who succeeded Aristotle as the director of a Lyceum from which

Friedrich Schlegel, much later, would have to emerge in order to found his *Athenaeum* . . .) of a moral genre which itself constitutes another version of the gnomic genre, and of the hortatory genre. Besides the fact that, unlike these latter genres, the genre of the *character* allies the "pleasant and picturesque portrait" with "moral painting"—to use the customary critical terms—this genre substitutes for the utterance of moral truths in the first person (albeit the first person of an anonymous and absent Subject) an utterance that is displaced and deferred through the staging of characters [*personnages*]. This is a genre in which mimesis supplants diegesis. A summary or sketch of a novel, perhaps, or in any case, a "romantic book," if we recall what this formula expressed in the *Dialogue.*

Character [*le personnage*] is essential to character. In German [and English], as in seventeenth-century French, the two words are identical, and the reader of the [modern French] translation of the *Dialogue,* among others, must beware of the fact that where the words "*personnage*" and "*caractère*" appear side by side, the German reader finds the single word *Charakter.* Which is surely not without consequence for linguistic sentiment or romantic sentiment.

Athenaeum fragment 418, as we have seen (in "The Poem: A Nameless Art"), makes the "presentation" of a character the fundamental merit of a novel—and examines this presentation in the most famous, most "phantastical," most "arabesque" characters of Tieck. In a *Charakter* like Tieck's Franz Sternbald, "the romantic spirit seems to be pleasantly fantasizing about itself." A character, or a character sketch, is a subject produced through *mimesis,* and capable (undoubtedly *for this very reason*) in its presentation or staging of re-producing or re-constructing the Subject, a Subject that is auto-constituting, auto-mimetic, auto-ironic, or in short, auto-fantastical in the sense of *Phantasie,* a Subject whose idiom is Phantasm—and that auto-imagines, auto-*bildet,* auto-illuminates itself: the Subject-Work. Such a Character owes nothing to the imitation of the "real"—or owes it only what it needs in order to be a re-construction, on the basis of an interior more interior than any psycho-sociological interiority, of the Figure absent from all figures. (And this is ultimately why the *nouveau roman,* as much as the old and perhaps even more than the Balzacian, in some respects, can aspire to the title of romantic.)

The character is what characterizes *itself*; and auto-characterization involves two poles. Either it refers to the literary-critical *topos* that requires a successful character [*personnage*] to be a person that is animated with its own life and that "escapes," as the saying goes, the novelist (once again, the novel or beyond-the-novel of our modernity carries this will to its most extreme point as it effaces the traditional imitative "character")—unless, at this same pole, the character can no longer be anyone but the author himself, who alone is capable of animating himself in the sort of "Confessions" celebrated by the *Letter on the Novel* ("and the author by himself" [*par lui-même*] will now, inevitably and rigorously, eventually come to imply "the critic by himself"[20]). Or—the second pole (which does not in fact exclude the first)—the character characterizes itself in that it becomes, as the distinctive sign or notable imprint of an essence, that which *characterization* requires as its minimal but sufficient condition: that is, the procedure—and above all the talent or genius—that allows one to "characterize . . . with a few strokes of the pen" the "physiognomy" of a "thought," as we have already learned from *Athenaeum* fragment 302.[21]

To characterize is to seize and present an essential vision of what constitutes the essence of an idea—and thus the "physiognomy" of its individuality. "On the Essence of Criticism" makes the characterization *of* the philosopher the fundamental critical task only because *philosophy* is properly what it is only in and through the individuality of a philosopher, through his originality. And from this, one understands that if the letter *On Philosophy* advances only one reservation with regard to Fichte, that he has not yet characterized himself,[22] it nevertheless formulates in this manner its most serious reproach: in the last instance, it means that philosophy up to Fichte has not yet attained its truth.

This truth, however, is neither in the discourse nor in the systematic exposition of philosophy; it is in the silhouette of the philosopher, "in a few strokes of the pen." It can only present itself, that is, through a form whose tendencies have been suggested to us, if not by the Fragments, then at least by the "fragmentary exigency." The critical imperative ("And besides, one can never be too critical," *A* 281) carries the fragmentary exigency to its greatest intensity: true criticism consists in the seizure of the Whole of the work (*KS* 396 and 398), and in simple, direct, essential characterization, which thus leads directly to characteristic traits—which are not so much traits of the work as traits of whatever or whoever is at work within the work. The necessity of the fragment or of ruin receives decisive confirmation here: what offers itself [*se livre*] only in fragments also offers its character, ready-made, as it were, for the characterizor. Or better yet, one suspects that in a certain manner the apparently external and accidental process of fragmentation—whether it concerns the fall of the ancient world or the chaotic state of modern poetry—actually constitutes the obscure and subterranean process that, in the collapse of external forms, gives auto-characterization its first impetus. Although no text verifies this suspicion literally, it nonetheless is authorized and solicited by everything that we have read and said up to this point. And surely nowhere else than in the shadow of romanticism could our modernity have thought of relating to literature even the supposedly most external accidents of its history: beginning, for example, with Novalis's death or Hölderlin's madness. These exemplary fragmentations—now "ontological" and no longer simply "literary"—have established for us (romanticism itself has compelled us to establish) the very character of literature; they have determined the entirety of our "literary criticism."

The beauty that criticism's task is to judge, or that criticism must complete in its form, is precisely that which is "impossible to imagine" "without character" (*A* 310). Character is the determination of "essential individuality" insofar as this latter is necessarily *embodied* in a precise and living form (*Athenaeum* fragment 310 is concerned with sculpture, with that type of *Bildung* and *Bild* in which the vigorous trait of characterization can be seen to best advantage). If criticism must be criticism of *art*—according to the exigency formulated in the epigraph to these pages—this is not primarily because it would be an activity specializing in the examination of works of art or of already given beautiful things. Or, to put it another way, it is not because there is art that there is criticism—and Schlegel's "On the Essence of Criticism" as well as Schelling's *Philosophy of Art* demonstrate quite clearly that, on the contrary, it is the romantics, and not Hegel, who in this respect did no more than follow them, who first found art to be a thing *of the past;* rather, it is only insofar as there will be a criticism that there will be an art, an altogether different art.

What is thus presupposed in the *past* of art—and thus in the entire historical schema that grounds all of romanticism, in its concept and even in its name, is its completion: the Individual, Epos, and Drama of antiquity are finished and can never return—except in the complex return of the re-construction of their essential classicity. Incompletion is thus implied along with and within completion; not incompletion within a continuity that would provide for the simple progressions of a modern art, but an incompletion of completion [*l'inachèvement de l'achèvement*] that continually renews the necessity for further critical perfection [*parachèvement critique*].

"The true critic is an author to the second power";[23] he is the author who perfects every work and every author, but this also means that what is not perfected—to the second power, squared, multiplied by itself—is not complete. And thus for the romantics there is nothing that is complete. Absolutely speaking, there never has been any completion, not even in the antiquity of Antiquity: "The deceptive image of a former Golden Age is one of the greatest obstacles to approximating the Golden Age that still lies in the future. If there once was a Golden Age, then it was not really golden. For gold neither rusts nor decays . . ." (*A* 243). And likewise for modernity, envisaged for example in its religion: "Christianity seems to me to be a fact. But only a fact in its first beginnings; in other words, one that cannot be presented historically in a system, but can only be characterized by means of divinatory criticism" (*A* 221). Thus it is the incomplete—the epoch *as such*—that harbors the ultimate fecundity of the chaotic in general, and thus also it is through what is least romantic about it (through what is most particularly German, as we know from several texts) that the epoch is disposed toward the romantic gesture: "Germanicity is probably a favorite subject for the characterizor, because the less a nation is finished, the more it is an object for criticism and not for history" (*A* 26).

But at the heart of critical desire, at the heart of the desire of and for the critical Subject, what matters is always the living unity of the individual. The formation of character, if it consists in the perfection of the author by the critic, is modelled on the most lively and intimate kind of exchange—the dialogue, or to an even greater extent, "sympoetry," which in turn inevitably suggests a sexual model:

> A whole new epoch of the sciences and arts would perhaps begin if symphilosophy and sympoetry became so universal and so interior that it would no longer be rare for several mutually fulfilling natures to create works in common [gemeinschaftliche Werke]. One is often struck by the idea that two spirits may properly belong together, like divided halves that can realize themselves only when joined [und nur verbunden alles sein, was sie könnte] (A 125).

Nevertheless, relative to the ideal of "sympoetry" (which in fact is always elusive in the texts, and whose importance tradition has often gauged inaccurately), criticism represents a necessity that is more complex, and whose emphasis corresponds to the latest period of romanticism's brief history. The Platonic fusion of "sympoetry" may well amount to a mere infinitization of the finite individual. Here too it is formation that, within idealism, distinguishes romanticism. Thus Athenaeum fragment 125 continues, in what is admittedly a somewhat incoherent manner, with the following lines:

> If there were an art of amalgamating individuals, or if wishful criticism could do more than merely wish, and it always finds occasions for that, then I would like to see Jean Paul and Peter Leberecht combined. The latter has precisely what the former lacks. Once united, Jean Paul's grotesque talent and the fantastic disposition [Bildung] of Peter Leberecht would yield an excellent romantic poet.[24]

Peter Leberecht is one of Tieck's characters—and these lines, if their interest lies in the models they choose for the romantic poet, may be more interesting still in terms of the critical operation they propose: the unification of the author with a character. If the character must take on personal autonomy, the author, in order to reach his "second power," must take on literary character: he too must become gedichtet,[25] composed, invented, written.

Neither author nor character: by 1800 literary criticism had volatilized the categories of literature, and traced the unaccountable contour of the literary character.[26]

In the end, what such a criticism must always re-construct and perfect, beyond all works, all authors, and all genres, is the "ancient criticism that has been lost."[27] Once perfected, ancient criticism will produce a criticism that would be less a commentary on a literature that is already present, completed, and withered, than the organon of a literature still to be completed, formed, or even begun. An organon of literature, and therefore a criticism that would not simply explain and conserve but that would itself produce, at least indirectly, as it directs, orders, and provokes.[28]

This criticism will thus perfect critical power itself, and will return to the deepest intimacy of *judgment* in order to reconstruct it—to that intimacy whose source Kant declared forever lost, to the bottom of the still-gaping hole of schematism. If the Kantian *schema* was the never *truly* explained union of concept and intuition, the romantic *character* is its explication and the figure provided for its truth. It fulfills the most proper power of the proper; that of engendering itself in [à] its proper form, and of grasping its unity and beauty in a single trait. It restores the *idiom* of judgment, that idiom which appears in the "mother tongue" whose fate "On the Essence of Criticism" links to that of "romantic poetry." Characteristics—as might have been suspected—is an idiomatics; and as an idiomatics, romanticism seeks to perfect eidaesthetics, according to the sole eidaesthetic motif to which it cares to respond. The literary genre is the idiomatics of the Idea.

But in this manner it brings into play the effects of the slow, imperceptible, and constant torsion that the motif of criticism (as we have constantly seen) and the motif of character have imprinted (this is indeed the correct word) on idealism. The idiomatic *Aufhebung*, which is undoubtedly *Aufhebung* itself, sublates meaning within meaning, and language within the Idea—a conjoint sublation of philosophy and of poetry—because it no longer restricts itself to the unique theme of pure vision or of theory; rather, it demands their putting-into-form and discretely directs this theory completed as literature back toward itself. In making the "highest task" of characteristics that of "constructing a concept . . . according to its becoming, . . . furnishing the concept's inner history along with the concept itself" [*KS* 400], romantic criticism opens onto that simple yet tortuous history in which Hegel's dialectical *Darstellung* proves closer than it seems to Nietzsche's artistic genealogy.

Closure: Romantic Equivocity

> This metaphysics should proceed through several cycles, ever greater and longer. Once the end has been reached, it should start again from the beginning, alternating between chaos and system, preparing chaos for the system, then a new chaos. (This procedure very philosophical.)
>
> —*Friedrich Schlegel, note from the posthumous "philosophical fragments" (1796–1806)* [*KA* 283, Frag. 1048].

We will not conclude: the conclusion, the resolution—the *Auflösung*—of romanticism has been repeated constantly in these pages. In all the texts in question, we have frequently pointed out the tireless return of the same pattern of resolution, unique in its abundance of motifs and in the "more than organic" imbrication of its functions. While this pattern may not exactly form Hegelian Logic's "circle of circles," it nonetheless constitutes the spiral of spirals that Friedrich Schlegel tried to sketch out in the note we cite as an epigraph. This spiral's alternation, infinitely resolved within itself, always leads back to the *center*, which was that of the *Ideas*—to a center itself animated by the spiralling movement of its own maelstrom: the center of the Work, of the Subject-Work and the Work-Subject, the poietic center of operation, or indeed of the operativity of the Work. Here, well in advance of the formation of any concept of the work, of any literature of genres, and of any philosophical subjectivism, the work operates itself; and perhaps even *it* operates itself, for although the romantics did not invent the Nietzschean usage of *it*, "what" else could be in question when the "true author" of the greatest work, the Homeric epic, is "nature" (*A* 51), but the "nature" of a thought that, as we have seen, is preoccupied with undoing all its links with any "naturality?"

In 1797, Rahel Levin described Friedrich as a "head in which operations unfold."[1] This could be the definition of the romantic Subject, that is, of the

121

subject of the literary genre, or of literature reduced to the Subject: it machinates, structures, mixes, engenders, fragments, poeticizes itself—but it took the *Witz* of a woman to characterize this head.

At the same time, however, we have pointed out that within this structure such a *Witz* continually errs—and even operates—between *system* and *chaos*, between the two poles of the *organon*. From the outset, we have attempted to point out not the place, but the play of a difference [*écart*] that separates romanticism from idealism (from the metaphysics that perfects itself therein). This difference appears in a supplementary complexity, hesitation, hovering— or *schweben*, to use a word that these texts are immoderately fond of, a word that may correspond to romanticism's infamous "vagueness," but that at times may also mean that romanticism constitutively involves a certain impossibility of exactly *accommodating* the vision of the Idea. Such an accommodation undoubtedly remains its goal, however, and the difference separating romanticism from idealism is minute. We must continually complicate the simple idealism/romanticism schema which we have nonetheless found useful. It is the difference of this "almost" that Friedrich would have liked to find in Kant, or most often it is probably no more than the slight commotion that is finally produced in idealism as a result of its abyssal auto-construction and auto-production. But once it has been established, as we hope to have done here without too many oversights, that romanticism *completes* idealism and opens up the ongoing history of its completion, it may be possible, albeit premature in a history that is not yet completed, to begin to discern what romanticism brings and brings back into play, both within and outside idealism (and as we have argued, this is above all not a matter of a relation between "literature" and "philosophy").

Let us repeat: each in its turn—the fragment, religion, the novel, criticism— reinstates the literary and literal *genre: Gattung,* species, the specific engenderment of the same specificity [*la specificité même*], the auto-engenderment of the mixture of same with same. Spontaneous generation, or, as it was called at the time, *generatio aequivoca,* which takes upon itself alone the two senses according to which, in every case, it engenders itself. —And from this fact, each in turn, each genre of genre, also confirms the equivocity of this generation, the equivocity of the *aequivoca*: the species is also the indistinct mixture without identity. At the very heart of the organic process of dissolution, something always resists—or escapes: something, for example, in Schelling's *Auflösung* always resisted Hegel's *Aufhebung,* and something of Schlegel's *novel* always escaped Schelling's *Auflösung.*

Mixture *as such* does not bring about a difference from idealism. Rather, it confirms it—as much by Roman satire as by the idea of philosophical art. To imagine that it would bring about such a difference stems perhaps, in some respects, from the illusion of a contemporary romanticism rather than from Jena romanticism. But what romanticism finally proves despite itself (and also, up to a certain point, because Friedrich's spiralling obstinacy says a great deal about what he "knew") is that there is no mixture *as such*. And thus that mixture neither makes a work [*faire oeuvre*] nor operates itself [*ne s'opère pas*]. Rather, at the very most, through its equivocity, the motif of mixture, without being or producing mixture itself (since it does not exist) leads to the extreme edge of what it mixes: genre, literature, philosophy. It may lead to the edge of what unmakes or interrupts the operation, to the edge of what could be called, with deliberate equivocity, the ab-solution of the literary Absolute.

Romanticism would thus have "known"—or would have made it possible for someone, such as Maurice Blanchot, to know how to read in it—this:

> Literature, nonetheless, beginning to manifest itself to itself thanks to the romantic declaration, will henceforth entail this question—discontinuity or difference as form—a question and a task that German romanticism, particularly that of the *Athenaeum,* not only foreshadowed but already clearly articulated, before passing them on to Nietzsche and, beyond Nietzsche, to the future (Blanchot 172).

It has now become possible to evaluate in an ever more rigorous manner what this involves—and this is possible precisely to the extent that Blanchot, as well as others we have mentioned or will mention, have enabled us to read the texts of romanticism.

"Literature's manifestation of itself to itself," a formula that strikes upon the essential character of romanticism, is an auto-manifestation only insofar as the *Gattung* of the work is incessantly un-worked within it. It is unworked, fundamentally, because the poetic *speculation* that so many texts of the *Athenaeum* call upon does not take place, or takes place only along with the decomposition of *Gattung*—the decomposition of genre, and of mixture. And thus, in this auto-manifestation, it is not only the identity of philosophy with literature and of literature with philosophy that never takes place, for the identity of literature with itself and philosophy with itself are absent as well. The Same, here, never reaches its sameness. And this is what something in romanticism, something that was already neither literature nor philosophy, *knew,* with a knowledge that exceeds any of the theoretical, poetical, or critical scientificities whose general program romanticism nonetheless initiated at the same time. To refer once again to Blanchot—and because, in the lines cited above, he acknowledges his debt to romanticism—this auto-manifestation of literature ought to be considered as a *neutral* manifestation, or as a *negative* [*pas*] of manifestation.

This would amount to saying that such a manifestation, rigorously speaking, is not a manifestation, not in any of the senses that philosophy can confer on this word. Obviously, it is not of the order of Kantian phenomenality—at least not according to the Kantianism that maintains, beyond the phenomenon, the agency of a "thing in itself," of which a kind of avatar or parallel is proposed, in opposition to romanticism, by Goethe, as we have noted.[2] We have also noted on more than one occasion that such a manifestation cannot be confused, however close it may be, with either a pure revelation according to the Shellingian motif, or with a process of Hegelian presentation. Something always seems to be missing, either due to a lack of Concept or to an excess of Form. But in the end it cannot be identified with putting-into-form either: because form is precisely what continually dissolves the problematic of genre.

The manifestation in question here, rather, seems to be one that can designate itself (and up to what point could this still be a designation) only through a peculiar eclipse of the manifest in its manifestation. It is indeed something of this genre that Blanchot tries to enable us to think, for example—to limit ourselves to one of the threads he has begun to draw from the romantic fabric—in his interrogation of "fragmentary writing." Something of this sort is also at stake in the most insistent of Heidegger's meditations, the meditation on language, which is largely undertaken with Humboldt (or in other words, along with a body of research that in many ways prolongs that of the Schlegels[3]), and which, citing Jean Paul and glossing Novalis and Hölderlin, leads, as if through the margins of romanticism, to the question of what, more "proper" than all propriety, speaks in language [la parole]. And Derrida's work on and around writing, the trace, and the dissemination of writing continues to proceed in the direction of this "thing"—if indeed it implies a direction to take. —Is it necessary to add that never for a moment did the romantics even imagine—if you will pardon the expression—a single one of these thoughts? They are instead eclipsed within romanticism. But perhaps this is why romanticism was able, in time, by maintaining its proper equivocity, to make them possible.

Is it also necessary to say that none of these thoughts can be possessed or manipulated as if they might be or had to be the resolution of the equivocity? In completing the closure of romanticism, they undoubtedly shake up the system with a sure hand [elles en ébranlent à coup sûr le système]. But then, too, this means that the epoch of solutions and resolutions, systems and chaoses, is also at an end. Let us say—in romantic terms, because fundamentally, we still have few others—that what romanticism "put off to the future," to a future that is still our own, constitutes only the "tendencies of the epoch" in the sense put forth in Athenaeum fragment 216, which is to say, as Friedrich explained elsewhere,[4] formless forms in the epoch's chaos, and our "fragments of the future." However, what we have perhaps begun to learn from this is that the future is fragmentary—and that a work-project has no place in it.

Thus, in the end, and insofar as it governs the entire question of "literature" up to the present, we can summon forth only romantic equivocity. The equivocity of the absence of the work. The purpose of this brief "Closure" is simply to draw it together and focus it once again around several testimonies concerning romanticism.

The first of these testimonies cannot be produced. Up to a certain point, it is the pure and simple absence of the Work: it is the obscure but certain failure of Schelling's project of the "speculative epos." It has been sufficiently discussed in this book, and we will not return to it here. Let us merely recall that such a failure is indeed the failure of a speculation that bestowed upon itself—albeit equivocally—the most proper place in the artistic auto-formation of the Idea. And that in place of this auto-formation we have offered the satiric *Confession of Widerporst*, at once genuine speculation *and* mockery of speculation—not because the genre is "low" but because it is not the Idea itself that engenders itself as satire. It would have had to satirize itself first—if indeed such a problematic could produce anything other, precisely, than mixture "itself," mixture as such, Satire as Identity. Philosophy confirms itself in the literary carnival.

The second testimony is Friedrich Schlegel's sonnet "The Athenaeum." Not without a certain deliberate brutality, we would willingly set it against all the texts of this same Friedrich, and against the extreme critical sophistication they demonstrate. This sonnet is one of a group that appeared in the last issue of the *Athenaeum*, and its subject is the review itself, romanticism itself, at the moment when it is about to dissolve. Along with Friedrich's handful of other poems—and his tragedy *Alarcos*—it constitutes everything "completed" that the "leader" of the romantics was able to compose. It is even completion as such, completion constructed *a priori*, one might say, that is represented by the sonnet, the most canonical of classical forms—and this particular sonnet, moreover, is absolutely regular and rhymed (for rhyme, as we read in *Critical Fragment* 124, is held by Friedrich to be the return of the Same . . .). The essence of the romantic project intends, if not to condense itself, then at least to accentuate its assertion in this microcosmic work: communalism, a desire to be free of limits, glowing formation, the satire of an epoch without romanticism, auto-presentation. It is not difficult to see that everything here is, in fact, less microcosmic than microscopic, tiny, insignificant, and all in all rather ridiculous, as the poem repeats the pomposity of its form in the pretentiousness of its contents. It would not be worth our attention if, despite everything he had written elsewhere, Friedrich had not written and published—in the *Athenaeum*—just such verses. Thus, this poem is not merely ridiculous, but raises the question of what profound equivocity inherent to the exigency of a "nameless art" could lead to this most laborious implementation [*mise-en-oeuvre*] of the most classical and classified of genres. An equivocity that here and elsewhere, right up to the present, always manages to renew an inextinguishable *faith* in words and in forms, and always in some confused and obscure magic of the verb, bringing about, where one least expects it, attacks of versification that even the romantics did not fail to ridicule—a *mania* for poetizing that cannot fail, at least momentarily, to suggest itself to anyone who sets out to write, in any genre, in the age of literature. This is nothing other, in the end, than being briefly fascinated by the Work, by the presentation of the absent and absolute Work.[5]

In conjunction with this text, finally, we refer the reader to the first two of Novalis's *Dialogues*, which were originally intended for the *Athenaeum*, although they never appeared there. These texts are usually grouped with Novalis's other unpublished dialogues (there are six in all), although they form a separate ensemble both by their subject and on the basis of manuscript evidence.[6]

It is therefore not the *poet* Novalis that we are discussing here, not the Novalis who (with an entirely different talent) believed even more strongly than Friedrich in the *poetic* arrival [*l'avènement*] and completion of "romantic poetry," just as he (aesthetically) believed in a religion that Schlegel and Schelling were carrying beyond itself. Rather, this is the Novalis who shared with Friedrich all the equivocity of *Idea* 95: the idea of the bible as a "system of books," "the infinite book," "the simple [*schlechtin*] book." This is the Novalis who, in a posthumous fragment, opposes the "*fragmentary*" world of books to the world of reality.[7]

What can be read in these *Dialogues* is the equivocity of the absence of the work in what is perhaps its most modern form, the form of "biblical" equivocity, or the equivocity of the multiplication of books. Like the proliferation of seeds in *Grains of Pollen*, this multiplication continually reunifies and reorganizes what it disseminates—and this is certainly in order to envisage multiplication (another form of mixture) *as such* and as an operation. For it is precisely the work's most "workmanlike" [*ouvrier*] and hard-working [*travailleur*] aspects that are staged by the *Dialogues*'s pretext (a "fair" that, as an "assembly of chance elements" [*Zusammenstellung der Zufälle*] is a true system of books) and by their metaphors of mining, industry, fabrication, and commerce. Insofar as these descriptions are ironic or humorous, Novalis might be said to be exhibiting the *commercial-spectacular* nature of literature. But he is also celebrating the work in its sheerly *economic* operation: art—*die Kunst*—as technique, production, and profit. And the exhibition of the conditions of production as the condition of production of "authentic" literature.

As part of this staging, the *Dialogues* take up all the great motifs of the Work: its auto-constitution to the second power, its obligatory presentation of the formation of man, the illimitation of the unique Subject. But at the same time, they lead these motifs toward the second Dialogue's somewhat different metaphorics—or mathematics, toward the "hyperbolic" *variation* that, one suspects, both recuperates and ironizes the *mathematical* ideal that idealism continually ignores—and yet depends on [*auquel l'idéalisme n'aura cessé de tourné le dos—et d'être adossé*]. In any case, the most radical irony would consist in the way that a mathematization of literature, building on an impossible Mathesis, would result in the futile and grotesque multiplication of *all* books, books by everyone and about everything, a multiplication of insignificance at the very locus of the operation. Which of course would not prevent these *Dialogues*, within the grotesque and the insignificant, from calling up a sort of bottomless generosity of the book and of books, a debauchery of works that would no longer make a work, a proliferation that could no longer be numbered.

This equivocity was at the center of the "Letter on the Novel"; and as Friedrich wrote, we are in the epoch of the book. —And *we* still are.

Notes

Translators' Introduction

1. Paris: Aubier-Flammarion, 1975.

2. *Institutio Oratoria*, IX. ii. 40.

3. See *Les Figures du discours* (Paris: Flammarion, 1968), where *hupotúposis* is discussed in the section "Figures of discourse other than tropes."

4. See the "Transcendental Analytic," Book 2, Chapter 1 in the *Critique of Pure Reason*, F. Max Müller, trans. (Garden City, N.Y.: Doubleday, 1966), 121–127.

   On the schematism of pure understanding, see Martin Heidegger, *Kant and the Problem of Metaphysics*, James S. Churchill, trans. (Bloomington: Indiana University Press, 1962), 93–117; Ernst Curtius, "Schematismus Kapital in Kritik das reinen Vernunft," *Kant-Studien* 19 (1914): 338–366; and Walter Biemel, *Die Bedeutung von Kants Begrundung der Aesthetik fur die Philosophie der Kunst* (Cologne: Kölner Universitäts Verlag, 1959), 94 ff.

5. Jean-Luc Nancy, *Le Discours de la syncope: Logodaedalus* (Paris: Aubier-Flammarion, 1976), 26–27.

6. For further discussion of Lacoue-Labarthe and Nancy's particular approach to the problem of presentation and its relation to the question of "literature," see Lacoue-Labarthe's remarks in "L'Imprésentable," *Poétique* 21 (1975): 53–95, and particularly in "La Fable," in *Le Sujet de la philosophie* (Paris: Aubier-Flammarion, 1979), 9–12.

7. Mary Shelley, *Frankenstein, or, The Modern Prometheus* (Oxford: Oxford University Press, "Oxford World Classics," 1980), 19.

8. See definition 9 in the article *keeping* in the *Oxford English Dictionary*, according to which the locution "in (or out) of keeping with" is derived from this particular usage of the term.

9. *Frankenstein*, 29.

10. At the point that Frankenstein is introduced, in a rescue of sorts, he is asked to account for himself, to explain why he was travelling alone on the ice, and why he was travelling in so strange a vehicle. He answers: "To seek one who fled from me" (Letter 4).

11. See also Nancy's articles on *Witz:* his introduction to a French translation of Jean

Paul's remarks on the subject, "Sur le trait d'esprit (Witz)," in *Poétique* 15 (1973): 365–406, and a more general treatment, "*Menstruum universale*: (Literary Dissolution)," in *Sub-stance* 21 (1978): 21–35.

Preface

1. R. Ullmann and H. Gotthard made this observation in the conclusion of their *Geschichte des Begriffes "Romantisch" in Deutschland*. We will make several references to this work in our "Preface."

2. Already in *De l'Allemagne*, to which we will return. Mme. de Staël opens the section on "literature and the arts" with the chapter: "Pourquoi les Français ne rendent-ils pas justice á la littérature allemande?" ["Why don't the French do justice to German literature?"].

3. Tr. note: *L'Absolu littéraire* was originally published in the Edition du Seuil's series "Poétique," directed by Gérard Genette and Tzvetan Todorov, whose journal bears the same name.

4. See "The Poem: A Nameless Art," herein.

5. Such cases have invariably been concerned with fantastic romanticism, which, as we shall see, is essentially exterior to or later than the romanticism of Jena.

6. See Benjamin 93.

7. For a historical study of this crisis in direct relation to Jena Romanticism, see H. Brunschwig, *Société et Romantisme en Prusse au XVIIIe siècle* (Paris: Flammarion, 1973), which is the revised edition of *La Crise de l'Etat prussien à la fin du XVIIIe siècle et la Genèse de la mentalité romantique* (Paris: Presses Universitaires de France, 1947), especially 228 ff. and 239 ff. This book's analyses are useful, even if we do not agree with all of the interpretations therein.

8. See *Athenaeum* fragment 421.

9. For one or the other of these reasons, almost all the Jena romantics experience difficult periods, precisely during the years of the *Athenaeum*. This did not prevent the leaders, Friedrich Schlegel above all, from going on to brilliant careers.

10. Letter to her son, cited in Ullmann 61.

11. Fragment 1073 [*Schriften* 3: 466].

12. For a detailed history of the formation of the group and of the foundation of the journal, see Ayrault 3: 11–95.

13. See J. J. Anstett's introduction to the French translation of Friedrich Schlegel's *Lucinde*.

14. With the exception of Schleiermacher, they will all meet for the last tine in Jena in the fall of 1799 and will serve as the protagonists of the *Dialogue on Poetry*. (See "The Poem: A Nameless Art," herein.)

15. Or when really successful, the journal sets off a genuine scandal, as was the case, for example, upon the publication of *Lucinde*.

16. See Ayrault 3: 42.

17. In *Poésie et poétique de l'idéalisme allemand* (Paris: Minuit, 1975), Peter Szondi characterizes the romantics' anticipation of Hegel. [Many of the essays that were translated for this volume are also translated in Szondi, *On Textual Understanding.*]

18. See *De l'Allemagne* (Paris: Garnier-Flammarion, 1968), vol. 3, part 3, chap. 9, 162.

19. With *Lucinde*, we will see what Friedrich Schlegel would attempt to forge as romanticism.

20. *De l'Allemagne.*

21. See the "Summaries of the *Athenaeum*," herein.

Overture: The System-Subject

1. We are using the text established by Horst Furhmann which, assuming that Hegel committed errors in copying, adopts certain corrections that allow grammatically correct readings of several passages. [H. S. Harris's study *Hegel's Development* includes an English translation of this same version of the text, as well as an appendix on its "curious background."]

2. A summary of the discussions concerning the attribution of this text may be found in the note that accompanies the "System-Programme" in *Frühe Schriften*, the first volume of Hegel's *Werke in zwanzig Bänden*, Eva Moldenhauer and Karl Markus Michel, eds. (Frankfurt am Main: Suhrkamp, 1971).

3. See "Closure: Romantic Equivocity," herein, and Lacoue-Labarthe and Nancy, "Le Dialogue des genres" (168–171).

4. It would be a long and difficult task to specify the place Hölderlin occupied or the role he played in the genesis of romanticism and idealism, between 1794 and 1796 (or even beyond) or, in other words, between the writing of *Hyperion* and the first two versions of *Empedocles.* He still maintains relatively close relations with Schelling and Hegel and, like most everyone else at the time, is influenced by Fichte (whose lectures at Jena he may have attended). His first essays, especially those on the poetic of genres, are inscribed within or, more accurately, begin to establish the future speculative dialectic (on this point, see Szondi's analyses). The essential aspects of the "System-Programme," as has long been observed in the criticism, are largely sketched out in the fragment of 1795 entitled *From Hermocrates to Cephalus* and in the September 4, 1795 letter to Schiller [*Sämtliche Werke und Briefe*, 2 vols. (Munich: Carl Hanser, 1970) 1: 841–842; 2: 667–668]. In particular, the idea of a completion of philosophy on the level of aesthetics alone—and not on the

level of knowledge, as Schiller affirmed at the time and as Hegel would always affirm—seems due to Hölderlin alone. In the letter to Schiller, he writes:

> I am attempting to develop, for my own use, the idea of an infinite progress of philosophy, and I am attempting to prove that what must be continually demanded of any system, the union of the subject and object in an absolute I (or whatever name one gives it), is undoubtedly possible on the aesthetic level, in intellectual intuition, but not on the theoretical level except by means of an infinite approximation, like that of the square of the circle. Immortality is just as necessary to realize a system of thought as it is to realize a system of action.

But none of this, it is true, will prevent Hölderlin's irreversible withdrawal from a "constellation" to which, as Blanchot puts it, he never really belongs (see Blanchot 165). Nor, above all, as his work on Greek tragedy and Sophocles indicates, will it prevent him from putting into question the dialectical model whose matrix he helped produce (see Lacoue-Labarthe, "Le Césure du spéculatif," in *L'Imitation des modernes: Typographies 2* (Paris: Galilée, 1986) and in Hölderlin, *L'Antigone de Sophocle* (Paris: Ch. Bourgois, 1978) [For an English translation, see "The Caesura of the Speculative."]

5. For the problematic of the System in speculative idealism, see Heidegger's *Schelling* 14–61, which from this perspective is clearly the best possible commentary on the text that concerns us here.

6. In greatest proximity to, but also maximally distant from, the "poetry of poetry" or "transcendental poetry" of the romantics (see "The Poem: A Nameless Art" and "Criticism: The Formation of Character," herein).

7. We are intentionally distancing ourselves here from the traditional presentation of the genesis of romanticism, which makes Fichte an obligatory stage. This gesture is in no way a "critique" of these geneses. Besides the fact that the development through Fichte has been well charted and offers few new insights (even with regard to the differing Fichtean and romantic treatments of the doctrine of the I, as analyzed by Benjamin, 18–40), it seems more urgent to relate romanticism, beyond Fichte and its dialogue with him, to the effective philosophical *crisis*, whose entire violence romanticism had to experience. As we will observe shortly, and as the previously cited letter of Hölderlin to Schiller attests, the "Earliest System-Programme" responds in its own way to the Fichtean idea of an infinite approximation of the three fundamental thetic judgments: I am; man is free; this is beautiful. Among other commentaries on this point, see Camille Schuwer, "La part de Fichte dans l'esthétique romantique" (in Béguin 137 ff.). The almost immediate articulation of romanticism and Kant has been well noted by Antoine Berman (89 ff.): "Imagine a post-Kantian, or even Kantian, poetry. It seems inconceivable that the development of poetry could be divided in two by a philosophy, but this is nonetheless the case. Novalis and Schlegel, like Hölderlin, Kleist, Coleridge, and Thomas de Quincy, were genuinely overwhelmed by Kantianism, which seems to me sometimes to be the philosophy of poets—but not of poetry. To philosophy's Copernican revolution corresponds a Copernican revolution of poetry. The former explores the vast territory of pure reason, the latter bravely pushes on into the mists

of the transcendental imagination. Novalis uses the words *fantastic* and *geniology* to describe speculation that returns toward the principle of poetry. Transcendental schematism, this *art hidden in the depths of the human soul* before which Kant halted in respectful fright, is its land of birth . . . ."

8. The world is thus understood here both as the effect of self-consciousness as representation and will (whence the idea of "creation out of nothing") and as the world itself, in a more "realistic" sense. Thus the "greater physics" programmed here sends its roots, short of Kant or even Descartes—and via Spinoza, whose *Ethics* finds an echo of its systematic status here—back to Bruno or Jacob Böhme. Recall that in 1795 Schelling writes the *Letters on Dogmatism and Criticism* in an attempt to move beyond the well-known quarrel over pantheism (see Heidegger's *Schelling* 62 ff. and Ayrault 3: 525 ff.).

9. The political radicalism of the "System-Programme" (Hölderlin?), its fairly clear anticlericalism (Schelling?), and above all its treatment of the question of the State merit a lengthy commentary. We limit ourselves to noting that the anti-State motif is relatively unusual in comparison to what will later emerge as the politics of German idealism. Compare this with Hegel, for example, for whom the State, as the "moral idea in action," constitutes the highest moment of ethics and thus—from the perspective of its realization—the final moment of the System. On this text and its echoes in Schelling's political thought, see Ayrault 4: 247–248.

10. Especially in the *System of Transcendental Idealism.*

The Fragment

1. Without forgetting the earlier-mentioned difference, which separates Hölderlin from all of Jena. But as will become apparent, this chapter is concerned, rather, with the initial proximity of the romantics and Hölderlin.

2. August Schlegel did not share his brother's ideal of the fragment and even seems, in a certain manner, to have practiced the genre in its traditional eighteenth-century form. Even within the group there was opposition to the "fragment," for example, on the part of Caroline Schlegel. The practice of the fragment was even more short-lived than the *Athenaeum* and thus figures as a sort of "avant garde" of the "avant garde."

3. See Ayrault (3: 111 ff.) for the history of Friedrich Schlegel's relations to the text of Chamfort, for the evolution of his conception and practice of the fragment, as well as for an entire analysis of the "genre," which we do not pretend to supersede here.

4. At least to the extent, which we cannot analyze here, that the *Discourse* itself does not belong, in its provenance and even its "genre," to what was established by the *Essays*. The simplified opposition that imposes itself here should not obscure the

degree to which the romantic "crisis" remains profoundly indebted to the Cartesian operation. This should become apparent often in what follows.

5. Epigraph: "Friends, the ground is poor; we must sow/Richly to reap even a modest harvest" [2: 413]. We will cite the last fragment further on in the text. *Faith and Love* appeared in 1798, in another journal.

6. See "The Idea: Religion within the Limits of Art," herein.

7. On this point also, see Ayrault [3: 111 ff.].

8. And the doubtful cases are indeed doubtful each time; that is, they encourage a double reading of the text, for example, in the fragment we have cited as an epigraph (*CF* 4) or in *Athenaeum* fragment 24: "Many of the works of the ancients have become fragments. Many modern works are fragments as soon as they are written." Ayrault sees in this statement only the pejorative value of the term (3: 120), but the irony here may well be accompanied by an awareness of the necessity of the fragment and, as we shall see, of "chaos" in modern poetry. Also, in conjunction with the theme of the fragment-project, see Szondi's interpretation of this fragment (64–65).

9. See also *A* 305.

10. To take only two examples, the *Physiognomical Fragments* of Lavater (who was, in fact, Swiss and not German) and Lessing's *Fragments of an Anonymous Person.*

11. On the motif of the "project," see the conclusion of the letter *On Philosophy* to Dorothea.

12. See Ayrault 3: 119.

13. To borrow this term from Gérard Genette. We will refer to his *Mimologigues* (Paris: Seuil, 1976) in connection with the romantic conception of the language.

14. Before the collective anonymity of the *Fragments*, the *Grains of Pollen* signed by Novalis already contained several fragments by Friedrich Schlegel and Schleiermacher, which Schlegel had added. At the same time, Friedrich Schlegel had also withdrawn certain fragments from Novalis's manuscript for later use in the collective publication. This practice of collective writing should therefore be approached with caution: it momentarily represented an ideal only for Friedrich Schlegel, essentially, and for Novalis. It seems, although this does not prevent one from analyzing its ideal as such, *also* to have corresponded to a somewhat dictatorial practice on Friedrich Schlegel's part. . . .

15. See also *A* 37.

16. But for the romantics, the (creative) potential and the meaning (in public) of genuine drama—ancient, then Shakespearean—are also what is most assuredly lost.

17. We refer here to the entirety of Heidegger's crucial analysis of the aims of *system* and of *Absolute Knowledge* in his *Schelling* (48 ff.). Our remarks will continually assume Heidegger's analysis.

18. See Benjamin, "System and Concept," 35 ff.

19. In his essay *On Naive and Sentimental Poetry*, published in 1795, of which Friedrich Schlegel speaks at length in his preface to *On the Study of Greek Poetry*. The "naive" would more precisely cover the renaissance or resurrection of the naturalness (lost) by art.

20. In the "sense" Jacques Derrida gives the word in *La Dissemination* (Paris: Seuil, 1972) [translated by Barbara Johnson as *Dissemination* (Chicago: University of Chicago Press, 1981)], of a sterile dispersion of seed [*la semence*] and of the semic [*le sémique*] in general; in other words, of sign and sense.

21. See *On the Study of Greek Poetry*.

22. See "The Poem: A Nameless Art," herein.

23. One should compare this with the motif of chaos as it appears in Kant, for whom the necessity of ensuring a regulative use of the Ideas—and a reflective use of judgment—without being able to go beyond this use—is a protection against the chaos to which finite reason, without this protection, would be condemned. (See in particular the first Introduction to the *Critique of Judgement*.)

24. *Kunstchaos*, in other words, chaos produced by art or philosophical technique. And consequently a chaos which is to genuine chaos somewhat as the "naive" is to the "natural."

25. In keeping with what Friedrich Schlegel himself wrote in "On Incomprehensibility" (that is, in the *Athenaeum*), published in the last issue of the journal, in which he expresses surprise at how little, given the fragments on irony, it had been understood that one must know how to decipher the irony in the texts of the journal. On the Schlegelian concept of irony, which we will only mention further on, see Bede Allemann (55 ff.). We will note, along with Allemann (60) that in Schlegel himself (as opposed to what would arise in the later systematization of Solger) the concepts of *Witz* and irony generally overlap.

26. As Benjamin emphasizes (24), this is precisely one of the essential points of difference between the romantics and Fichte. Whereas, in opposition to Descartes, Fichte postulates the primacy of the substantial Self [*Moi*] over thought, the romantics hold, despite Fichte, the primacy of reflection, of the self-reflection of every thing, over the Self. "For Fichte," writes Benjamin, "consciousness is 'I' [*Ich*], for the romantics, it is 'itself' [*Selbst*]."

27. On *Witz*, see Ayrault (3: 139 ff.) and Allemann. On the theme of the "*chemical mixture*," which is completely informed by *Witz*, see Peter Kapitza's *Die frühromantische Theorie der Mischung* [*The Early Romantic Theory of Mixture*] (Munich: W. Fink, 1968).

28. Thus Heidegger, after defining the dialectic in the manner to which we referred earlier, can write: "Friedrich Schlegel once said (*Athenaeum* fragment 82) that 'a definition that is not *witzig* is worthless.' This is only a romantic transposition of the idealist dialectic" (*Schelling* 82). This affirmation nevertheless raises the question,

clearly, of what is in fact at stake in this *transposition*, or of the "play" that subsists between idealism and romanticism.

29. On the privilege of *writing* in general, the reader is referred, as far as Schlegel is concerned, to the letter *On Philosophy*, and as far as Novalis is concerned, to Novalis's *Dialogues*. Whatever the nature of this privilege might be, it never really leads to a meditation on writing in romanticism comparable to that of our modernity, or more specifically to that of Blanchot and Derrida. This is evident, for example, if one follows the motif of "the Spirit and the Letter" through these texts, where it always functions in an at least ambivalent manner. If romanticism nevertheless admits the possibility of opening up something like a meditation on writing—as we will soon point out—it is in function of the motif of fragmentation rather than of the motif of writing.

30. Tr. note: In "The Architectonic of Pure Reason" in the first *Critique*, Kant speaks of "intussusception" as the form of growth proper to the system that knowledge, under the sway of reason, must become: "The whole is articulated (*articulatio*), not aggregated (*coacervatio*). It may grow internally (*per intussusceptionem*), but not externally (*per appositionem*), like an animal body, the growth of which does not add any new member, but, without changing their proportion, renders each stronger and more efficient for its purposes." *Critique of Pure Reason*, F. Max Müller, trans. (New York: Doubleday, 1966), 530.

31. Tr. note: See Aristotle, *Metaphysics*, 1048a–1051b.

32. For this citation and for those that follow, see Maurice Blanchot, "The Athenaeum."

The Idea

1. Which is to say, into the essential. Here again, the reader is referred to the irreplaceable work of Ayrault; see in particular 3: 111 ff.

2. In fact, the composition of *Lucinde*, the letter *On Philosophy* to Dorothea, and the *Dialogue on Poetry* (the first part of which appears in the same issue of the *Athenaeum* as the *Ideas*), all occur between the publication of the *Fragments* and that of the *Ideas*. Also in 1800, Friedrich publishes the poem "To Heliodora," and of course the final issue of the journal will include a group of sonnets.

3. As for example in the case of August (who from 1801 on will be delivering his *Lectures on Art and Literature*) and even Schelling.

4. As Anstett in particular emphasizes, in Béguin 234 ff.

5. See the May 20, 1798 letter to Novalis (cited in Ayrault 3: 119).

6. See "The Poem: A Nameless Art," herein.

7. Amalia or, in other words, Caroline. The exact title is *Letters on Poetry, Meter, and Language*. These letters were published in 1795 in Schiller's journal *Die Hören*.

8. Twice converted: first to Protestantism when she married Friedrich, and subsequently to Catholicism when Friedrich himself converted. The essential reference for the literary figure of Dorothea is *Lucinde*.

9. See the "Note on *Heinz Widerporst's Epicurean Confession of Faith*," which is appended to this chapter.

10. See *Über die Philosophie. An Dorothea* (*DA* 459). Schlegel adds: "In this sense, understanding is nothing other than natural philosophy itself, and hardly less than the highest good" (460). For the role of the understanding in Schlegel's thought, see Szondi 97 ff.

11. In other words, in relation to the problematic of the "mixture of genres," which originates in Cynicism.

12. Essentially in the *Aesthetics:* in the Introduction (Chapter 3, 3: "Irony and Romanticism"), as well as in the exposition of the history of art (second part, chapters on the dissolution of Greek art in satire and of romantic art in the novel. In these passages, the motif of what could be called bad dissolution (non-"relevant" dissolution) serves to articulate a blanket condemnation of the dissociation of form and content, prosaism and unilateral subjectivism, the profanation of the sacred and divine, the mixture and confusion of genres, etc., which are exemplified in Roman art as well as in "romanticism" in the narrow sense.

13. On the role played by the paradigm of Aristotle's *Rhetoric*—and its "modernization" into an example—in the constitution of aesthetics (Baumgarten) and of the theory of art in the eighteenth century, see Alfred Bäumler, *Kant's Kritik der Urteilskraft, Ihre Geschichte und Systematik* (Halle: Niemeyer, 1923).

14. On the history of the concept of the mediator from Lessing to Novalis, see Ayrault 3: 353 ff.

15. On this point, see "Overture: The System-Subject," note 7, herein.

16. See *Athenaeum* fragment 234: "It is very narrow and presumptuous to maintain that there should be only one mediator. For the perfect Christian, whom in this respect Spinoza probably resembles most, everything would have to be a mediator." Here, as one can see, a veiled criticism of the specifically Christian usage (in Novalis' manner) of the concept of the mediator is already seen.

17. *Über die Diotima*, which appeared in 1795 in the *Berlinische Monatsschrift* [see *DA* 277–311]. The letter *On Philosophy* also contains a number of themes that were developed earlier in the study "On the Feminine Character in the Greek Poets" (*Über die weiblichen Charaktere in den griechischen Dichtern* [1794. This study was republished in Schlegel's study *The Greeks and Romans: A Historical and Critical Essay on Classical Antiquity* (1797) under the title "The Representation of Femininity in the Greek Poets" (*Über die Darstellung der Weiblichen Charaktere in den griechischen Dichtern*).]

18. See, in particular, the "Earliest System-Programme."

19. The word "oath" (*Eid*) is the only word in the *Ideas* that is underlined: linked to the motif of the alliance (*Bund*), which recurs quite often in the *Ideas* (*I* 49, 140, 142, etc.), it clearly alludes to the practices of Masonry, whose—symbolic and real—importance in this period is well known. On this point, the reader is referred to Jacques d'Hondt, *Hegel secret* (Paris: Presses Universitaires de France, 1968), especially to the third part (236–253).

20. See *I* 19: "To have genius is the natural state of man. Nature endowed even humanity with health, and since love is for women what genius is for men, we must conceive of the Golden Age as a time when love and genius were universal."

21. The letter *On Philosophy* brings up the *topos* of a necessary reconstitution of primitive androgyny [*DA* 448–449]. See also *Lucinde*, of course, on which these texts are ultimately a perpetual commentary (if not the inverse), as well as *Athenaeum* fragment 364.

22. The fragment continues as follows (and we cite it in order to emphasize the distance that separates Schlegel from Christianity): "But that women should, as it were, believe more in God or Christ than men do, that some good and beautiful habit of freethinking should suit them less than it does men, is probably only one of the infinite number of commonly accepted platitudes that Rousseau built into a systematic theory of femininity; and in which nonsense is so improved and developed that it simply had to gain universal acclaim."

23. In other words, also of the entire tradition that lies behind the Kantian "anthropology"—for which, it must not be forgotten, woman was the privileged object (which a note in the *Athenaeum* denies, however): not only post-Wolffian aesthetics, but also the tradition of the English Moralists, or of Hume (with which Kant was largely familiar, thanks to Mendelssohn . . . the actual father of "Dorothea").

24. See *I* 127: "Women have less need for the poetry of poets because their very essence is poetry."

25. Tr. Note: For a discussion of the term "re-mark," a "concept" elaborated in the writings of Jacques Derrida, see Rodolphe Gasché, *The Tain of the Mirror* (Boston, Mass.: Harvard University Press, 1986).

26. See the praise of writing at the beginning of the letter *On Philosophy*, which also appears in the *Ideas* and *Lucinde*.

27. More so than the "people," although the idea of an education of the human race, as the "Earliest System-Programme" notes, undoubtedly implies this as well.

28. Fontenelle's *Entretiens sur la pluralité des mondes habités* was considered a model of the exposition of a difficult science in a form suitable for ladies. Algarotti was an Italian poet and critic (1712–1784), the author of *Newtonism for Ladies*. The association of Fontenelle and Algarotti to which Schlegel refers in the letter *On Philosophy* (*DA* 449) was first made by Kant, in the same context but with opposite intentions, in section 3 of the *Observations*.

29. Which Kant himself was the first to recognize (because of his concern for popularity, precisely). The affirmation that religion is in fact genuine popularity, an

affirmation that appears throughout the *Ideas,* descends directly from the Kant of *Religion within the Limits of Reason Alone.* Its direct echo appears in "idea" 42, where, in conformity with the Schlegelian "dialectic," only religion can ensure the reconciliation of philosophy and poetry, a condition indispensable to genuine popularity.

30. The only piece of work that nonetheless remains for me is the search for a means of presenting the necessary and natural character of the philosopher in general. For if Fichte, with all the faculties his being reunites, is a philosopher and if, for our age, he is also, by his mode of thought and his character, the model and representative of a genre, he cannot be understood except by knowing these things, not just philosophically, but in a historical manner as well [*DA* 464].

31. It is also necessary to remark, not only that it is indeed Montaigne who opens (or re-opens, in the "modern" age) the tradition of the Moralists, but that the movement of "dissidence" with respect to Authority is inaugurated in the *Essays,* as the "break" in Book 3 in particular reveals.

32. Particularly in the letter *On Philosophy* [see *DA* 451].

33. In *Europa,* 1803 [cited in Benjamin 96].

34. See *Ideas* 112 and 138, for example.

35. All these texts must constantly be read with reference to Schleiermacher's *Discourses on Religion* [*Reden über die Religion*], Schlegel's hommages to which are always, at the very least, ambivalent. It is also well known that it is from Schleiermacher that Schlegel borrows the word (but not the concept) "cleric," with which he designates the artist who has made it [*parvenu*]—if you will excuse the expression—to the stage of religion.

36. See the "Note on *Widerporst*" following this chapter.

37. See the second of the "Paralipomena" to the *Disciples at Saïs*: "Someone arrived there—who lifted the veil of the goddess, at Saïs.—But what did he see? He saw—wonder of wonders—himself" (*Schriften* 1: 110).

38. So come all of you, you other Philanthropists and Encyclopedists, come in to the Den of Peace. . . . I want to lead you to a brother who will know how to speak to you in a way that will open your hearts. . . . He made a new veil for the Saint, so supple and caressing that it betrays her heavenly beauty, and yet covers and clothes it, revealing it all the while, with even more modesty, than any other. The veil is to the Virgin what the spirit is to the body: it is the indispensable organ whose folds form the Letter of her most gentle annunciation . . . (3: 520–521).

[Novalis's text involves a transparent allusion to the name Schleiermacher, which literally means "veil-maker," from *Schleier,* a veil or screen.]

39. See *Widerporst* 184, lines 262–264. ["Reden von Religion als einer Frauen,/Die man nur dürft' durch Schleier schauen,/Um nicht zu empfinden sinnlich Brunst"—"Speaking of religion as of a woman,/That can be gazed upon only through a veil,/So as to avoid surrendering to sensual lust."]

40. [*DA* 458; Schlegel uses the term *Härte*, hardness, harshness, roughness.]

41. From *Über Lessing*, published in the *Lyceum* in 1797 [see *KS* 381].

42. Tr. note: "The Decii, a noted Roman family in which grandfather, father, and son freely gave their lives for the greater glory of Rome" (Firchow 253n).

43. See part two of the thesis on irony: *The Concept of Irony: With Constant Reference to Socrates*, trans. Lee M. Capel (Bloomington: Indiana University Press, 1965). On the relation between irony and sacrifice in Kierkegaard, see Sylviane Agacinski, *Aparté* (Paris: Flammarion, 1977).

44. See *Athenaeum* fragment 121:

> But to transport oneself arbitrarily now into this, now into that sphere, as if into another world, not merely with one's understanding and imagination, but with one's whole soul; to freely relinquish first one and then another part of one's being, and confine oneself entirely to another; to seek and find now in this, now in that individual the be-all and end-all of existence, and intentionally forget everyone else: of this only a spirit is capable that contains within itself simultaneously a plurality of spirits and a whole system of persons, and in whose inner being the universe which, as they say, should germinate in every monad, has grown to fullness and maturity.

The finitude of the poet, however, is understood at once as the annihilation or dissolution of the subject in the absolute Subject *and*—as Benjamin demonstrates (77)—as the limiting condition of the form imposed on the author no less than on the work. The ideal poet is not (as in the model of a certain French romanticism) a subjectivity that overflows all contour: he is an artist who is *gebildet*, in every sense of the word. (On irony and auto-limitation, see also Szondi 106 ff.)

45. Benjamin 77 ff.

Note on Heinz Widerporst's Epicurean Confession of Faith

1. A complete analysis of the circumstances of the poem, of its content, and of its relations with Schleiermacher and Novalis, as well as with the thought of Schelling himself, can be found in Ayrault 3: 525 ff. and 4: 13 and 528.

2. See F. Lion's article in Béguin 367. [See Schelling's *Night Watches of Bonaventura*, trans. Gerald Gillespie (Austin: University of Texas Press, 1971).] On satires and parodies in romanticism, see *Satiren und Parodien*. For a more precise description of the Schellingian motif of the philosophical poem, see the "Dialogue des genres" in *Poétique* 21, where one will also find, among others, an extract of *Clara* translated into French.

3. See lines 288–291: "They advise whoever has read it,/in order to recover from depravity,/to take a beautiful child onto a sofa/and explicate "Lucinde" to it."

The Poem

1. Tr. note: Lacoue-Labarthe and Nancy distinguish *Gespräch*, which they translate as *Entretien*, from *Dialog*, which they translate as *dialogue*. For Schlegel, the latter, they note, "always refers to the ancient genre (and above all, to the dialogue as practiced by Plato)" and is to be distinguished from Schlegel's practice in the *Gespräch über die Poesie*.

   To aid the reader of this chapter, the authors provide the following breakdown of the *Dialogue's* parts: (1)Introduction, 53–55; (2)Narrative: the "staging," 55–59; (3)Andrea's talk: "Epochs of Poetry," 60–75; (4)Discussion 1, 75–80; (5)Ludovico's "Talk on Mythology," 81–88; (6)Discussion 2, 88–93; (7)Antonio's text: "Letter on the Novel," 94–104; (8)Discussion 3 (Summary), 104–105; (9)Marcus's talk: "Essay on the Different Styles in Goethe's Early and Late Works," 106–113; (10)Discussion 4, 113–117.

2. In 1802–1803. But Schelling had already set forth his view in a number of texts, notably in the last of the *Letters on Dogmatism and Criticism* (an analysis of Greek tragedy) and in the final section of the *System of Transcendental Idealism* (1800). This latter text, moreover, served as the basis of certain developments in Schlegel's *Lectures*.

3. The willful pedantry of this philological term, which Andrea used in his "Epochs of Poetry" (63), is later mocked by Marcus in the discussion following the "Talk on Mythology" (89).

4. See "Criticism: The Formation of Character," herein.

5. It appears notably in "idea" 95, where it designates the organic ensemble of modern books—compared and opposed to the "single poem" formed by the reciprocal relations of "all the classical poems of the ancients": "In a similar way, in a perfect literature all books should be only a single book. . . ." One should note that the word "literature" is the final word of the *Dialogue*.

   On the history of the word "literature," see R. Escarpit et al., *La Définition du terme "littérature,"* a paper delivered at the Third Congress of the International Association of Comparative Literature, Utrecht, 1961.

6. See *A* 121.

7. See the two dialogues that August contributed to the *Athenaeum* (the second in collaboration with Caroline): *Languages: A Dialogue on Klopstock's Grammatical Dialogues* and *The Paintings [Die Gemälde]*. Both of these texts—even if the second includes lengthy descriptions—are simple dialogues, that is, dialogues without narrative. [On *The Paintings*, see also Ayrault 3: 324–336.]

8. See the *Dialogues* (numbered 1 through 5) that Novalis composed for the *Athenaeum*. These, too, are simple dialogues.

9. For historical analyses that cannot be developed here, we refer the reader to our "Dialogue des genres" in *Poétique* 21.

   For the relation between dialogue and Roman satire and, consequently, the novel, see *Critical Fragment* 42, *Athenaeum* fragments 146, 148, 239, and 448, among others, and "Epochs of Poetry" in the *Dialogue on Poetry.*

10. See *On Philosophy* and the earlier analyses in "The Idea: Religion within the Limits of Art." See also *Lucinde*, "Julius to Antonio," 121–125.

11. See "Epochs of Poetry."

12. Or, in other words, to the tradition that we have traced to Montaigne and that the romantics knew essentially through English or eighteenth-century French "literature."

13. On this point, see Gérard Genette, "Frontières du récit," in *Figures* II. [(Paris: Seuil, Collection "Tel Quel," 1969), 49–70. English trans: "Frontiers of Narrative," in *Figures of Literary Discourse*, trans. Marie-Rose Logan (New York: Columbia University Press, 1982), 127–144.]

14. Aristotle, *Poetics* 1447b.

15. Since writing these pages, we have become aware of Gérard Genette's fundamental study "'Genres,' 'types,' 'modes,'" in *Poétique* 32 (1977): 389–421. From the perspective of the history of poetics, this study decisively clarifies the process by which romanticism, as it completes a movement extending at least as far back as Abbé Batteux, tends to project a distinction of *genres* (lyric, epic, and dramatic) onto ancient poetics (Plato and Aristotle). This distinction of genres:

    (1) does not appear as such in either the *Republic* or the *Poetics* (and, in particular, no fate is reserved for the lyric); and

    (2) actually corresponds to a distinction between *modes of utterance* (direct, or in the first person: *diegesis;* indirect, or through a third person: *mimesis*).

    Thus, it becomes clear that what romanticism names, or desires, in the name of "genre," results from this double distortion. Likewise, one can understand why, as we point out at the end of this text, the "generic speculation" of romanticism comes up against the particular problem of the lyric. In all that follows, it goes without saying that we employ the word *genre* in the sense the romantics attempted to give it.

16. See for example the *Dialogue's* discussion of Goethe's *Wilhelm Meister* (in the "Essay about the Different Styles in Goethe's Early and Late Works"). The first of *Wilhelm Meister's* qualities is that "the individuality that appears in it is refracted into various rays, distributed among several persons" [112]. See also *Critical Fragments* 78 and 89, among others.

17. See Ayrault 3: 71.

18. Tr. note: In *Friedrich Schlegel* (New York: Twayne, 1970), Hans Eichner translates the Schlegel brothers' *Charakteristiken und Kritiken* as *Pen-Portraits and Reviews.* In his article entitled "Friedrich Schlegel's Theory of Literary Criticism," in *Romanticism Today*, ed. Reinhold Grimm (Bonn: Inter Nationes, 1973), 17–26, he suggests that the "closest English equivalent" to the *Charakteristik* is an *interpretation.* We have translated the term as *character sketch* in order to emphasize the fact that such interpretation is intended to provide a succinct representation of the total "spirit" of an author and his works.

19. See Ayrault 4: 294 ff. [On pages 296–297, Ayrault asserts that in the *Dialogue* "there is only the unilaterality of (Friedrich's) thought," and argues against reading the dialogue's "characters" as representations of the members of the *Athenaeum* group.]

20. See *Athenaeum* fragments 22 and 418, as well as "Criticism: The Formation of Character," herein.

21. Amalia had already been Caroline's pseudonym in August Schlegel's *Letters on Poetry, Meter, and Language.*

22. In *Wilhelm Meister,* as Ayrault points out (4: 290), Lothario symbolizes problems related to economic activity, and was found by Schlegel to be "the most interesting character in the entire work."

23. Or at least certain of its central motifs—beginning with that of an "erotic" pedagogy. It is nevertheless clear that the relation to Caroline is not comparable to the one that can be glimpsed in *On Philosophy* and above all in *Lucinde* (where Friedrich's "Platonic" passion for Caroline is recalled in the section "Apprenticeship for Manhood" (77–103); this is why no trace of the initiatory theme is found here. The *Dialogue,* oddly enough, is a *Symposium* without Diotima.

24. Which in fact contains, in the section entitled "Allegory of Impudence" (53–63)— and in the form of a "walking dream"—a sort of theory of the novel. It would not be difficult to demonstrate that *Lucinde* is constructed on the principle of auto-engenderment, although the important thing is still, perhaps, that the book should never have been completed or, if you will, that once begun, it should have been aborted.

25. We can only refer here to Peter Szondi's fundamental study, "Friedrich Schlegel's Theory of Poetical Genres: A Reconstruction from the Posthumous Fragments" (75–94). Relying particularly on the posthumous "fragments" collected in the *Kritische Friedrich Schlegel Ausgabe* and the *Literary Notebooks* (ed. Hans Eichner), Szondi attempted to reconstruct a "system" of Schlegelian poetics oscillating between a "critique of poetic reason" and a sort of pre-Hegelian synthesis that would reconcile subjective and objective poetry in and as the novel. Nonetheless, Szondi's analysis stops at a recognition of Schlegel's contradictions and a paraphrase of *Athenaeum* fragment 116. Moreover, Jean Bollack, the editor of *Poésie et poétique de l'idealisme allemand* (Paris: Minuit, 1975), a translation of selected essays by Szondi, reminds us in a note, [which Mendelsohn translates (77)], that "Peter Szondi did not ignore the objections that were raised against his inclusion of the novel in the genre that Schlegel defined as objective/subjective . . . and especially against his linking of the two oppositions: poetry of nature/artificial poetry and Antiquity/Modernity." Benjamin, on the other hand (94 ff.) has shown that the novel is an "ideal" only insofar as it authorizes the fulfillment of poetry as prose ("The idea of poetry is prose,") or, in other words, the fulfillment of what, for Novalis, would define "romantic rhythm." This motif reappears explicitly in August Schlegel's *Lectures:* "A genre has opened up in romantic poetry that not only can do without verse, but that even in many cases forbids versification: the

novel." This ideal of prose, of *oratio soluta*, should be related to what we have been calling "the fragmentary exigency"—and to everything, in other words, that has thus far fallen into place around the speculative motif of the Ab-solute (on the Ab-solute, see Heidegger's *Schelling* 43).

26. The *ghedh-* root reappears in *gatten* (to unite oneself to or to come together) or in the couple *Gatte/Gattin* (husband/wife), and refers to the idea of jointure or connection. Perhaps to the idea of system?

27. See "The Fragment: The Fragmentary Exigency," herein.

28. From "On the Combinatory Spirit," the introduction to the second part of *Lessings Geist aus seinen Schriften* (1804) [*Lessing's Spirit in his Writings, KS* 425–426].

29. See Benjamin 104 ff.

30. In relation to the question of academic exploitation, it is worth noting that August appropriates fragments of his brother's work, without ever giving the slightest indication of their source.

31. This same expression—inherited from Kant, as the *Lectures* point out—also appears in the "Talk on Mythology" and in Schelling's *System of Transcendental Idealism*, which was the inspiration for the *Lectures*.

32. See "The Idea: Religion within the Limits of Art," herein. In the Age of Subjectity, *Mimesis* is *Poiesis;* hence the Promethean motif that appears both in the *Lectures* and at the end of the *Dialogue*.

33. See Genette, *Mimologiques*, particularly 227 ff., and Todorov, *Théorie du symbole* 179 ff.

34. See "Epochs of Poetry" in the *Dialogue* 60–75.

35. See also *CF* 117. We will return to this question in "Criticism: The Formation of Character," herein.

36. See Benjamin 104 ff.

37. See the entire development on the Alexandrine "Idyllion" and on the Roman satire in "Epochs of Poetry." In decomposing its art, Antiquity actually destroyed the genres themselves.

38. On this point, see the beginning of "Epochs of Poetry," as well as Schelling's *Philosophy of Art* and *Athenaeum* fragment 50.

39. See Szondi, "Friedrich Schlegel's Theory of Poetical Genres" (75–94).

40. Especially in the different versions of the apogee of Greek art found in the *Phenomenology* (in "Religion in the Form of Art" ["Die Kunst-Religion"]), the *Aesthetics*, and the *Philosophy of Religion*.

41. But, contrary to what Szondi thinks [see "Underwindung des Klassizismus: Der Brief an Böhlendorff vom 4 December 1801" and "Gattungspoetik und Geschichtsphilosophie: Mit einem Exkurs über Schiller, Schlegel und Hölderlin" in Peter Szondi, *Hölderlin-Studien: Mit einem Traktat über philologische Erkenntnis* (Frankfurt am Main: Suhrkamp, 1967), 95–169], nothing is less certain. None-

theless, this does not mean that one must automatically and unreservedly endorse the Heideggerian interpretation of Hölderlin, which moreover pretends to ignore Hölderlin's poetics. On this point, see Lacoue-Labarthe, "The Caesura of the Speculative."

42. See "Criticism: The Formation of Character," herein.

43. But which is not unrelated—although in a quite ironic mode—to the problems raised in the letter *On Philosophy* to Dorothea or in *Lucinde*, to say nothing of the way in which it clearly remarks Friedrich's own obsession with being an artist.

44. See *I* 95 and "Closure: Romantic Equivocity," herein.

45. See also *Lucinde's* "Prologue."

46. See also note 25, above. Here, as Szondi pointed out in "Friedrich Schlegel and Romantic Irony" (58–59), this conception of "chemism" must be referred to the profound ambiguity that surrounds the notion of *understanding* in all the texts of the *Athenaeum*. As was seen with respect to the praise of understanding in the letter *On Philosophy* to Dorothea, the entire relation to Kant is involved here. Note also that August Schlegel, in his *Lectures*, makes understanding itself the origin of the prosaic, and hence of the novel: "Whence, then, does the prosaic in language originate? From the fact that understanding takes possession of signs that imagination has created."

47. In *Athenaeum* fragment 196, on the contrary, autobiography and particularly Rousseau are condemned.

48. Behind these lines, for Schelling, is above all Goethe's *Faust* which, along with the *Divine Comedy*, is seen by the *Philosophy of Art* as the great model of the completed work of art. We should note that Goethe himself dreamed of a sort of "musical drama" and that it was only because he could not find a musician that suited him—Mozart being dead and Goethe's relations with Beethoven being less than ideal—that he renounced giving a sequel to the *Magic Flute* or treating *Faust* as a true "libretto."

　　We must also point out here that a final paragraph follows the lines we are citing (we alluded to them earlier). Schelling designates the Mass as an "interior drama," and opposes it to the total work that tragedy represented for the Greeks. And this time one is reminded less of Wagner—despite *Parsifal*—than of Mallarmé.

49. In a posthumous note of 1802 is also found the following, which is perfectly clear on this point: "Novels, *witzig* and epic poetry are nothing but elements of and preliminaries to a *mythic* poetry, as tragic, comic, and musical theatre are for historical drama. The same thing applies to lyric poems. Nevertheless, they must already be very close to mythical poems."

Criticism

1. That is let us recall, Novalis; we will return to the distinction thus made between Novalis and the others (see "Closure: Romantic Equivocity," herein).

2. Because we shall be concerned with one of Friedrich's texts here, let us content ourselves with recalling the interrelation of "genres" in his work. Before *Lucinde* in 1799, which is left unfinished, Friedrich had published at least seven critical essays, the "Critical Fragments," and his portion of the *Athenaeum* fragments. Subsequently, apart from the poems of 1800 (including a few sonnets in the *Athenaeum*) and the "Trauerspiel" *Alarcos* (1802), Friedrich's activity will be exclusively critical (in 1801 the two brothers jointly collect and publish their *Charakteristiken und Kritiken* [*Characteristics and Critiques* or, as Hans Eichner translates this title on one occasion, *Pen-Portraits and Reviews*], and then, until his death in 1829, simultaneously critical, linguistic, and philosophical. His only book will be *On the Language and Wisdom of India* (1808); otherwise, besides numerous courses and individual talks, his "genre" will always be the practical genre of criticism *par excellence*, that of the journal, which he either contributes to or founds (*Europa* in 1804, *Deutsches Museum* in 1812, *Concordia* in 1820). The superficial obviousness of the observation, usually treated either with irony or regret, has up to now elicited no rigorous analysis of the romantic concept of *criticism* save that of Benjamin, to which we have constantly referred in this chapter.

    [For a succinct and reliable account of Friedrich Schlegel's literary production and public career, as well as bibliographical information on the numerous nineteenth-century translations of now unavailable works, such as the later lecture courses in history, philosophy, and criticism, see Hans Eichner, *Friedrich Schlegel* (New York: Twayne, 1970).]

3. See Schelling, *Philosophie der Kunst* 379.

4. The reader will have noted the frequency of this motif throughout all the texts we have examined, beginning with the *Critical Fragments*.

5. Their father, J. A. Schlegel, a pastor, was for some time co-director of the *Bremenish Contributions to Recreation, Understanding, and Witz* . . . and, above all, translated, with additional critical commentary, the celebrated treatise of Batteux, *Les Beaux-Arts réduits à un même principe* [*The Fine Arts Reduced to a Unique Principle*].

6. "In the sense in which it has been defined and used in Germany, aesthetics is a word that notoriously reveals an equally complete ignorance of the thing signified and the signifying language"; see also "The Idea: Religion within the Limits of Art," herein. One should note, on the other hand, that the term is not depreciated by the author of the "Earliest System-Programme."

7. We are, of course, simplifying matters, particularly by neglecting the authors who count most for the romantics, notably Lessing, Diderot, and Hemsterhuis.

8. As we have seen in "The Poem: A Nameless Art," herein, in relation to the origin of language.

9. Fragment 101 of the first version of *Grains of Pollen* [2: 460].

10. See Schelling, *Philosophie der Kunst* 379.

11. Tr. note: For Schelling's discussion of the concept of *Potenz*, its relation to determination and form, and its place in the project of a "philosophy of art," see *Philosophie der Kunst* 385–389.

12. On the theme of the relation between criticism and reflection, see Szondi, "Friedrich Schlegel and Romantic Irony" (61 ff.).

13. It also suggests a proximity to the early Hölderlin, although this Hölderlin might be better characterized by his maintenance of and insistence on the Kantian critique, in the *margins* of idealism.

14. This "supplement" undoubtedly belongs to the epoch and logic of the *supplement* that Jacques Derrida has elucidated in relation to Rousseau in *De la Grammatologie* (Paris: Minuit, 1967) [*Of Grammatology*, trans. Gayatri Spivak (Baltimore, Md.: Johns Hopkins University Press, 1976)].

15. Which implies a critique not only of classical conceptions of imitation, but also of Goethe's conception, according to which art offers a "resemblance" of the *Urbilder* (or "original forms," which are situated in the order of the "original phenomenon," the *Urphänomen*, that plays a key role in Goethe), yet does not pass them over into "objectivity." Herein lies the major difference between Goethe and the romantics, despite all their similarities. This also explains why Goethe does not call the "genres" into question—except in *Faust*, as we saw in "The Poem: A Nameless Art." On the comparison of Goethe and the romantics, see Benjamin 105 ff.

16. See also Friedrich's posthumous "philosophical fragments," where he writes: "Critique of philosophy and philology are the same thing. —Since philosophy has criticized so very much, yea, has criticized just about everything in the heavens and on the earth, it certainly ought to tolerate being criticized in turn" [*KA* 40, Frag. 228].

17. The term "characteristics," already adopted by the romantics, plays an important role in Goethe's *Propyläen*, which appeared in 1799.

18. *Critique of Judgment* 222 ¶59. In the background of everything that follows, one should also also note the importance of the Leibnizian idea of *characteristics* as a language or combination of signs producing all the properties of the system of the Universe.

19. On this point, see Benjamin 102.

20. Tr. note: This parenthetical remark alludes to the series "*Ecrivains de toujours*" (Writers of Forever, for All Time; or Eternal Writers), published in France by the Editions du Seuil. Each volume in this popular and quasi-encyclopaedic series (which at present contains more than one hundred titles, from Apollinaire and Aristophanes to Voltaire, Virginia Woolf, and Zola) is a short biographical-critical essay on a canonical author. Each volume's title consists of the author-subject's proper name, followed by the phase "par lui-même" (by himself), for example, *Châteaubriand by himself, The German Romantics by themselves, Colette*

by herself, etc. This "by himself" serves to emphasize the specific nature and aim of these "critical" texts, which do not provide specialized or particularly academic commentary on the author in question, but rather restrict themselves to the more generally informative and educational function of introducing the author as a "personality" or "character" to a general (but nevertheless cultivated and seeking to be cultivated) audience.

The point of the parenthetical remark here—that Romantic criticism's auto-biographical and generally "auto-" conception of the author eventually leads to the becoming-critic of the author and the becoming-personality and -work of the author-critic—corresponds not only to the implicit "logic" of the "*Ecrivains de toujours*" series, but is also very specifically illustrated (quite literally, because each volume in the series is not by accident copiously illustrated with "personal" documents, portraits, photographs, and "pictures" of every description, all of which serve to reinforce the notion of the author-subject as a personality "expressing himself" in his "life and work") by the example of Roland Barthes who, it is here suggested, might be said to "personify" this tendency. Lacoue-Labarthe and Nancy have already cited Barthes as an example: "the critic himself (lui-même) and as such must be an author (Benjamin, Barthes, Genette)." (112).

Early in his career (in 1954), Barthes wrote the *Michelet par lui-même* volume in the series, and twenty years later (in 1975, shortly before the composition of *The Literary Absolute*), having become a "personality" himself, auto-biographically wrote his own volume for the series, *Barthes par lui-même.* With this text, the first and only genuinely autobiographical volume in the series, Barthes foregrounds, carries to its logical extreme, and thus both fulfills and parodies the "idealistic" critical logic of the series to which Lacoue-Labarthe and Nancy allude.

21. See "The Fragment: The Fragmentary Exigency," herein.

22. See "The Idea: Religion within the Limits of Art," herein.

23. See Friedrich's posthumous "philosophical fragments" of 1796-1806 [*KA* 106, Frag. 927].

24. On the place of Jean Paul, see "The Poem: A Nameless Art" and the *Dialogue's* "Letter on the Novel." This is the moment to recall that all subsequent literary history emphasizes that romanticism produced only one "treatise" on poetics that claims to be exhaustive, Jean Paul's *Introduction to Aesthetics [Vorschule der Aesthetik]* (1804). Jean Paul's text is, in fact, no longer romantic, but rather characterizes the romantics (as "nihilists": whence the fortunes of the word). But on the other hand, the charge that is always levelled at this *Introduction* is that it is only . . . an auto-characterization.

25. One sees all that Nietzsche could have taken from romanticism, from the *Dichtung* of great literary and philosophical figures to *Ecce Homo,* by way of *Zarathustra.* But it is surely the theme of the *philosopher-artist* that is most fundamentally, romantic in his work.

26. See *Athenaeum* fragment 439, which bestows an extremely general literary significance on the character sketch.

27. "On the Essence of Criticism" [*KS* 396 ff.].

28. "On the Combinatory Spirit" [*KS* 424 ff.].

Closure: Romantic Equivocity

1. Cited in Ernst Behler, *Friedrich Schlegel* (Rowohlt: Reinbek bei Hamburg, 1966), 164.

2. See "Criticism: The Formation of Character," herein.

3. On Humboldt, see Todorov 203 ff. On Heidegger, see in particular "The Way to Language," the final text in his *On the Way to Language*, trans. Peter D. Hertz (New York: Harper and Row, 1971).

4. In "On Incomprehensibility" (that is, on the *Athenaeum*), which appeared in the last issue of the journal.

5. All things considered, this also confirms the enigmatic status that the romantics ascribe to lyricism, before or beyond all *poetry* (see the last pages of "The Poem: A Nameless Art," herein).

6. Tr. note: Richard Samuel's introduction to the *Dialogues* (Novalis 2: 655–660) discusses the manuscript evidence and thematic differences that distinguish the two "Athenaeum" dialogues from the other four.

7. Tr. note: This fragment is number 237 of the unpublished fragments grouped together as "Vorarbeiten zu verschiedenen Fragmentsammlungen" ("Preliminary studies for various fragment-collections") in Novalis 2: 578–579.

Bibliography

Allemann, Bede. *Ironie und Dichtung: F. Schlegel, Novalis, Solger, Kierkegaard, Nietzsche, Thomas Mann, Musil.* 2nd ed. Pfullingen: Neske, 1969.

Ayrault, Roger. *La Genèse du romantisme allemand.* 4 vols. Paris: Aubier-Montaigne, 1961–1976.

Béguin, Albert, ed. *Le Romantisme allemand.* "Bibliothèque 10/18." 1949. Paris: Union Général d'Editions, 1966.

Benjamin, Walter. *Der Begriff der Kunstkritik in der deutschen Romantik.* In *Gesammelte Schriften Werkausgabe.* Eds. Rolf Tiedemann and Herman Schweppenhäuser. 12 vols. 1972–1977. Frankfurt am Main: Suhrkamp, 1980. 1: 7–122.

Berman, Antoine. "Lettres à Fouad-el-Etr sur le romantisme allemand." *Le Délirante* 3 (1968).

Blanchot, Maurice. "The Athenaeum." [From *L'Entretien infini* (Paris: Gallimard, 1969). 515–527.] Trans. Deborah Esch and Ian Balfour. *Studies in Romanticism* 22 (1983): 163–172.

"Earliest System-Programme of German Idealism." ["Ältestes Systemprogramm des deutschen Idealismus."] Trans. H. S. Harris. In H. S. Harris. *Hegel's Development: Toward the Sunlight, 1770–1801.* Oxford University Press, 1972. 510–512.

Genette, Gérard. *Mimologiques.* "Collection Tel Quel." Paris: Seuil, 1976.

Heidegger, Martin. *Schelling's Treatise on the Essence of Human Freedom.* Trans. Joan Stambaugh. Athens, Ohio: Ohio University Press, 1985.

Kant, Immanuel. *The Critique of Judgement.* Trans. James Meredith. 1928. Oxford: Oxford University Press, 1980.

Lacoue-Labarthe, Philippe. "The Caesura of the Speculative." Trans. Robert Eisenhauer. *Glyph* 4 (1978): 57–84.

Lacoue-Labarthe, Philippe and Jean-Luc Nancy. "Le Dialogue des genres: Textes de Shaftesbury, Hemsterhuis, Schelling." *Poétique* 21 (1975): 148–175.

Müller, Andreas, ed. *Satiren und Parodien.* Reihe Romantik 9. Darmstadt; Wissenschaftliche Buchgesellschaft, 1970.

Novalis. *Schriften.* Ed. Paul Kluckhohn and Richard Samuel. 3 vols. 1935. Stuttgart: Kohlhammer, 1960.

———. *Blüthenstaub. [Grains of Pollen.] Schriften* 2: 412–470.

———. *Die Christenheit, oder Europa. Schriften* 3: 497–524.

———. *Dialogen. Schriften* 2: 661–671.

———. *Glaube und Liebe. [Faith and Love.] Schriften* 2: 475–503.

———. *Heinrich von Ofterdingen. Schriften* 1: 183–369.

———. *Die Lehrlinge zu Saïs. [The Disciples at Saïs.] Schriften* 1: 71–111.

Schelling, Friedrich W. J. *Epikurisch Glaubensbekenntnis Heinz Widerporstens. [Heinz Widerporst's Epicurean Confession of Faith.]* Müller 177–186.

———. *Philosophie der Kunst.* In *Werke.* Ed. Manfred Schröter. 6 vols. Munich: Beck and Oldenbourg, 1927–1928. 3: 375–508.

Schlegel, August W. *Die Kunstlehre. [Lectures on Art and Literature.]* In *Kritische Schriften und Briefe.* Ed. Edgar Lohner. 6 vols. Stuttgart: Kohlhammer, 1962–1967. vol. 2.

Schlegel, Friedrich, *Dichtungen und Aufsätze.* Ed. Wolfdietrich Rasch. Munich: Hanser, 1984. [Cited as *DA.*]

———. *Kritische Schriften.* Ed. Wolfdietrich Rasch. Munich: Hanser, 1970. [Cited as *KS.*]

———. *"Lucinde" and the Fragments.* [Also includes "On Incomprehensibility."] Trans. Peter Firchow. Minneapolis: University of Minnesota Press, 1971.

———. *Lessings Geist aus seinen Schriften. [The Spirit of Lessing in his Writings.] KS* 384–451.

———. *"Philosophische Lehrjahre, 1796–1806."* Vol. 18 of *Kritische Ausgabe.* Ed. Ernst Behler. Munich: Ferdinand Schöningh, 1963. [Cited as *KA.*]

————. *Über das Studium der griechischen Poesie*. [*On the Study of Greek Poetry.*] *KS* 113–230.

————. *Über Philosophie. An Dorothea.* [*On Philosophy. To Dorothea.*] *DA* 444–468.

————. *Dialogue on Poetry and Literary Aphorisms.* [*Gespräch über die Poesie.*] Trans. Ernst Behler and Roman Struc. London: Pennsylvania State University Press, 1968.

Szondi, Peter. *On Textual Understanding and Other Essays.* Trans. Harvey Mendelsohn. Minneapolis: University of Minnesota Press, 1986.

Todorov, Tzvetan. *Théorie du symbole.* Paris: Seuil, 1977.

Ullmann, R. and H. Gotthard. *Geschichte des Begriffes "Romantisch" in Deutschland.* [*History of the Concept of the "Romantic" in Germany.*] Berlin: E. Ebering, 1927.

Appendix:
Topical Index to the Fragments

Tr. note: Although this volume does not include English translations of the *Critical Fragments*, the *Athenaeum* fragments, or *Ideas*—see Firchow—we include the authors' valuable subject index to the fragments.)

Aesthetic
CF 40.
A 202, 256.
I 72.

Alliance
CF 114.
I 32, 49, 124, 136, 139, 140, 142, 144, 146.

Antiquity (Ancients/Moderns)
CF 11, 39, 44, 84, 91, 93, 99, 107.
A 8, 24, 69, 121, 143, 145, 147, 148, 149, 151, 155, 159, 164, 185, 191, 192, 193, 194, 239, 242, 248, 252, 271, 273, 321, 393, 402, 440.
I 35, 59, 85, 95, 102, 138.

Art
CF 12 (philosophy of), 51, 115, 117.
A 60, 68, 71, 167, 252, 255, 302, 310, 339, 360, 364, 432, 444.
I 11, 41, 48, 68, 102, 106, 109, 111, 119, 120, 123, 135, 145, 148.

Artists (Author-Public Relation)
CF 1, 24, 32, 33, 35, 37, 58, 63, 68, 70, 81, 85, 89, 94, 98, 110, 111, 112.
A 20, 109, 117, 253, 255, 287, 327, 381, 419, 432.
I 13, 16, 20, 32, 42, 43, 44, 45, 49, 54, 64, 92, 113, 114, 122, 131, 136, 142, 143, 145, 146, "To Novalis."

A   13, 26, 44, 47, 56, 59, 66, 67, 89, 116, 125, 167, 205, 221, 238, 259, 281, 403, 404, 426, 439, 448.

Dialogue
CF   37, 42.
A   37, 77, 221.

Divinity (*see* God)

Drama (Theatre, Tragedy/Comedy)
CF   30, 45, 49.
A   17, 36, 42, 110, 123, 126, 129, 138, 140, 141,154, 187, 244, 245, 246, 251, 253, 307, 383, 424.

Energy
A   375, 378, 445.
I   23, 132, 153.

Enthusiasm (Inspiration)
CF   37, 63.
A   88, 220, 246, 364, 394, 427, 445.
I   18, 102, 131, 137, 144.

Epoch
CF   38, 53, 120.
A   26, 135, 216, 243, 275, 277, 285, 334, 421, 424, 426.
I   35, 50, 56, 112, 124, 134, 139.

Family
A   314, 364.
I   122, 126, 152.

Fantasy (*see* Phantasie)

Fragment
CF   103.
A   22, 24, 77, 206, 259, 302, 424, 451.

Friendship (*see* Love)

Geist
CF   28, 82, 92.

History
CF 25.
A   28, 45, 80, 163, 166, 217, 219, 223, 224, 226, 432.
I   70, 123, 139.

Humanity
A   180, 223, 262, 315, 336, 355, 363, 364, 396, 426, 441.
I   21, 24, 33, 41, 50, 51, 55, 57, 64, 72, 80, 87, 102, 107, 122, 152.

Humor (*see* Witz)

Idea (Ideal)
CF 23.
A   49, 121, 198, 202, 236, 238, 336, 364, 369, 406, 412.
I   10, 15, 17, 82, 95, 117, 118, 155.

Individual
CF 46, 81.
A   22, 51, 55, 81, 82, 121, 125, 195, 225, 242, 248, 406, 415, 426, 427, 451.
I   6, 22, 24, 47, 60, 64, 65, 95.

Infinite
CF 47, 87.
A   116, 227, 363, 364, 394, 406, 429, 432, 448.
I   3, 13, 30, 42, 80, 85, 86, 98, 131.

Inspiration (*see* Enthusiasm)

Intuition (Intellectual Intuition)
A   76, 102, 342, 443, 448.
I   44, 78, 102, 137, 150.

Invisible
I   2, 6, 16.

Irony
CF 7, 42, 48, 108.
A   51, 121, 305, 314.
I   69.

Novel
CF   18, 26, 78, 89.
A   111, 115, 118, 124, 146, 170, 216, 252, 364, 380, 398, 426.
I   11.

Organization (Organism, Organic)
CF   14, 21, 103.
A   116, 192, 214, 245, 304, 338, 340, 352, 355, 412, 426, 447, 451.
I   8, 24, 48, 64, 75, 86, 95, 97, 152.

Orient
I   133, "To Novalis"

Painting
A   174, 175, 176, 177, 178, 179, 181, 182, 183, 184, 185, 187, 188, 189, 190, 193, 253, 302, 308, 309, 311, 312, 313, 314, 365, 372.

Person
A   27.
I   24.

Phantasy
A   250, 330, 350, 364, 414, 418, 429, 433.
I   8, 26, 109.

Philology
CF   75.
A   93, 147, 231, 255, 391, 403, 404.
I   119.

Philosophy
CF   12, 42, 83, 95, 108.
A   1, 3, 28, 43, 44, 48, 52, 54, 56, 75, 82, 84, 93, 94, 95, 96, 98, 99, 103, 104, 112, 137, 161, 164, 216, 220, 245, 264, 266, 269, 270, 274, 281, 303, 322, 327, 343, 344, 345, 346, 347, 355, 358, 384, 387, 388, 389, 398, 399, 412, 416, 417, 431, 444, 446.
I   1, 25, 34, 42, 89, 105, 117, 134, 149.

Poetry
CF   4, 7, 14, 21, 23, 62, 65, 84, 87, 100, 107, 117.
A   9, 60, 67, 100, 101, 114, 116, 123, 129, 132, 140, 172, 173, 174, 193,

Sacrifice (Auto-Destruction)
CF 28, 37.
A 15, 51, 195, 286, 292, 305, 328, 422.
I 44, 113, 131.

Science(s)
CF 61, 108, 115.
A 75, 77, 82, 89, 92, 125, 169, 220, 255, 259, 280, 302, 365, 381, 400, 412, 437, 443, 444, 445.
I 11, 32, 41, 68, 97, 99, 106, 111, 120, 135.

Sculpture
A 180, 185, 187, 191, 310, 365, 372.

Sinn
CF 63, 69, 111.
A 78, 252, 273, 329, 336, 337, 339, 350.
I 5, 20, 44, 51, 79, 80, 124, 144.

Sociality (Urbanity)
CF 34, 42, 103.
A 5, 34, 146, 152, 170, 204, 257, 344, 425, 426, 431, 436, 438.

Subject
CF 28, 29, 37.
A 15, 51, 74, 77, 99, 132, 151, 196, 201, 252, 284, 328, 331, 338, 345, 352, 375, 433.
I 41.

System
A 46, 53, 66, 72, 77, 91, 116, 142, 168, 242, 247, 290, 371, 383, 384, 432, 434, 439, 451.
I 12, 95, 150.

Theatre (*see* Drama)

Tragedy (*see* Drama)

Understanding
A 300, 366.
I 8, 91, 93.

Urbanity (*see* Sociality)

Witz (Humor, Grotesque)

CF   9, 13, 16, 17, 22, 34, 39, 41, 43, 51, 56, 59, 67, 71, 90, 96, 97, 104,
     109, 111, 126.
A   29, 32, 37, 58, 82, 106, 116, 120, 121, 156, 217, 220, 237, 245, 289,
     305, 366, 383, 394, 421, 426, 429, 438, 445.
I   26, 59, 109, 123.

Woman
CF   106.
A   30, 31, 49, 102, 133, 134, 170, 196, 235, 313, 337, 363, 364, 374,
     420, 421.
I   19, 115, 116, 126, 127, 128, 137.

Work
CF   103.
A   45, 60, 117, 168, 206, 283, 295, 297, 336, 367, 432, 451.
I   33, 44, 136.

Index

Note: In listing references to the three fragment-collections, *Athenaeum Fragments*, *Critical Fragments*, and *Ideas*, we have given the pages references for each fragment separately, following fragment numbers indicated by an *f*. Thus *f10*, 51, for example, indicates a reference to fragment 10 on page 51.

Printed in the United States
1162000005B/190-204